AF656747

Gulam Mandi

Gulam Mandi

A Throbbing Market of Sex Slaves

Nirmala Bhuradia

DK
PRINTWORLD
Publishers of Indian Traditior

Cataloging in Publication Data — DK
[Courtesy: D.K. Agencies (P) Ltd. <docinfo@dkagencies.com>]

Bhurāṛiyā, Nirmalā, 1960- **author.**
Gulam mandi : a throbbing market of sex slaves / Nirmala Bhuradia.
pages cm
Novel.
Also published in Hindi.
ISBN 9788124609538 (paperback)

1. Human trafficking – Fiction. 2. Prostitution – Fiction. 3. Indic fiction (English) I. Title.

LCC PR9499.3.B48G85 2019 | DDC 823.914 23

ISBN: 978-81-246-0953-8
First published in India, 2019
© Nirmala Bhuradia

All rights reserved. No part of this publication may be reproduced or transmitted in any form or by any means, electronic or mechanical, including photocopying, recording or any information storage or retrieval system, without prior written permission of both the copyright owner, indicated above, and the publisher.

Printed and published by:
D.K. Printworld (P) Ltd.
Regd. Office: "Vedaśrī", F-395, Sudarshan Park
(Metro Station: ESI Hospital), New Delhi - 110015
Phones: (011) 2545 3975; 2546 6019
e-mail: indology@dkprintworld.com
Website: www.dkprintworld.com

Foreword

Gulam Mandi, my novel on human trafficking, has already been published in Hindi. Here is an earnest attempt to reach out to a wide audience having its English version. I would say "version" since I did not translate it by putting the Hindi manuscript alongside. Rather, I recreated or rewrote it, following the same sequence of events and the same plot in mind, with only a few changes here and there. My guru Adrian Khare helped me to a great extent in picking up the threads, polishing the language and removing glitches that came to his notice.

Gulam Mandi would mean a market where some unfortunate human beings are put on open display to be picked up as slaves. Living at the mercy of their masters, these men and women would be made beasts of burden or prostitutes.

If, we, the people of twenty-first century, believe that we have left behind this agony of the Middle Ages, we are mistaken. In reality, the practice is still prevalent, in different hue and shade. Of course, it is banned across the world, at least in legal parlance, and it is beyond one's imagination that people of flesh and blood, like us, could be put on display in a bazaar. The poor, vulnerable and gullible people are still lured, cheated, trapped and forced into slavery. The only difference is that their perpetrators, while at large, operate elusive.

The business of slavery goes on so subtly and secretly that one cannot see it in open. This modern-day business is popularly come to know as "human trafficking". Of this business, sex trafficking holds a huge sway in which a commercial sex act is induced by force, fraud, coercion of a person, below the age of eighteen, is induced to perform a sexual act. Also, the recruitment, harbouring, transportation, provision or obtaining of a person for labour or services, using force, fraud or coercion for the purpose of involuntary servitude, peonage, debt bondage or slavery come under the label, human trafficking.

Governments world over are trying to fight this malice, each one in its own way. I came across one such initiative when I visited the US in 2006, on an invitation by the US Department of State under the International Visitors Leadership Program (IVLP). That year, the subject of study under the Program was "trafficking in persons". The IVLP, launched in 1940, seeks to build mutual understandings between the US and other nations through carefully designed professional visits to the US for current and emerging foreign leaders. With this objective, naturally we were introduced to several policies and strategies to prevent and actively combat "trafficking in persons". To help us acquire a background on trafficking issues we were taken to four cities in the US: Washington DC, Seattle, Dallas and New York.

In Washington DC, we were taken to the US Department of State. Here we had appointments at the office that monitors and combats trafficking in persons, the Bureau of South and Central Asian affairs, the Bureau of Democracy, Human Rights and Labour. The journey continued with the visiting of the

US Department of Justice, particularly its criminal division and civil rights division. Then were the visits to Department of Homeland Security, the US Immigration and Customs Enforcement and various other government offices. One day we had an appointment with Mr T. Kumar, Advocacy Director for Asian in the Amnesty International, which was followed by the visit to the US Helsinki Commission and the office of Senator Patty Murray.

Senator Murray, a campaigner for the rights of women and families, had helped write and pass the historic Violence against Women Act, 1994. In Seattle, we met former state Senator Jeralita De Costa and even a detective, Harvey Sloan, of the Seattle Police Department and other police officers. In Dallas, meetings were arranged with not-for-profit organizations that help immigrants and refugees of victims of human trafficking, the local media, Dallas Police and others. In New York, meetings with organizations like Sakhi for South Asian Women, Safe Horizon and Human Rights Watch were arranged. Even the United Nations' office in the Empire Estate building was on our agenda, where we visited the United Nations Development Fund for Women (UNIFEM) office to discuss agendas like women's empowerment and gender equality. A senior advisor on child labour in the child protection section of UNICEF discussed international efforts to combat child labour.

In Dallas, when I conveyed to the police department that I intend to work on a novel on the subject of human trafficking and wanted to visit a strip show, they took me seriously. The next day, they arranged for two guards to accompany me to a joint in Dallas.

Naturally, during this visit to the US, I could gather crucial information on the "trafficking in persons". I was observing the scenario of human trafficking in India for a long time and in 2005 had attended a national seminar on Trafficking Women and Children organized by Madhya Pradesh Police. So the visit to the US served as a trigger and my novel had moved from just taking notes to writing properly with a plot, scenes and sequences. But it did not mean that some academic book on "trafficking in persons" was taking shape using all the references at hand. On the contrary, the references remained only at the back of mind and fantasies began to weave the story or a stream of stories on their own around the scaffold, by the characters that had confiscated my keyboard. So what I present here is totally a fiction, of course, with a tint of truth in it.

Right from my childhood I had wondered as to why there is a separate community of hijaras (eunuchs) in India! Why is it that they cannot live and mingle with the mainstream? As I grew up to a teenager, some more questions began to prop up. Why are they treated with dreadful contempt? Why are they marginalized? Why are they social outcastes who are forced to live a life of penury in ghettos? Is it their fault that they are born with an ambiguous gender status? Is it a crime to be born that way? If not, why are they not treated well? The third gender people are also human beings with flesh and blood and they deserve to be treated with the same dignity as others. In order to raise these issues I have portrayed the characters of hijaras in this novel. I was careful enough not to give an account of hijaras from our side. For this it was important to know their minds, their psyche, their environs, their way of life. For this, I visited their homes, conversed with them and accompanied them from place to place. The story of *kinnar*s runs along the main story and ultimately gets merged with the main theme.

My story has two protagonists, Kalyani and Janki. The

resultant story takes us mainly to a turbulent world of human trafficking. But many other issues are interwoven with the main story: like a society where the caste system is still prevalent, untouchability still persists, life of a beauty queen, who fears ageing, and is jealous of her own daughter who is at full blossom. Then there is this girl who comes from an oppressed class and faces rejection from some people who believe that they belong to a higher stratum than her in social status. India's ancient caste system, ingrained in the social framework, is thus exposed.

Then there is Meera, a female elephant and the world of elephants and people from exotic India, who understand animal language.

However, as an unknown author once said, people like a story and like it being told well. It is in the telling of the story that the writer's entire resources and skills to be employed. But it is ultimately left to the readers to decide whether a real story has been told really well.

Nirmala Bhuradia

One

STICKING HER tongue out, the woman closed her eyes. Jamunalal brought a cobra, wound tight around his wrist, close to her mouth. In response, the cobra angrily inflated its hood. Jamunalal, as if waiting for this moment, with a quick blow, struck its head with a pincer, annoying the snake even more. In a fit of rage, the hissing cobra embedded its fangs on the woman's tongue.

"*Aaahh* ...!" She unleashed a soft cry, in pain and ecstasy, and put her tongue back into mouth. The cobra too withdrew springing back to its position around Jamunalal's wrist. The woman dragged her feet unsteadily toward a nearby bamboo chair. Seconds later she began muttering, though she could not continue it for long. Her head was spinning and she could do nothing but bend forward onto a wooden desk.

"Next ...!" Jamunalal called out to the waiting people.

Jamunalal lived within this shanty-gully, yet maintained a luxurious lifestyle. He occupied two rooms, side by side, one of which indicated opulence and the other, sheer deprivation. The interior air-conditioned room had a TV and a refrigerator, with vinyl flooring. The outer room was ill-furnished in comparison.

It had rough mud walls and a low roof, supported by wooden beams. This was no irony at all. The rich–poor combo was very much intentional, a deliberate design. The luxurious room was for personal use and the farm hut-like ambience to lure customers who sought romance in rustic charm.

Snakes of various kinds hung from the wooden poles in the hut, as if the latter were serving as mall windows or showcases of this "snake bite" bar. Serpents were on display so that customers could see for themselves and choose whether they would like to be bitten by a fierce viper, a bad tempered cobra or a simple natured green water snake. Like the snakes of various species, an eclectic mix of people also filled up this place. A white German with green marble eyes stared at the yellow mud wall. A Madrasi with his lungi hitched up the knee-line, scratched his calf; a young lad skimming through a glossy, girlie magazine waited for his chance. He stared unblinkingly at a picture of a girl in lingerie.

A snake charmer squatted on the floor near the door, keeping beside him three baskets, each full of coiled snakes. He awaited his turn to meet Jamunalal, keeping a hopeful gaze on the man, so that as soon as Jamunalal finished business at hand, the charmer would be able to bargain for a good price and sell the snakes he had captured from the woods.

A middle-aged woman, wearing a low-necked blouse, persistently rubbed the portion below her neckline. Two youngsters, pointing mischievously at her, passed remarks, "Would she like to be bitten over there?"

They were close to the truth in fact. Everybody did not want to be bitten on their tongue. They chose to receive it on their palm, heel, big toe or even solar plexus. But Kalyani was firm on being bitten on her tongue alone by a poisonous snake whose potent venom could nullify the poison which life had injected into her.

For long Kalyani had been thinking of visiting Jamunalal's gully, but was not able to, because she feared entering an obscure, mysterious lane which she had to cross before making her way to this one. God bless Anguri, whose help ultimately made this possible. Anguri knew the topography of the place well and was totally devoid of fear. Kalyani simply held her hand and went along.

Anguri was not an old friend. Kalyani got acquainted with her fairly recently when Anguri, along with a few members of her hijara fraternity, came for a ritual dance performance in the neighbourhood, on the birth of a male child. Though this also was almost a ritual that they come uninvited to celebrate such an occasion and perform a dance which is hardly rhythmic. This time also they were hopping and jumping while trying to sway their hips, singing in their masculine, frog-in-the-throat voice. To add music to it, they were thumping the floor, clapping hands in a way singular to hijaras.

After this self-proclaimed felicitation programme, they asked for a hefty amount of money as tip, which the family refused to give.

The verbal tussle was growing with every minute, with the hijaras demanding a whopping 5,000 rupees for their "precious blessings" and the family not ready to give a *naya paisa* above 100 rupees. Both remained unyielding and adamant. At last the family said a firm "no." Seeing thcy outwitted, Anguri took her last card out and said defiantly, "Meet our demand or else ... watch me with my skirt up!"

This took a serious turn. Here Kalyani had to step in.

That day the problem was solved with Kalyani's help. Instead of calling Anguri a shameless, graceless whore like others would have in such circumstances, Kalyani came forward with an offer of a peaceful solution. She called for the best crockery from her home and served tea to Anguri and the others. Anguri was overwhelmed with the respect of the sort she could never have seen or imagined in her life. That was Kalyani's first introduction to Anguri. (Though on another occasion Kalyani met Anguri at a place completely unexpected and was taken aback to see her there.)

Kalyani was doing a documentary on AIDS. In the AIDS ward of a government hospital, she encountered Anguri and was shocked to see her there.

Let's set aside that incident for now. Coming to the present, where Anguri is guiding Kalyani through a *mohalla* maze with narrow lanes. It is so much like a honeycomb that neighbours in facing buildings can dry their clothes on each other's balconies merely by extending their hands. Windows and balconies are so close and within reach that people easily gossip and exchange goods. Houses seem to be internally connected to each other with staircases running through one house and leading to the next. Joint roofs make it easier for an aspiring thief to steal into any house. But because of the *mohalla*'s nature, even the boldest burglar would not dare set foot here.

In this interlacing web of abodes, Anguri took Kalyani to the house of Rekha Albeli, from where she would lead her to her own household, as if a direct entry was not possible.

Rekha Albeli was sitting on an extension outside her home. She was constantly swinging her legs while munching on a corn cob. When Anguri introduced her, "Meet our Kalyani didi, she wants to visit our home," Rekha Albeli stopped biting into the corn and stared sternly at Kalyani.

Kalyani folded her hands in a *namaskar* and smiled meekly at Rekha Albeli who paid no attention and resumed swinging her legs and eating, all the while paying total disregard to Kalyani.

Kalyani now entered the house. Inside, in a passage, there were two or three hijaras chopping vegetables for their next meal. On the right of the passage was a room with a parquet floor, giving the impression of an outsized chessboard. Across the room were the stairs running upward. These were almost lost to sight. The mysterious atmosphere was enhanced by a heavy aroma which seemed to descend from the stairs. As Anguri and Kalyani started up, one of the eunuchs called out from where she was sitting, "Put on the light." Anguri came down a bit to switch on the single naked electric bulb. Before this, there was no hint of such a light. The stairs without the light gave a mystery-shrouded air to the murky surroundings, wrapped in the heady aroma.

As soon as the bulb illuminated the expanse, there came in sight a tomb covered with a green silken cloth. Going along the flight of stairs was a whitewashed wall with a niche in which the tomb was placed. The strong aroma which was descending from here was of incense burning near the tomb. The former guru of the Albeli clan was buried here.

While Rekha Albeli's former guru had been laid to eternal rest in a grave, her present guru was taking a siesta in her room; so Kalyani and the others went ahead without even meeting her. After crossing a small open air passage, they came to another flight of stairs, this time leading downward. As they started descending, Kalyani heard a loud cawing, as if of crows, approaching them. She looked up suspiciously toward the sky. But the sky was free of any crows. Puzzled, she continued the journey downward. After a few steps came a right turn. A few more steps and they reached a courtyard; its flooring was uneven with broken tiles at places revealing the ground below. A water-filled earthen pot was resting in a corner, near which lay a decaying wooden chair, alongside which were five cages placed in a row. The caw-cawing was rising from here. There were black ravens, not crows, kept in these cages.

Surprised, Kalyani threw a quizzical glance at Anguri, to which the latter answered, "Don't stare at me like a buffoon. My guru owns the ravens, these are her dear pets."

"But why ravens only …!" asked Kalyani.

"So what do you think we are going to raise? Mynas and parakeets?"

This caustic comment came from another hijara entering the courtyard from the inner gate. The hijara continued, "Crows are the ones who belong to us. They are our true kin. We raise them with love and care. We don't despise them like you do. …"

"This is Kalyani didi, Hamida!" Anguri tried to introduce Kalyani to the new entrant. But Kalyani didn't pay much attention to the introduction and tried to pitch a crisp retort to Hamida. "You are forgetting that we offer delicious *kheer-puri* to crows during 'shraddha'," replied Kalyani.

"That's it. You yourself have spilt the truth, that you give them *kheer-puri* 'only' during the Shraddha period. That is your selfishness. You want to appease your ancestors and disincarnate beings. But otherwise if a crow sits on your head, you will call it an ominous portent and carry out sacred ablutions. Your approach is the same toward us," said Hamida, "we can sing, dance and get the *neg* for blessing a couple on their marriage in your family but if we cross your path on an ordinary day, you will look with disdain, calling us 'hijara' in an abusive manner," said Hamida with their signature clap.

This deliberate sound of a clap made by Hamida was meant to emphasize that "We know this gesture of ours is a point of ridicule for you." Through her body language, loaded with sarcasm, she wanted to say, "We know you call us scruffy, unkempt hijaras behind our backs – the word hijara itself is unwholesome for you."

Closing the topic, Hamida then went toward the exterior. After she had gone, Anguri hastily grabbed the opportunity to clarify and apologize on Hamida's behalf. "Kalyani, please forgive Hamida for her sharp tongue. She has turned bitter over the years because she has had to face a lot. You know, misfortune befalls us wherever we go. Our lives are a multitude of agonies; storms brewing within us are always on the verge of breaking out."

Kalyani responded with a faint smile. Along with sympathy for Hamida, a nagging fear began to gnaw on her. She was apprehensive – was it alright for her to enter this den? Had she breached the line which common perception had drawn between Kalyani's world and that of Hamida's? Had she dared to wade into shark-infested waters? As rumours have it, hijaras are people with serpentine intelligence, whose cunning is familiar with magical manipulations! They even go to the extent of emasculating young boys to increase their numbers.

"Would you like to see our temple, Kalyani?" Anguri's voice disrupted her train of thought. Amazed, Kalyani repeated what she had just heard, "Temple? Really? Do you have a temple?"

"Yes, we have a temple and stupid people like your Anguri believe in God also. Go and see more proof that we too are people of flesh and blood; we are human beings." The answer came not from Anguri, but from Hamida who had returned from outside.

The three entered the house together. On the right, there was a room with the TV on. A few eunuchs, with a layer of fresh green henna on their hair, were watching TV. There was a small balcony connected to this room. Two small drums were lying on the floor of the balcony. Colourful skirts and blouses were spread out to dry on them. There was a wash basin in the corner of the balcony where a eunuch was trying to slip glass bangles onto her wrist, using soap lather.

A big almirah stood along the wall near the balcony where there was a full length mirror on one of its doors. While crossing the space in front of the almirah, Kalyani suddenly saw the reflection of a woman with a double chin, eyes drowning in black patches and permanent furrows across her forehead. Kalyani almost shrieked in horror, but managed to stifle the scream. It was her own reflection, which saddened her to the quick. This abrupt invasion of reality reminded her of the purpose of her coming here. With this realization, a knot of anguish arose from the pit of her stomach, darting through her system; it exploded in her heart with a mute boom. These days, a thousand such burning orbs blew up inside her, over which she had no control. In order to douse them she had come to this gully. Maybe the fatal venom from Jamunalal's snake bar would stem the bloody grief inside her – or perhaps act as an antidote for her present toxic state of mind ··· that is, before the next orb arose in her stomach. ··· Anguri's voice diverted her attention, "Come in, Kalyani."

Kalyani went in. It was a damp room with a single closed window. An earthen lamp barely lit the room. A wooden bracket was nailed to the wall, on which was placed a framed photograph of a deity riding a rooster. Before the photo, in a glass chalice, lie a few small, sugary *chironji* balls as an offering. The photograph was adorned with a red hibiscus flower, probably as part of some ritual.

"Bow to Devi. She is Bahuchara Mata, our family goddess," said Anguri to Kalyani in a voice which sounded more like a command.

The moment Kalyani arched her neck in a move to bow before the Devi, she heard a heart-rending scream coming from somewhere within the house. Frightened, she quickly stood upright, now completely alert. The shrieks mounted and after a few high-pitched screams though, the voice descended in pitch; the sharp yells gradually becoming feeble, slowing down till they eventually ceased.

Anguri tried to console Kalyani, "Don't be afraid dear, she is Rani, one of us. She is not well and is in chains. She screams when she is in this condition. Otherwise, she is friendly and kind. She would have offered you a cup ofcardamom tea had she been all right."

"Rani? Who is Rani? Where is she from?" enquiring, Kalyani saw her past in flashbacks. Her own father was chained to a pole ··· the very day little Kalyani was to give a school exam. To fare well in exam, she needed to keep her mind unruffled but how could she? There was this disturbing reality. That morning, in an uncontrollable frenzy, her father tore off the clothes he was wearing and was scurrying about the house totally unclad.

Shame, pity, helplessness ··· she could not describe her feelings and looked at her mother who was silently crying. Tauji eventually overpowered her father and struggled to push a kurta over his neck, wrapping a towel around his waist. Taeeji was holding a cane in her hand, in case she had to hand it over to her husband. With the help of the domestic help, Ramjiram, they fastened him to a pole in the veranda. But he stopped screaming only when Dr Gaud came and gave him an injection. Now came the most difficult part which Kalyani had to face; watching her father defenceless, with beseeching eyes looking at the people around him.

After a short pause, Rani started screaming again, which disrupted Kalyani's train of thought, at the same time triggering an intense surge of emotions inside her as waves of stress washed over her. Her father's illness was suddenly a fresh wound again and filled her with great uneasiness. She felt a shortness of breath, palpitations and tingling in her fingers. But this was a state of being which she would rather not share with anyone around; for fear that people would stigmatize her. After all, she is the "daughter of a father who was considered mad!" She remembered well when, for the first time, she got a panic attack like this and someone very close to her told her in mock seriousness, "Oh, genes are at work!" Though any normal person, in the event of a stressful situation, could suffer such an attack.

"What are you thinking about?" Anguri broke into her thoughts. Before Kalyani could say anything, Anguri herself answered her question, "So you are thinking about Rani na? Right! She has lost her mind due to the trauma she had undergone for a long while. My guru brought her from Moradabad." "Moradabad" was said in a tone as if her guru had brought a lota from Moradabad ··· "Come, I shall introduce you to my guru", Anguri suddenly said.

Kalyani and Anguri came downstairs again. Across the broken tiled quadrangle was a room with a creaky wooden door. Inside on a cot was sitting the hijara guru who was one hundred years old. The guru held a rosary in her hand, her lips moving with the beads.

"Kalyani, touch her feet, be blessed and book a good boon in your name! A hijara guru's blessings are considered very auspicious, particularly when she is a hundred years of age. You know, people throng here to get her blessings."

Perhaps the guru was hard of hearing, but was smiling back at them; having lip read what they were saying besides their gestures.

Kalyani almost lusted for the guru's blessings if such there be a description. She desperately needed blessings – let them come from anyone. So, for her, this one was particularly priceless and to earn this privilege, she bent toward the guru's feet; albeit from the corner of her eye, she was trying to find hijara peculiarities in the guru's attire. But there was none. A flat chest below the blouse made it clear that, like other hijaras, the guru was wearing no false bra beneath the blouse. There was no sign of pan chewing or lipstick on her lips, nor was she wearing earrings, bangles or even a necklace. She wore a drab sari, with the *pallu* covering her head. Despite this, she was not looking like a model grandmother in Indian society, but more like a grandfather in a dhoti next door.

After being blessed, Kalyani left the place and took the route down Jamunalal's gully.

• • • ● • • •

Two

JANE COULD GUESS where she was right now. In Texas, in a bar room, dancing almost in the nude! Was this the American dream she was longing for? She had no respite to even think about her situation but was destined to glide and flutter incessantly, like the other girls, who were gesticulating on their platforms, set close together. Their bodies writhing to thunderous music under flickering lights. Jane was tired but could not stop. Bald bear-like Mac's red eyes were scaring her.

Wicked, heartless, hirsute Mac was standing a little away from the platform where the girls were performing – leaned against the bar, closely watching the girls. He had a few goons spread out in the big hall. All the girls were not dancing; a few were serving at the bar. They were almost naked like the dancers. But there was a difference. The girls, who were above twenty-three, were serving at the bar while the teenagers were literally "made to dance."

While dancing, Jane had a fleeting glimpse of Su-Bin who was merely fifteen. This Korean girl knew no English. Actually, on the stages there was a riot of races. There were girls of various colour lines – African-American, Mexican, Asian and European, but the men who drooled lecherously over their naked bodies were of one race – villains! There was no bias. Every girl was merely a piece of flesh for them. The irony was that the girls were made to dance to lure these bloodhounds. The way they were moving and shaking their bodies could not exactly be called dancing. Their movements imitated love-making. Lotharios hilariously hooted and whistled at this voyeuristic meal. Some of them tried to get near the girls. But even getting a little bit closer to any of the girls or touching them in passing, required a fee. A man, like a dog, sniffed a half bent girl's buttocks for a second and had to stuff dollars into her belt. Another man took his lips close to the bosom of a girl and retreated immediately, not before slipping a few crisp dollars into the band around her thin waist. In the middle of the performance, a girl came down the platform to the audience and sat down on the lap of one of the drooling viewers. The man rewards her by sticking some bills into the thread around her midriff.

This practice had given birth to an altogether new development. Gradually, the bands around the waists of the girls were becoming festoons with dollars. But the girls were not going to get their hands on these dollars. Instead, the bills will be marked for the goons, hustlers and pimps ultimately filtering down to the mafia running the show.

Jane and the girls were wearing four-inch high stilettos. Dancing with these shoes for never-ending hours was an excruciating experience. But they could not refuse. Any protest would invite further torture by their handlers. Adela from Mexico was running a fever for two days. She was totally fed up with wearing stilettos. She said "No!" Her refusal enraged Mac, who twisted her arm savagely to the extent that brought on terrible pain and she produced colourful expletives in Spanish. Mac's reply to this was a brutal pinch to her ear and he informed her about something in Spanish. This silenced her immediately.

Probably he had threatened to harm her family which she had left behind in Mexico. That was his ploy. He would never chance to torture a girl in a way that could disfigure her body, which could destroy a girl's physical appeal, making her less worthy. He would rather apply emotional pressure on her.

Adela and two other girls from Mexico crossed the border illegally with the help of Mac's gang who helped those using fake documents, evading guards and even supplying transportation. Lara, a woman from Mac's gang, used to come to Adela's town in Mexico. She coaxed her into joining them by painting a rosy picture of opulence and opportunities in the States. "You will be the Golden Goose of your family. Not only will you save them from penury, you will even provide them with luxuries."

The idea was good enough to lure Adela. In fact, she had no qualms doing any work if she earned dollars in return, whether it was dancing, prostitution or anything else. But when she saw the true colours of her "sweet Lara" of the past, she became apprehensive and lost trust in her.

Now she was not sure whether this vixen, or the gang she was working with, was sending money back home. Adela was worried that her "consensual exploitation" was worthless.

The coquette Lara was standing at the bar, engaged in bantering with a reed thin man. Her cackling showed up her black gums. "Why could I not see her black heart beyond those black gums," Adela thought, "I was terribly naïve and trusting. ..."

Trusting ··· to a lethal extent. Wasn't that the thing with Jane too? She trusted JoJo. She thought Kalyani was jealous of her!

• • ● ● ● • •

Three

"THE TRUTH IS that I was getting jealous of Janki," Kalyani said to herself as she walked toward Jamunalal's gully. "But this was not the kind of jealousy that people ordinarily feel toward others when the later grows in maturity or prospers."

Looking back, Kalyani knows those pangs had not grown from malice. They were rather like Kalyani once became jealous of her own self!

This was a new phenomenon that the once narcissistic Kalyani had become self envious. The microcosm of her own images, which used to fill her with a sense of pride, was beginning to push her into an unnamed dread! Her own photographs were giving her heartburns! Posters of the film *Humsaya* – the film she starred in – seemed to mock at her. The film was never taken out of the can, even as Kalyani's run of luck seemed to dry up.

Despite this frustration, Kalyani preserved the relics with great care. Photographs taken during the shootings, stills from the movie, its posters and, snaps from her special photo session for the portfolio – all are now adorning the walls of her study-cum-living room as a part of an aesthetically done decor.

Two of the walls of this room are chosen for the display of her photographs; on the third wall is hanging an oil painting which Kalyani herself had done.

Kalyani did not paste her pictures casually on the walls, but had carefully put them up under the supervision of a well-known interior designer. The choice of colour for these walls is in accordance with the mood of the snaps. Carefully selected colours are made to complement the pictures. Contrast and symmetry are in aesthetic collusion. The layout of the snapshots is such that a few are presented in a collage, while others are dispersed separately on the walls. If a photograph shows a close up of Kalyani's plump-lipped pout, the other covers her large bewitching eyes, shot from very close. A still from the movie, taken in long shot, shows Kalyani happily roaming in a picturesque valley of a hill station – Manali. Placed above this is another still from the film, taken in mid-shot.

Pictures selected for display on the second wall are the close-ups of her mobile face, showing every change in countenance. If in one picture Kalyani flaunts her white teeth in a frozen lightning smile, in another, she has her hand under her chin, wearing a serious expression as if pondering over something. In a comparatively smaller snapshot she is simply smiling, while in the other, she seems to be in a pensive mood. A medium-sized duo-tone photograph shows her sticking her tongue out as if she is trying to make a child laugh!

A very large close-up of her face shows a solitary, tear-like drop of translucent glycerine, which allows her flawless, exquisite complexion to be seen by the onlooker. The close-up is so sharp and aesthetically right that the tear appears to be a glacier! Behind the transparency of this see-through artificial tear one can get a glimpse of the unblemished, clear skin Kalyani is blessed with. No wonder that these pictures have been so close to her heart all these years.

Looking at her own photographs for minutes has been a great passion for her till now. Though many a time she had rankled and resented the fact that her producers prohibited her from giving any press interviews before the release of the film. But the film was never released, therefore, she had lost the opportunity of getting publicity to be realized. Many of the posters, pictures, snapshots and other publicity material were prepared by the producer himself, but could never be launched.

Despite this ever looming trace of resentment, Kalyani never allowed these pictures to be moved from her sight, rather she developed a sense of pride every time she looked at herself staring back from the photographs. Looking at the beautiful girl in the pictures had been an absorbing passion for her.

But now, Kalyani had increasingly begun to see this fetching seductress in the pictures as not herself but someone else. She had started growing envious of the young and beautiful girl looking back at her from the snapshots. Burning jealousy was troubling her.

This was not the only thing. Much more was changing within Kalyani. Once as free spirited as a bird, Kalyani was now becoming a stereotypical self-conscious woman. Her growing insecurity was making her somewhat superstitious too.

Now here was the Kalyani who now was changing her spots and was ready to meet a Kapaldarshi Baba, in Jamunalal's gully.

Going by hearsay, Kapaldarshi Baba is able to read and tell one's future by merely looking at the forehead as if the forehead is a television screen, where a coherent train of future events of one's life is running.

• • • ● • • •

Four

WHEN KALYANI WAS leaving for Kapaldarshi Baba's *kuti*, Anguri made a suggestion that she would take any red flower as a gift to Milarepa, the Kapaldarshi Baba.

Why red only, Kalyani wondered! "Go and see for yourself and you will know why," Anguri said with a mischievous smile on her face.

As Kalyani entered the *kuti*, she was astonished by its curious setting. Milarepa was wearing a red dhoti and a matching red jacket. His tresses, beard and whiskers were all red, not henna crimson but deep red, as if washed in blood.

Kalyani soon found a corner and sat down on a mat which was also red. Once she made herself comfortable and poised for a while, she began to see more reds in the room.

Walking into the room were four or five disciples of the Baba. They too wore red clothes in sync with the setting. Though in a dire need to stand out sparkling among his apologists, the Baba's clothes were given a different cut altogether.

It was like a scene in a group dance from some Hindi film in which extras wear clothing that is one of a kind. The protagonist, on the other hand, being the main dancer, wears apparel that sets him apart from the others, both in cut and colour. This gives him highly individual characteristics and makes him the focus of everyone's attention.

Kalyani remembered a dance she performed in her film *Humsaya* where she wore a sky-blue gown.

The others in the group wore knee-length saris of the same hue. She was the mermaid in the scene ··· the extras were fisherwomen. During the shooting, while the song was being filmed and moving into the stanza white smoke from a fog machine billowed across the stage. From its midst Kabir the protagonist emerged. In the *kutir* too, Kalyani seems to see a similar scene. The only difference this time is that the smoke is not white, but tinged with red.

As the smoke settles down, a casket is seen. This casket is also red and it has been placed before Milarepa. Within this casket there is a man lying very still. When Milarepa asks questions to the man, his lips begin quivering. It is only then that Kalyani realized the man is not dead!

The walls of the room are cream coloured, with red stripes. The ceiling is red. Milarepa is sitting on a low wooden platform, which is also red. The small carpet on which seat is placed and the bolsters against which it rests are a uniform red. Scenes of the Himalayas on the wall are all framed in red. On a red stand next to Milarepa is a selection of fruits, all in red: two red apples, a bunch of red cherries and two red plums. From the low red seat, where he sat, there is a red carpet which has been unrolled similar to those that are rolled out for visiting VIPs. There was a red thread around his neck from which hung a same coloured talisman; a red thread was wrapped around his right wrist. For Kalyani this scene became a matter of slight amusement. In her mind she imagined a red draw string hanging from Milarepa's red underclothing. But her amusement turned to astonishment when Milarepa began to speak with the man in the coffin whose tongue was also red.

Milarepa in a deep, hoarse voice called for his speaker. Hearing this, the dwarf, clothed in a red surplice got up and quickly made his way toward the coffin holding a red-covered book. Meanwhile, a woman came and seated next to Kalyani. In a low voice she asked Kalyani if she had received her token. To this, Kalyani asked "what token?"

"If you have a token you would know where you are placed in the series of patients. You have come to have your dreams interpreted, your forehead read or your shadow measured?"

Hurriedly, Kalyani answered, "any of these, I have no idea of anything, but tokens, numbers and registration, this sounds like a doctor's clinic." "Exactly, you are here to get rid of your maladies. Milarepa is going to treat you. Today, he is first going to ask about your problems. If he believes that you can be cured by dream analysis, you will have to keep a ten-day record of your dreams. You will go to sleep only after taking one dose of his red herbs. If he decides to read your forehead then you will have to cover your brow with red sandalwood paste, given by him, at least for an hour. And if he thinks measuring your shadow will be the proper thing, then you will have to come tomorrow at twelve forty-five sharp, near the red wall in the backyard. …"

"What melodrama?" Kalyani thought. But this was one thought. Another thought was in a flux with this red flow; she was quite excited at the prospect of being analysed by Milarepa's method.

"… my wife was shuddering. I could see her cracked heels trembling violently … no, no it was not her heels, it was a wall with cracks … the cracks were widening with each shudder. And so! she started trembling so violently that it … brought about an earthquake." This was the elf reading out the dream of the man lying supine in the casket. Kalyani couldn't get to know the analysis Milarepa had made of the dream. The same woman came calling her after sometime and informed Kalyani that it's all right if she could not decide for herself, whether she wanted to be analysed through her dreams, forehead reading or by shadow measurement. Milarepa himself would decide on her behalf what should be the method of diagnosis.

Now Kalyani sat cross-legged before Milarepa. The guru, in a manner as if trying to assess something, touched Kalyani's ear, then her forehead, tip of her nose and then removed his hand and brought it back to his lap. Taking a deep breath, he closed his eyes and went into a meditative mode. After a few minutes, he opened his eyes and fixed them on Kalyani. Holding his gaze on her he asked Kalyani:

"Now, lady, let me know what your sorrow is?"

"My sorrow? My sorrow? I have no sorrow that I can put my finger on …."

"Then what …?" asked the guru.

Kalyani answered, "I am sorrowful, but …."

"But what?"

"I have no such sorrow, yet I am feeling such as if a single pea is hurting me though it is under seven mattresses."

"A single pea?" Milarepa asked sarcastically, "laced with the incredulous …"

"Yes indeed! A single pea beneath seven mattresses is what is hurting me …"

"*ohhhhssss*, a single pea! A red pea, a pea which is red…. And this hurts you …!"

Milarepa then broke into Homeric laughter. His laughter

caused people present to turn and look at him with startled surprise. Milarepa, meantime laughing all the while, applied red sandalwood paste to Kalyani's forehead.

After reaching home, Kalyani opened the paper pouch to see the red herb Milarepa gave her. It was a finely ground red powder with a pungent smell. As Kalyani brought the powder up to her nostrils, its peculiar odour reminded her of Rani Lantarani. The latter got her rich name from her habit of spinning tall yarns. "Gapodi" *bua* had another facility – she kept a small container in her blouse pocket which contained red powdered tobacco, strong enough to make the nostrils tingle. This was Rani Lantarani's *nasvar.* Just before she would begin to unleash her storytelling, she would open her little magic container and take a sniff of the powder. She would inhale it and grandiosely pass over her head. Then she would sneeze and it felt (to her) that all the doors of her perception had been opened. With this, she unravelled stories like a seasoned globetrotter.

"Gapodi *bua*, you have never been to a school, have never travelled in a train or crossed the boundaries of this city, then how come you know so much about the world?" you ask her. She will tap her index finger on your head or hers indicating, the cosmos! Our brain is not merely the size of a small hemisphere. It is the cosmos.

All three worlds lie herein. It is a suprafilled universe of your dreams, desires and phantasmagoria.···

So, that red powder used to take *bua* around and across the globe; she could trot the universe riding on the winged horse of her own waking hallucinations.

Bua whiled away her time gossiping, taking substantial pinches of snuff and consuming rotgut. She would sit in the *kalali* with menfolk and relish sips of the liquor, intermittently popping hot, spicy chana-chat with red chilli. Smoking bidis was another avocation. Lantarani was honest and courageous, something which her husband was not. Time to time she would unleash a steady barrage, of choicest "blessings" on her no good, freeloading husband. She would openly thrash her brother Ghunghru too, who was a master in sleight of hand. Nothing in the house was safe from his nimble fingers. As for employment, it was below his dignity to work. But *bua* had clean hands and she would never let herself to get into the smallest debt. It was in her lot to work and earn for herself. And this gave her the permission to talk authoritatively even when the son of the proprietor was present.

This reminded Kalyani of her parent's home known as the Lord's bungalow. When the original inhabitant returned to England following India's Independence, Kalyani's grandfather bought the bungalow. His lordship had long gone but the people continue to refer to it as the Lord's bungalow. The design and layout of the bungalow was typically English in style. Attached to this was a piece of land which could not be called a garden, it was really a farmland on which the Englishman had planted not just fruits and flowers but also vegetables. Mango, jamun, tamarind, *kabit* and plums grew there. This avid sahib also grew figs and mulberry with equal fondness.

During summer, *gulmohar* trees would appear covered with a fastidious crimson. In winter, the aroma from the rose garden would blow through the house with their royal perfume. An ancient banyan tree, which had found itself on the wrong side of the fence, sheltered a small temple of Shiva which the Laat Sahib had not removed. At the entrance of the farmland, there was a grove of neem trees within which was a sweet-water well. There was a canal running from this well, which went down, irrigating the rows of splendid rose bushes. Amidst this hybrid burgeoning "garden" the lord thought it fit to set down a small crop of sugar cane.

Sometimes he would grow local vegetables like gourd, cucumber and green gram. He, himself, would abstain from these, as his delicate constitution revolting at the thought of digesting raw grams. Ironically, since the sahib of the manor could not enjoy the bounty of his land, it was left to Lantarani's mother and father and their extended family to enjoy the fruit of his labour. Fate, it seems, was kind to them. From time to time Lantarani's father would fill a basket with gourd and sell it in the market. From say the two pennies he received from the sale, he would give one to the lord and pocket the other one. A typical example of the latter's attitude toward money was that he would toss his "share" into his pocket and perhaps continue reading his book, lying languorously in his rocking chair.

But when Lantarani's father Buddhuram and mother Hansiyabai's landlord changed, Buddhuram also changed. He became much wiser. The new landlord Basahib was sharp despite his years. Besides, he had an acute knack at keeping track of every penny that was earned or spent. Realizing the awareness of the new master, Buddhuram also shifted tracks and did not give an account of what had been earned. Similarly, the basket of vegetables was now carried by Hansiyabai. She was sly and conniving and made for the market while it was still dark and Basahib was performing his morning ablution.

But Lantarani was unafraid of Basahib because she had played with him in his lap. Basahib's son, Dadabhai (now Tauji) and with him Lantarani would play *gulli-danda* with gusto. One time, the sharp-edged *gulli* hit Dadabhai on the forehead. Dadabhai later narrated the incident to his mother, the way it had happened. This was alien to Lantarani, who thought that there was enough scope to live the incident with sufficient spice. Lantarani visualized to herself as to how she would narrate the mishap. She was dying to tell somebody and not finding anyone, the untold story seemed to grow within her stomach. Why provoke the ailment to increase? She urgently needed an audience to get rid of the growing ache. This desperation would drive her to find listeners in creatures like pigs and herons; in the immediate surroundings, riding for free on buffalo backs. Even a buffalo would do, its devil-may-care attitude would not deter Lantarani; she could jabber incessantly before the beast. Once there was demise in a family in the neighbourhood. Lantarani was called there to carry out ritual cleaning of the floor. There she was even hired for crying! This bizarre practice was a usual source of income for her! There, while sweeping and mopping the floor, she could hear the *Garud Puran* narrated by a pandit. An account of *Garud Puran* is one pertaining to heavens and hells, which, according to Hindu mythology, one has to face after death. Lantarani found it so scary and fascinating as well that she needed an immediate outpouring in front of somebody, anybody. While returning to her shanty she had to cross fields. Here she saw a scare crow and she decided that it was the one who could listen to her with an absorbing passion without being distracted! As Lantarani was growing up, many more household chores were given to her. And now she had enough people to listen to her narration.

• • •

Jane was in the process of being moved from Texas to somewhere else in America. For obvious reasons, the wannabe mafia types kept the girls on a short leash, shadowing their every move. When the girls moved, a fresh set of handlers, the crude hard men and equally rough middle-aged women, took over the job of keeping the girls on "their best behaviour." With the change of place, these handlers would also change. But for their names and features, inside, they were all the same in doing cruelty. If we called every such man a Mac, then every woman would definitely be called a Moll, a Lara. This would make them all alike and they are all organized too. Theirs is a big network, which is involved in trafficking woman and pushing them into prostitution. This network is spread far and wide from Europe, Asia, India, Nepal and Bangladesh to Russia, Romania, Herzegovina and Latin America. All the Macs and Laras are well connected with each other. Every Lara and every Mac wire rarely short circuit because of the skilled organizers. That is how transnational traffickers manage to run their shadowy business under the very nose of their own governments. Changing the locations of the victims also is an attempt to blindside administration.

Every time, Jane was made to change her place, she would also have to meet and mingle with a new herd of girls of different races. This time, the apartment in which the girls were being kept was bigger than the previous one. A wooden-floored room, in the middle of the apartment, was the one in which the girls usually slept and rested when they were allowed to do so. You could not see the clear sky from this room. It was devoid of any windows or maybe the windows were sealed. Though adjacent to this room was a staircase leading to an attic with ventilators. Beyond the stairs was a balcony with glass windows. Two guards, appointed by Mac, were constantly posted there to keep a watch over the girls. Sometimes the girls got a glimpse of the outside world through this window. During such moments they could see a small tree full of pink flowers, which, Fang told Jane, was a cherry tree.

Fang knew English. She reminded Jane of Lantarani *bua* and like her, she also liked to weave stories. But there was a difference between the two. Lantarani's yarns were spiced, inflated and full of entertainment while Fang's accounts were true and full of horror. She had one day recounted the hair-raising story of Lidia of Moldova, which Lidia herself had told the girl upon digging a little.

Lidia was rather a silent person. She would prefer to keep her thoughts to herself and let things remain unspoken. But, one day, she was utterly upset, so much so that she lacerated one of her customers with her fingernails. Her handler Mile had punished her for this by cutting KM 50 from her already meagre payment and left her to her own devices with a woolly-headed British customer who had a reputation of torturing the girls with burning cigarettes. That day Lidia went out of her mind because of that disturbing incident.

Through force or coercion, the mafia would bring in new girls almost every day, but that day the one they had brought in was merely a ten-year old kid. They had picked her up along with her teddy bear, for those special customers who relish the tender flesh of kids. Such devils pay unbelievable amount for their perversions, which they call their special choices. But this little girl was so unfortunate; they not only forced her to "serve" the favoured customers, but also the regulars. She was kept confined to a small cot in an equally small cell, her teddy bear placed nearby on a stool along with a toilet roll. This made it easier for Mile to come in at regular intervals and wipe her clean.

The child was put into this brothel for merely two days. In quick succession, she was being shifted from one place to the other, as a piece of human cargo.

Lidia was also being shifted to different locations within Romania. Now Lidia was not aware of the location and fate of the child but she was unable to forget her face, like she would never forget the face of her own daughter, Olga, whom she had left behind in Moldova. Ironically, it was for Olga's bright future that Lidia took the big step of leaving home. Now again it was Olga's future which worried her the most. The child reminded her of her own little Olga. She wondered how her Olga would be able to survive in this utterly selfish, dog-eat-dog world!

Lidia had been desperately hunting for a job, when she was in Moldova, but had always been left behind in a slough of despond. She would complain constantly and voice her grudges to anybody who was ready to lend an ear to her; in the same breath, she would ask the sympathetic listener to help her get some work, of whatever nature.

One day in a local shop Lidia chanced upon a woman called Natasha. Natasha was looking very stylish; her attire also said something about her high life, she was holding a handsome, costly handbag and was waving it around with an air of sophistication. Lidia looked at Natasha's dress with a covetous glance and then touched her bag as if with a deep yearning. Natasha was sharp enough. She asked Lidia in Romanian, "Yearning to own a smart bag like this for you?""

Y a ss ··· don't know ··· but yes, my daughter would definitely wear good clothes when she grows up," said Lidia.

Natasha started laughing mockingly, then stopped and looked at Lidia's drab clothes with a sneering smile, as if saying, "That is out of your limit."

Natasha knew that her sneering glance would be accurate enough to touch Lidia's weak spot with laser-like precision. As was expected, Lidia became conscious of her own fading lacklustre apparel. So while consciously trying to remove creases with her hands from her skirt she asked Natasha about the prospect of earning well. Natasha, as if waiting to come to this point, gleefully explained to Lidia that if she could make it to Italy and there become a waitress in a club then she would definitely be able to make a lot of money and there will be no dearth of food and clothes for her and her daughter.

"But I don't have the passport or documents required nor do I know any other language except Romanian," Lidia expressed her concern.

"Not to worry about that," Natasha assured her, promising to make all the arrangements. "After all, it is a good thing to help people in distress." Saying this, Natasha held out a slip of paper from her pocket, wrote a phone number on it, handed the slip over to Lidia and went away.

Merely a week after Lidia made a phone call to Natasha and arranged a meeting with her in a city near her own town. Natasha had told her to bring along her birth certificate, which she did but Natasha was not there at the place fixed for the meeting. Some other woman was waiting for her.

Lidia was disappointed, "What to do now?" she wondered, but not for long. Soon she gathered courage and boldly shook hands with the woman before her. Lidia considered her position, mumbling to herself, "What if the woman is not Natasha?" After all, she has been sent by Natasha. If the woman knows her job well then there was no harm in taking her help; she understands Romanian and will definitely aid in fulfilling her desire. Now Lidia was sure and decided to ask for help. She directly came to the point.

"How will I get my passport? Shall I have to pay for it?" asked Lidia. "No, give me your birth certificate and everything else will be taken care of," replied the woman, with a cold expression on her face.

Lidia extended her birth certificate. In return, the woman handed Lidia a scrap of paper and instructed Lidia to reach the address written on it, exactly after ten days.

As required, after ten days Lidia reached the place. A woman was already waiting for her there. But she was not the woman who had taken her birth certificate. Again this was someone else, other than the one she needed. But there was no reason to complain. The woman was in possession of the documents Lidia was expecting. Of course, she did not show them to Lidia but again Lidia did not want to spoil the mood of that helpful woman by asking her to show the documents, so she kept quiet. Now the woman took Lidia along and boarded a bus going their way. At check post the woman showed the documents to a border officer who seemed acquainted with her, ultimately they crossed the Romanian border.

In this new place, the woman took Lidia to an apartment where they stayed for the night. In the morning, the woman entrusted Lidia to a man and went away. The man took her to the bank of a river. There they met two more men. The foursome crossed the river by a row boat. Now they were in Serbia.

Lidia was tired and hungry; she had not been given anything to eat for a long time. She asked one of the men, in which direction her supposed destination Italy lay.

"When are we going to reach Italy? How far is it from here?" she asked but received no reply from any of them. After an hour or so, they gave a sandwich and a water bottle to Lidia and left her in an empty, single-storeyed house.

She was all alone in that house. Lidia spent the afternoon there with fear in her heart. She ate the sandwich and tried to catch some sleep. It was a broken sleep. Nightfall brought two unknown men with it. They were armed with two big, battery operated torches. Again they got ready to cross a river, in the dark of the night. By midnight, they reached a place which was buzzing with activity despite the late hour.

There were many bars in the locality, smelling of stale food and peopled by heavily made-up girls, decked out in frills and cheap, shiny clothes. Other birds were roaming the narrow alleys and alert to danger streets. Many young and old men were hovering around the bars or standing below street lights with or without girls in their arms. Also, there were men in regimental uniform, probably foreigners to this country.

The two men left Lidia with a man whose name was Marco. Marco told Lidia with a straight face that he had bought her from them for KM 3500, which she had to give back by sleeping with customers.

Marco had kept Lidia in an apartment with another ten girls. Each of them was given a small cell, which could just about hold a narrow cot. Lidia was sleeping with at least ten customers a day in order to reach the target forcibly thrust upon her. What was the option? She had no documents, no passport and no identity. She was lying at the bottom of hell's abyss. There seemed no escape. Instead, she had been shifted from one abyss to another. Marco sold her to Mile and she was taken to Mile's den. Mile was the person who had brought that little girl, who clutched onto a teddy bear, into the brothel he was running. This was the case which had spun Lidia's head.

"Poor Lidia, her story is really sad, but where did you meet her?" Jane asked Fang. Before Fang could answer the question their handler Lara rushed in. She did not like their talking to each other and her anger exploded with her landing a punch on Fang's solar plexus. Then she turned to Jane and in a stern voice ordered her to get ready with a towel and massage oil. A customer was coming for a massage.

That night, Jane could get very little sleep. At last, when she managed to, she and Fang both curled up on the same cot.

They were so tired that even the talkative Fang preferred to catch a wink instead of talking. In her sleep, Jane saw a big, pink teddy bear and a little girl playing very happily with it. She was very happy. This happiness was very soft, soft like a melting ice cream. She wanted to enjoy this superlative soft happiness. But suddenly somebody jabbed a pointed sharp knife into the tender, melting happiness. No, not into happiness but into the chest of the Teddy bear, ripping it open. Shreds of cotton dispersed into the air. Muttering "no, no, no ···," Janki started kicking and throwing her legs in her sleep. This might have disturbed Fang sleeping nearby. In response Fang nudged Janki. The poke of her elbow knocked Janki out of her sleep. Now wide awake, she realized where she was, thousands of miles away from her country. She felt very lonely. Yearning for home made her heart heavy. She pined for her people to the extent that not only the fond memories of her mother, sister and Lantarani *bua* came back to her, but also her ruthless father Ghunghru's images began to fill the space of the sad, empty heart. Of course, she longed for Kalyani and Gautam too.

In fact, it was Kalyani didi who gifted a pink teddy bear to Janki when she was a little child. Janki had liked it and had held it close to her chest saying, "My doll." Kalyani had corrected her immediately, "It's not a doll dear, it's a teddy bear." To which Janki had clutched it even closer and had asserted, "Okay teddy bear, but it's all mine and I am not going to give it to anyone."

More than eighteen years had passed since then; still Janki remembered the cut and the colour of the teddy. Even its soft touch was heavy in her memory.

Maybe in Janki's dream, the image of her own pink teddy slipped in with other motifs, the little girl with a teddy as recounted by Fang.

• • • ● • • •

Five

SITTING UNDER HER garden tree, Kalyani sniffed the red powder given to her by Kapaldarshi Baba. As she took the sniff it hit her brain and she remembered many old accounts. She recalled a day from her past when Lantarani *bua* paid a visit to her home. That day, Lantarani brought along not only her unique brand of *nasvar*, but also something more special, her pet mongoose Choo-choo. *Bua*'s five-year old niece Janki too had come along with her. Janki was a sprightly child with a spring in her step. She was wearing a frayed, calf-length *ghaghra*, a printed blouse, without a dupatta. The little girl's hair was long but jaded and dry, tied back in a single plait. Her skin was on the darker side but she had the large eyes of a houri; attractive eyes lined with antimony, which her mother thought was a secret protection from the evil eyes of others! "Come on Choo-choo, let's take a round," saying this, Janki was trying to ride the mongoose which was scurrying here and there, continuously. Riding it was difficult. After all, it was not a horse, but a mere mongoose.

"I found it on the farmland when it was tiny," said Lantarani.

"Whom, what?" asked Kalyani.

"Oh dear! I am talking about the mongoose, not about Janki. I did not find her on the farm; she is the daughter of that *chaddi-chor* (underwear stealer), Ghunghru!"

Kalyani started laughing at this description of Ghunghru, because she knew that Lantarani used curse words in full measure. Her language was often decorated with expletives; though she may not have meant it, still, Kalyani wanted to know why was Lantarani calling her own brother a *chaddi-chor*?

Kalyani knew that Ghunghru had a knack for nicking. In her maternal home – Lord's bungalow – Ghunghru was a distinguished character for lifting small household items. His feats of infamy included pulling off Kalyani's mother's and aunt's saris drying on the clothes line and selling them off in the market. He would not spare even petty things like a toilet mug or a chutney-grinding stone. While dusting and brooming, or spring cleaning the attic he would swipe small household articles.

But selling things off was a far bigger passion for him than merely stealing them.

He was not dependent on the saleability of the articles. Anybody can sell a diamond nose ornament in this world – but selling a stolen, old, tyre-slipper for a reasonable price would be a master stroke which only Ghunghru could pull off.

Coming back to his expertise in stealing not only things like utensils or shoes; Ghunghru was able to steal and sell animate objects like a cow from the home-dairy or an owl holed up in the notch of a neem tree on the farm.

Ghunghru's mother Hansiyabai, in her lifetime, tried her best to encourage Ghunghru to take some job up. Once she had sent Ghunghru to join a brass-band in which her brother was working. By Hansiyabai's standards Mama Bajaram Bapu was earning well as a drummer in just such a band. He could play other instruments, too, when required to. But when sent there, Ghunghru learned nothing except sounding metal rattlers in his hands. Yes, when he had returned from the so-called training in the band, two sets of band uniforms were spirited away hidden at the bottom of his tin trunk.

Of course, Ghunghru returned home without becoming adept in any of musical instruments of the band but, Mama bandwala's company propagated his knowledge of something else. Here, he met a Tantric and got to know that an owl is a precious commodity when it came to Tantra. But why would someone steal an underwear? Who would buy a stolen, used underwear? And what is the value of an old *chaddi*? Kalyani could not comprehend all these puzzles. So she threw questions at Lantarani asking why she called Ghunghru a *chaddi-chor.*

Who were the owners of such shoddy inner garments? There were males, females, both or the third ...!!!

Hearing the question Rani Lantarani burst into gales of laughter. Then she stopped, but her face flushed with a little embarrassment. After all Ghunghru was her brother.

Lantarani's face was like that. If you racked your brain a little, you could comfortably read it. It guided you more than her words. And it was really essential to read her face, along with listening to her, because you needed to make out when she was exaggerating and when she was serious.

The chart to understand her language was drawn on her face. The vocabulary said that when she was spinning yarns, her face would become round like a clock, eyes wide open and sparkling, with a gleam of some unknown pleasure; her lips would spread in an arc across her face. When she was lying, she frequently needed to fortify her conversation with an affirmation

"I promise", pinching the skin of her neck, between her thumb and index finger. But when she was actually speaking the truth "I promise" was not there, her eyes crinkle at their edges, the jaw drops and a sincere effort made her facial muscles to twitch. In her case the reverse was true. While speaking the truth, a nervous tic manifested itself on her face.

At the moment Lantarani was just talking. So her face was neither round nor elongated, and with a rather flat expression, she asks a simple thing to Kalyani, "How is Gautam babu? Does he live with you or ···?"

"Lantarani *bua* you are avoiding my question. I am talking about Ghunghru and you are bringing in Gautam instead," Kalyani got irritated.

"I am trying to answer your queries only," *bua* smiled, "When you were not here then also Gautam babu used to come here to the Lord's bungalow.

When Gautam babu got to know the odd actions Ghunghru had been performing, he burst out laughing at first. But when he stopped, he concluded quietly, "He is sick. Stealing undergarments is an ailment." Afterward Gautam had taken Ghunghru to some "lapolatory" where he attached a network of wires and threads to his head and had the waves on a plain paper.

"You know, I myself had seen that wave chart. It was looking like ··· you know as if a ghost with strings attached to his feet would have run up and down over that blank paper!"

Bua had been describing the brain waves with the words "up and down." While her eyes were moving round and round her face elongated at intervals.

Kalyani became amused. "All right *bua*, I have got it." So Gautam did not spare even Ghunghru from his experimentation.

What you are describing must be wave charts which Gautam might have had by putting electrodes on Ghunghru's head ··· but this question still remained unsolved, as to why Ghunghru had this curious habit of filching panties. What could be the purpose, who were the victims of his odd behaviour and who would buy such things from him?

"Nobody", and as *bua* said this, both the ladies started giggling helplessly. When the laughter stopped, *bua* spilled the secret, closely guarded till now, "he never sold the stolen undies. He would just smell them and throw away."

Even a bold woman like *bua* turned red as she suddenly spoke of the embarrassing fact. Both women stopped talking. An awkward silence ensued between the two filling the air.

A few seconds of silence was broken with the mongoose nearing them, making a "quack-quack" sound and Janki chasing it saying, *hush-hush*! All efforts failed. Janki could not ride the mongoose as she had intended to. So, exhausted and bored, she came back to the red-faced ladies. As Janki seated herself near the two, the mongoose followed suit and settled down next to them. The foursome was now sitting quietly together as if they were posing before the lens. And see, came the click! Rani Lantarani was the first to open the shutter of her mouth.

"So Kalyani will you go back to Bombay to work in the cinema?"

"Oh, no! Lantarani *bua*, it is not that easy to get work in the movies. My first and only film never got released. But definitely I will go back to Bombay and try my luck again," said Kalyani.

Before Lantarani could move the talk further, little Janki interrupted, "Take me along didi, I will also dance in the cinema."

"Do we need to tear open the screen to get into it?" she

asked innocently.

"Get away from here, stupid ··· see your face into a dirty water pond and you will know what your face is worth," said Lantarani; these bitter words were couched in what she thought was a charming smile.

"*Hee ··· hee*". Instead of sulking, Janki started giggling on what *bua* had said. Though a child, Janki knew it well that *bua* loved her and using expletives was a way of speaking for her, she was not cursing Janki. When her expression was particularly loaded with affection it would also be charged with added expletive.

Srr ··· rrr ··· Once again the mongoose was skittering out of the room. Seeing this, Janki too ran behind it and went out. Leisure crept back into the room. Moments of freewheeling chat returned like a coverlet pulled off the two women. Lantarani had brought out her tobacco pouch from the pocket of her blouse. While mixing the tobacco with her thumb on her palm adding a dash of lime, she started talking, "Oh Kalyani, I feel like smoking a bidi but I have finished a packet in the morning itself, so I have to be satisfied with this meagre thing tobacco." With a pause, Lantarani started again, "Can I please smoke one or two bidis here?"

"*Bua*, when you don't have the packet, where is the question of smoking or asking for permission," asked Kalyani.

"I will send that little idiot Janki to the corner pan shop and get a bundle of bidis for me. You know, right from the morning she was freaking around, rather than going to work with her mother" declared *bua* in a very melodramatic tone.

"Oh *bua*, after all, Janki is a child of just five years. Let her play. What work can she do at such a tender age?"

Bua's arrow was ready, "No, no, if she will not develop the habit of doing something worthwhile from childhood, she will turn sophisticated like you! We don't allow our girls to become fragile, in case they have to face domestic violence or are thrown out from their homes, they should be independent enough to look after themselves. In any case, Janki does not have to work full-time since she is small; she only assists her mother, maybe in dishwashing or things like that. Poor Saoo! She has to earn her own bread. As you know, her husband in just another freeloader."

"If you want to make her independent you should send her to school, *bua*, I will pay her school fees," said Kalyani.

Bua had the answer for this, too. "Flaunting money is not enough dear. You don't know our reality. Her father will snatch the money or misuse the other comforts offered by you," *bua* stopped with a sigh.

Meantime, Janki was back with a bundle of bidis. *Bua* fondly planted a kiss on Janki's cheek, then, holding hands both went away.

Six

IN SEATTLE JANKI was preparing for her next performance in a night club. Four Russian strippers accompanied her. The day before, there were two more girls in their group, one from Bangladesh and the other from Mexico. But today, only Russian girls were there with Janki so they were talking among themselves in their own language leaving Janki out. Naturally, Janki couldn't follow a word! Meanwhile they, including Janki, were all busy putting on make-up and readying themselves for the show. Just ten minutes earlier, Mac had given them a large can of moisturiser with the instructions that the girls need to apply it all over their bodies.

There was a large dressing table in the room. The make-up palette and shelves were holding a lot of lotions, serums, correctors and other paraphernalia.

The Russian girls were using the products quite carelessly, spilling them all over. One of the Russians had poured pink face foundation, almost nonchalantly, in a used tea cup! The other one, who was largely built, had freckles on her right arm, left thigh and on small of her back. The colour of her skin had a deathly pallor which was making the spots all the more pronounced.

In the morning Lara had given a concealer stick to this girl to cover the freckles carefully. While this girl was applying the concealer on her body, another one was lying on the floor, stomach down jutting out her derriere! An Indian boy, with a mane of shoulder length black hair, was tattooing her back. She was giving small cries with each piercing stroke.

The presence of a person from her own country gave Janki a sense of assurance, which soon turned into disappointment as the boy did not show any interest in talking. Perhaps he did not want to get into a scrape. He made his dollars, shook hands with Mac and went away.

Rising from the floor, the girl was now putting a belt around her waist, for customers to hang dollars. Trying to do so, she reached toward her back, with her head turned. This gave others a chance to get a glimpse of the tattoos freshly graven on her back.

Janki was the first to see the images and was highly amused. The boy had engraved the images of Ganpati and his vehicle "a mouse" along with a plate of his favourite sweet, *motichoor laddoo*s held by Ganpati, on the Russian girl's back. The other three Russian girls found it quite curious and were cackling, giggling and falling over each other to closely see the image. Perhaps they were appreciating the art work. But the girl with the tattoo was not at all amused. She seemed a bit sullen and peeved. She got irritated with Janki, too, at which her companions, in their broken English, tried to explain her predicament.

They informed Janki that her name was Tanya and that she was a chain smoker. In Russia the madams had to give her a fraction of her earnings to spend on whatever she wished.

There, she could buy cigarettes and puff on them regularly like a steam engine. From the time she began roving with different troupes in various countries, she was almost unable to indulge in her addiction. She rarely got a chance to smoke. "As you know, we are paid a pittance from our own earnings and, sometimes, not even that," said the Russian bitterly while rubbing concealer on her arm.

"What do you do with your money? Do you send something home?" Now the girl was inquiring from Janki.

"Home?" The question always perplexed Janki. A home is one's heart, one's core, an individual's reference point. What was her reference point? To whom did she belong? Janki thought but no sooner had her thoughts began racing than they came to an abrupt halt. Something else cornered her attention. It was the chain smoker. She was behaving strangely. She had opened a tea bag and collected from it the dried tea leaves and emptied them into the hollow of her palm. Now she was wrapping the contents into a paper, rolling cigarettes out of them. Her Russian companions almost pounced on her in an effort to snatch the rolls. The girl was shrieking in protest but, ultimately, her friends were successful in grabbing and holding on to the prized tobacco sticks!

"Why are you grabbing it from her, it's only tea, it's not harmful", Janki tried to side with the smoker, at which the other Russian explained why they had so suddenly snatched the rolls. "You do not know Jane. We can't let Tanya loose with those rolls. It's dangerous, we know her. She will go to the kitchen and try to ignite the roll directly from the stove."

The incident reminded Janki of almost the same kind of rolls, designed by her father Ghunghru. All sorts of weird people use to visit him to buy those rolls. On a small piece of land behind their shanty, he had grown a mysterious crop. His well seasoned hands would collect a kind of grain from those plants and wrap them into the rolls, using a special type of paper. Janki was too small to understand what the paper was really meant for but this much she knew that this was something like the *bidi*s she brought for Lantarani from the pan shop.

Ghunghru used to smoke only one or two of these hand-made cigarettes, the remaining would be arranged neatly in cardboard boxes. Such a box filled with rolls of these mysterious granules cost hundred rupees each.

• • •

One day Mama Bajaram came home and expressed his desire to smoke one of those special cigarettes. But characteristically, Ghunghru didn't oblige, being notoriously parsimonious. Mama did not have money to pay for the smokes. Mama kept quiet at this unspoken refusal. Fussing over could have spoiled the chances further; Mama was smart enough to know this. Unflappable, he was instead, chalking out a strategy.

Janki's mother, Saoo, was making rotis on the *chulha*, to be eaten warm and fresh. Janki was rolling the rotis. Mama and nephew were eating sitting cross-legged in front of them. Finishing the meal, Ghunghru lighted a home-rolled cigarette for himself from the log fire, without offering Mama even for courtesy's sake. But Mama was the guru; he smiled inside, laying down a plan.

After a few pulls, when his nephew's eyes had begun rolling upward, Mama looked at him slyly from the corner of his eyes, just to assure himself Ghunghru was flying and now would not be able to understand much of what was happening around him, maybe even till the morning.

After the meal, both of them went out to wash their hands clean of the dal which they had relished using their fingers. Janki followed them with a small jug of water. Mama, with his eyes, signalled Janki to pour water on Ghunghru's hands first. So she did. With his hands cleaned first, Ghunghru quickly went in. Now Mama washed his hands but did not follow Ghunghru into the house. Instead, he asked Janki to bring more water from inside. Janki went in and dipping the jug into the water bucket returned with more water for Mama.

Mama took off the thin, soft, red-lined *gamchha* draped around his shoulders and soaked it with water, immediately rinsing the *gamchha* by twisting it tightly. Then, holding it in his hands, he flicked the cloth once into the air. Out of curiosity, Janki remained there, watching him.

Mama went toward the crop and spread the *gamchha* to dry on it and then returned inside, humming to himself. In the morning, Mama and his nephew sat together sipping hot tea sweetened with jaggery chatting with each other. Janki was given her tea in a small brass bowl. As soon as he had finished the tea, Ghunghru felt the first rumblings building up in his stomach, and quickly he made for the open spaces to clear his system. Anticipating this moment, Mama who had finished his ablutions before dawn, took his *gamchha* and scraped off the granules of the crop adhering to the cloth. Janki and Saoo were silent witnesses to this delicate operation. Mama collected this mini crop into a piece of paper, folding it carefully and placing the *pudia* in his shirt pocket.

When Ghunghru returned, Saoo divulged nothing. She was apparently used to keeping her mouth shut.

She was well aware that there was a Mama–Bhanja hand in glove connection. They would favour each other to a great extent but, when the time came, they could cheat and blackmail each other or even set each other's tail on fire!

So he was afraid Mama may carry this to the Lord's bungalow. Mama was capable of doing this if he did not get his share; after all he was Ghunghru's Mama.

Imitating what Mama had done earlier, one day Janki tried to roll marijuana grains for herself in an ordinary piece of paper and was about to pull on it when Saoo saw her and gave her a stinging slap. That day, Janki's desire remained unfulfilled but soon one more opportunity arose, again by the "good grace" of Mama Bandwala. Thanks to Ghunghru, too, he would send his girls on any random job under the sun, through which they could earn a little money for him.

That day, the girls got the job of carrying gas lanterns on their heads in a wedding procession. Mama himself was going to perform with the band playing for the cavalcade. He also requested the band owner to give a piece of work to bone idle Ghunghru so that the nephew would do something and rake up a few rupees for himself. Though Ghunghru was utterly unskilled, he never tried learning play any instrument, so he was given the job of merely using the maracas. Uniformed bandsmen were at the forefront of the procession dressed in red coats with gold buttons and gold lace on the borders, red trousers and caps. There was a pink feather in each one's cap. Sixteen bandsmen constituted the group with an array of instruments – trumpet, clarinct, saxophone, shajaphone, baras, bass drum, side drum and *shehnai*. Beyond them was a *rath* fashioned out of a push cart, embellished with some tacky silver-coloured metal. In addition, two loud speakers were fixed on the cart along with a music system. The band master was seated on a chair placed upon the cart. He had a mike in his hand and was singing Bollywood hits in rapid succession. The band was playing along with him. Sometimes he would stop singing but order the band to play a particular Hindi filmi number. Occasionally, the *barati*s requested a song through him for the bandsmen to play.

In the procession, immediately following the band and its cart, were the gentlemen of the *barat*. Following them was the bridegroom on a mare's back, especially trained for the occasion. The mare made its way slowly, kept in control by the stableman walking along holding the reins. It was a sultry summer evening; there was a fire in the wind. Despite this the groom wore a full three-piece suit with a heavily brocaded necktie and a many layered traditional headgear and heavy leather shoes. He was repeatedly lifting and throwing the strings of flowers, the *sehra*, hanging over his face to wipe out the sweat running off his forehead. This showed a smile plastered on his face, despite the blistering heat.

Immediately preceding the bridegroom were the ladies. The womenfolk constituted the female family members, guests and women who were hired for singing wedding songs. They were not accompanying the brass band. But since they were part of the ritual, singing dutifully, they were not in tune with the band. It was a parallel affair. Though their voices never reached above the band, their singing was hardly melodious.

Following the women, was a decaying, discoloured wooden push cart; mounted on it was a diesel generator.

The generator had also seen better days, now old and rusting it was continuously emitting an unpleasant, low humming. A confusing mesh of electric wires was running the length of the generator to the heads of the children carrying the road lights. Janki and Laxmi were among them with these lights on their heads.

The street was narrow and the *barat* party was big. Still, it was proudly marching right down the middle of the street. The drivers of scooters, mopeds, cycles and other vehicles on the road were trying to cut from the left or right side of the *barat* crowd. Unable doing so, they took to honking and blaring horns sharply in desperation. It was already very noisy and adding to the clamour the groom's father was ordering the bandmaster to play dance tunes.

With this, the procession took a pause and the enthusiasts among the *barati*s came forward, formed a circle and started dancing in a frenzied abandon, amidst the shouting, whistling and clapping of the others. The fervour easily captured the bandsmen who then started playing even more vigorously and louder.

The earth-shaking dance, with almost *hoi halla* volcanic eruption of music added to the pell-mell and the already snaking traffic was caught up in a honking snarl. People getting prickly stuck on the road were cursing the *barat.* ··· A few blamed themselves for choosing this particular route and resigned themselves to that unique Indian belief in fate. The opportunistic ones saw this as an opening to boast about their *barat*s which, in their opinion, had created a bigger jam than this and consequently was a bigger achievement.

Unperturbed by the mess they themselves had created, the *barati*s kept dancing incessantly. This gave the light carriers a much needed moment of relaxation. They gave a sigh of relief while putting the lights down from their heads. One of these labourers was a pregnant teenage girl. She was so tired that after putting the lights down, she deposited herself right there, on the ground, cross-legged. Laxmi and Janki, as if on queue, put their lanterns down. Seeing no hope of the congestion melting away, a pedestrian lit a cigarette and started smoking.

But he could enjoy only a few puffs, before someone among

the unruly crowd nudged him heavily and the smoking cigarette was flung from his fingers. Janki was watching him keenly and, as if waiting for this moment, she darted toward the glowing butt to pick it up from the ground. The frustrated smoker was determined to stop her, so he quickly put his foot down, literally, and crushed out the cigarette beneath it. Janki had jerked her extended hand back, to save it from being trampled.

Alas! Once more an opportunity to hold a cigarette slipped through her fingers but as if this blow was not enough, she received a hot five finger slap from her sister Laxmi.

The opportunity presented itself again. This time in a new garb, though the bandsmen were the unchanging factor. A few days after the carnival, Janki and Laxmi again got a job along with the bandsmen. But, this time, they did not have to carry road lights, nor was it a marriage procession. Now they had to go with a funeral procession. The job was easier, too.

An old, rich man had died and his sons had hired the band. They wished to bid adieu to their father with pomp and evidence of circumstances. Mama bandwala was aware that on such occasions the family of the deceased generously throw coins, for the purposes of benefaction, along the route of the procession. Mama saw a job prospect in this, for Ghunghru's daughters, who would pick up and collect the coins, flung along the funeral route, and make a little money.

The job was merely a picnic for Janki. She rhythmically walked along with the procession, almost dancing with *raghupati raghav raja ram* ···, the signature tune for a funeral procession.

Laxmi would not do such a thing. She was beyond the age of innocence, far more elder to Janki. Saoo had conceived a few more times between Laxmi and Janki but none of the progeny had survived; they either ended in a miscarriage or for some reason, died in infancy.

So while it was mandatory for Laxmi to wear a grave countenance, people paid no attention to how Janki was comporting herself.

Laxmi was holding a regular, blue polythene bag and both the sisters were putting the coins collected into this bag.

The family of the rich man was throwing coins generously or so it seemed. But actually, the denominations of the change they selected were low. The misers were trying to fool the gods in the havens, by their false generosity. Maybe they were trying to show off their wealth and benevolence to the common people without spending much.

There was another reason that the sisters were unable to make much money. There were competitors, too, in the fray. The beggars, the kite runners and the street urchins also crowded around to loot whatever freebies were available. Seeing not much opportunity here, Laxmi decided to walk along the procession till it reached the cremation ground; Janki of course followed her.

The dead rich man was influential indeed, and his four sons were no less. It seemed they must have also been very rich and powerful, no wonder, the many enthusiasts were gleefully extending their shoulders to support the bier, also, there were some who prostrated themselves before the bier. Maybe the rich man was charitable and used to donate a lot, so when the procession passed through the bazaar a few shopkeepers came forward and paid homage to the deceased by quietly laying fresh marigold garlands on the bier. It was getting a reception at every corner, such that a marriage procession would!

When they were about to reach the cremation ground, Janki observed that one of the sons of the rich man started falling back behind the procession. She was wondering, why. But, very soon, she got the answer. The son had lit up a cigarette. More wonders were waiting for Janki. The cigarette in his mouth was neither like a bidi nor an ordinary cigarette. The colour of the cigarette was blackish brown! Janki was more amazed when she saw that the man was not using any match box to light his cigarette rather, he had kept the fire in a small metal container from which he could bring out the flame at a mere click of his thumb! Naturally, it was very easy for him to light a cigarette and he was lighting and smoking incessantly. But he would not finish them down to the fag end, thus smoking all the cigarettes but only half. In the process he had thrown quite a number of stubs as he went along. Happy and excited, Janki gathered the stubs and stored them in a polythene bag.

The family and relatives of the deceased had now entered the cremation ground with the bier, leaving the bandsmen and others outside.

There was a narrow stream running alongside the cremation ground, behind which was a temple to Shiva with a big *bilva-patra* tree in the courtyard. At the base of the tree, there was a circular stone platform, surrounding the tree. In order to unwind, the bandsmen sat down on the platform, relaxing and stretching their limbs. If one man was buffing his "baras" to a bright sheen with his vest, the second one sat propped up against the bass drum. One of them took off his uniform, folded in into a pillow and resting his head onto it, dozed off.

Laxmi wanted to count the coins in the blue polythene bag, but did not know how to calculate, so she sat down cross-legged on the platform and began piling the coins into stacks, according to their sizes. But she couldn't enjoy keeping money in her hands for long. Ghunghru while peeing on a wall nearby, happened to turn his head and saw the piles of coins. Naturally, as soon as he had finished, he swept the coins from the floor and put them in his pocket. Laxmi was highly disappointed but could do nothing. Surely, this was an alarm for Janki. She anticipated it was her turn next if Ghunghru got the clue, he would snatch the polythene bag from her and forcibly take all the cigarette stubs, perhaps, even by slapping her, if she resisted. She promptly started searching for a secret place to hide her possession. Finding an anthill in the recesses of the roots of the *bilva-patra* tree, she placed her bag there behind the anthill.

Since this was the temple to the lord of the ghosts, and was situated near the cremation ground on the outskirts of the city, the place was rather desolate. It was not yet dark but dusk had gradually begun to fall. A mahout on his elephant was returning to the elephant camp, situated behind the cremation ground. The tusker was tired, ambling along in its second nature. Whatever may have been the reason, the animal's saunter was producing a strange, halting sounding from the bell hanging from its body. This was making the ambience all the more mysterious. As he came close to Ghunghru, the mahout stopped by, as if there was some acquaintance between them; yes, there was. They exchanged meaningful glances and what one wanted was promptly understood by the other. Ghunghru drew a small pouch from his pocket and placed it on the trunk of the elephant. The elephant raised his trunk to hand over the pouch to the mahout sitting on its back. The mahout took the pouch; in return, he had set a currency note into the grip of the elephant's trunk, which the elephant gave to Ghunghru, bringing its trunk down. The two men smiled at each other.

Ghunghru was overjoyed to receive the money, so much so that he had forgotten the daughters still sitting under the *bilva-patra* tree, waiting for him to go home together. Though the band had stopped now, *raghupati raghava raja ram* which the bandsmen had played for hours, was still reverberating in Ghunghru's mind. So, crooning this desi requiem in the ecstasy of getting money, he left for home. The bandsmen had also collected their belongings, and had put on their uniforms again. Hanging their drums without playing this time, they too had left for the next destination. The sky was getting dark; the twilight *arati* began to toll in the Shiva Temple. As the sound of the *arati* bells started reverberating in the silence, the two sisters enthusiastically ran toward the temple to join the *arati*. They were the only devotees from the outside. The rest were the members of the priest's family.

After the *arati*, the priest distributed *chironji prasad*, which the girls gleefully accepted on the extended palms of their right hands. In a corner was lying a brass cup filled with *bhabhuti* (the sacred ash). The girls took a pinch of *bhabhuti*, licked it, as was the custom and came out again.

At the same time, when they were coming out of the temple, the cremators of the rich man were also leaving the *shmashan ghat*. Night was about to fall, so there was no possibility of more cremators coming to the ground.

This time, too, the chain-smoking son of the rich man was walking a few steps behind the others. As the man lit a cigarette bringing out an orange blue flame from inside his tiny tin box, it became a question to Janki, how would she smoke the stubs without fire? She looked at the temple with hope. A small earthen lamp was burning there but the priest was sitting near it like a guard.

Moreover, Laxmi was getting anxious now and was pulling Janki's hand, trying to drag her home. Actually it was time for Laxmi to assist Saoo in the kitchen. She would be needed there to roll rotis and grind green chilli and ginger chutney. Laxmi wished she could find a few *karonda* berries somewhere there so that she could bring a sweet sour flavour to her chutney. There were ripe *karonda* berries on their farm till yesterday. But Kalyani didi's aunt had collected them all to make *karonda* pickle from them, only today.

Laxmi hopefully looked around; maybe she could find some *karonda* shrubs here. But there was none. There were mostly *besharam* shrubs, forming almost a boundary wall around the cremation ground. Besides, there were a few thorn-apple shrubs laden with the fruits. Maybe, these fruits remained unplucked as these were offered to Lord Shiva. Perhaps some necromancer was practising his rites with these fruits at the *shamshan ghat.* Searching *karonda* shrubs, Laxmi's roving eyes fell on a strange tree in the cremation ground. The tree was dwarf, but the fruits growing on it were extraordinarily large and were red in colour. While she was looking at the tree, the priest came out of the temple and appeared in the courtyard. Pointing at the red fruits Laxmi casually inquired from him, "What kind of fruits are those?" Laughing at the question, the priest said, "No, not fruits, those are earthen pots carrying fragments of bones left after the cremation. The Dom picks the mortal remains from the extinguished pyre and puts them in these earthen pots. He wraps the pots in red cloth and hangs them on that tree. Each pot carries a marking, identifying the remains of the departed. When family members will come asking, the Dom will entrust the pot to the person concerned. Got it girl? If yes, then say *bam bhole* with me!"

Bam bhole, both the girls chimed in while looking at the tree with its earthen pots in astonishment. And this was the moment when Janki discovered what she was looking for. As the winds blew Janki could see flames erupting from a pyre.

"Fire!" she exclaimed and promptly plunged her hand into the hollow of the *bilva-patra* tree's base, toward the anthill, behind which she had hidden the polythene bag with its cigarette stubs. She pulled it out successfully, but, along with the bag, a few fire ants came scurrying onto her hand. The ants were biting her and irritated she started flicking the insects off her hand. Amid this chaos, Janki had lost her grip on the bag and it came down on the ground, scattering the stubs all over. Undeterred by the fire ants, Janki picked up one or two stubs and raced toward the pyre. Watching all this, meantime, Laxmi understood the matter clearly and she immediately ran after Janki to stop her from doing what she wanted. That day, Laxmi brought Janki home pinching, slapping and cursing her all the while. So that day, too, Janki had missed the chance to smoke.

• • •

Bam bhole Janki muttered to herself and came back to the present where she was sharing space with the Russian girls. The Russian who had tried to light her cigarette, on a burning stove, holding it in her mouth, was now sitting on a chair with her head down. Janki looked at her and a sudden wave of sympathy surged through her. She felt she could empathize with her. After all, trying to light a cigarette from a burning stove was no less reckless than trying to light it from a burning pyre, which Janki was so eager to do that day. That first time, long ago, Laxmi had stopped Janki, but Laxmi was no more there to dissuade her. Though Kalyani didi was present, Janki had never paid heed to her.

• • •

As Milarepa had recommended, Kalyani had started recording her dreams regularly. Before this she used to perceive dreams as merely meaningless hallucinations and wondered how

Milarepa would ascribe any meaning to them. He assured her though that he knew how to interpret her dreams and find their hidden meanings. Still, Kalyani would continue puzzling over their weirdness. For instance, she could not stop smiling while writing this dream.

"She is in London. ··· Wants to return to Delhi. She is looking for an autorickshaw which could drive her off from London to Delhi; instead, she gets a buffalo for the ride. One passenger is already sitting on its back. This is Kabir. Kalyani too, mounts the buffalo, setting herself behind Kabir. By pressing his foot down on the stirrup, Kabir kick-starts the buffalo. The animal gallops. Kalyani is apprehensive ··· since she has taken a buffalo for the ride, tigers or lions may attack them. ···"

The impact of the dream took Kalyani down the memory lane. She could feel the pull of the few days spent in London, while shooting for her film. "It was a long time ago, almost twelve years. London must be a different place now." She thought as she googled Hyde Park London, clicked on the option of the images and pressed "ENTER". Immediately, myriad images of Hyde Park began to appear on the laptop, awakening real pictures of that wondrous place on her mind's screen.

There was this pathway outside Hyde Park, flanked by sprawling trees. A romantic duet on Vishakha and Kabir was to be shot on this spot.

The situation did not demand that Kalyani be there. Since she was not required in the scene, the director had suggested to her that she could opt to remain at the hotel and enjoy a full-fledged holiday. But she did not. She came along with the unit to the shooting spot. Smitten, she did not want to miss even a single glimpse of her beloved Kabir. It's awkward, she understands, still she could not take her eyes off him. It was written all over her face, like everybody else in the unit, Kabir could sense that, he was still quite rude to her. Maybe he wanted to keep Vishakha under the impression that there was nothing going on between Kalyani and him. He was not in a serious relationship with Vishakha, though it seemed he was clearly inclined toward her. He kept flirting with Vishakha all the time, much to the chagrin of Kalyani. And today a licence for flirtation between Kabir and Vishakha presented itself. But it seemed as if Kalyani had taken leave of her senses; despite knowing the equation between Kabir and Vishakha, Kalyani was here to watch the shooting. Was she losing her mind? Yes, indeed! What else could it be?

There was no ebb in the tide of her madness toward Kabir, even after all these years. "One day Kabir will recognize my love and will reciprocate," she believed! But how? She did not know and meantime wove fantasies about him.

Just now, while putting down this dream her eyes fell on her own hand and she realized a truth dawning on her.

Though her hands were still silky and butter soft, a subtle change had come about. A maze of swelling green veins was appearing on them, souring her fantasies. Like, for instance, this romantic fantasy she often wove when she felt the need to muse upon something beautiful – Kabir and Kalyani are having a candlelight dinner in a famous restaurant. They are sitting across each other at the table. Kalyani is unable to keep her eyes off his sharp features. He, too, looks into her eyes. A waiter intrudes with a plate of golden baby corns and places it on their table.

Now Kabir is looking at Kalyani's delicate fingers which are moving in a languid, graceful manner toward a fork and then sophisticatedly picking up a baby corn.

Bewitched, he reaches for her hand which is all peaches

and cream.

Before she could feel the thrill of the fantasy she was immersed in, the realization about the green veins shook her from her reverie. Though she could not lure him even when she was still in the freshness of youth, Kalyani had a unique charm that strangely ignored by Kabir. Why did he find Vishakha's appeal hypnotic? Kalyani would never understand. What was so special with Vishakha, a little plump girl with a bronze complexion! One day, she suddenly grew such a large ugly pimple on her cheek that the poor director had to postpone a close-up shot for four days in succession. Still, Kabir had fallen for Vishakha's charms. "Maybe, because of her large bosom!" Kalyani had concluded out of sheer jealousy.

In her small town, Kalyani was considered the resident beauty like her grandmother, who had become a legend in her lifetime. Kalyani had inherited that beauty from her, besides the awareness and pride about her own good looks.

Kalyani was habituated to sit on the mountains of praises heaped on her. She was used to seeing people in awe of her.

Kabir's indifference was making her even more desperate. It was now a challenge for Kalyani to break his arrogance. This attraction, she thought, was a great passion, for which she was mentally ditching her husband Gautam. Her fantasies were the vehicles to adultery which carried her across the moral landscape in which she would live with Kabir instead of Gautam, in this ongoing fantasy of many years.

Their age was also a constant in these "delicious" home-cooked reveries, which were time warped in her twenties. There was more to this adultery – while the film was being shot, Kalyani never disclosed her marital status, to the unit, rather she gave the impression of being an unmarried prima donna.

Kalyani vividly remembers, the film unit had been put up at Hotel Prince, London. That day the shooting was scheduled for Piccadilly Circus.

Some local extras had been included in that particular shoot. Instead of directly reaching the spot, they had been called to Hotel Prince and since they were Londoners they had all reached in time. Scattered around, some were present in the hotel lobby, lounging on couches; others were standing around at the square chatting to one another, whereas some enthusiasts strolled into the casino nearby.

Now that things were running late, it would be difficult to recollect the extras, again particularly the extras who were the toffee-nosed whites. They were getting grumpy and would not obey even the unit head, though they were merely extras.

In a few minutes other members of the unit also came down. Everybody was ready to move and all were just waiting for the unit vehicles to pick them up.

Those who were in the lobby kept their eyes on the square, through a glazed glass wall dividing the two.

Kalyani, Kabir and Vishakha were sitting on a large sofa being Kabir in the middle, with Kalyani on one side and Vishakha on the other. Kalyani sat erect and alert, while Vishakha slouched and relaxed, leaning slightly toward Kabir, reflecting the closeness and reciprocation that existed between them. They seemed intent on playing games. Kabir would whisper in Vishakha's ear and both would fall apart laughing at their shared secret. Kalyani would die from a sinking heart but did not know how to draw Kabir's attention.

The reception in a corner of the lobby was attended by three English girls.

Suddenly one of the girls came darting toward Kalyani and told her in an irritated tone that she had a phone call from India, a certain Mr Gautam was on the line.

Kalyani got up to receive the call. Neither Kabir nor Vishakha wanted to know what the matter was, yet Kalyani loudly said, airing the information, "My cousin Gautam from India."

Kabir paid no attention to what was being said, neither had he any interest in knowing who the caller was. Indifferent, Kabir remained expressionless. Though Vishakha, being a woman herself, comprehended Kalyani's gesture discerning how pathetic it seemed. She smiled sarcastically. "Country cousin," Vishakha vented her spleen silently.

With a fire burning inside her, Kalyani went to receive the call. While she was talking, the fire ball exploded in her when she saw one of the unit vehicles reaching the square, and Kabir and Vishakha boarding it. Through the glass partition, she could see them taking the back seat, sitting close to each other.

That night, Kalyani had a dream! She had turned into a sticky spider. Running after a red ladybird-like insect; secreting a mucilaginous substance to catch the insect. The insect was running from the spider, which was mired in its prey's sticky gel!

But in those days, Kalyani did not practise documenting her dreams, though she used to make mental notes of her reveries and gave certain numbers to her specific daydreams which came to her regularly. The reveries, which became her favourite guests, used to be repeatedly woven and each was given its own title like the dream number three, which was titled, "The Dust of Gold." The first time Kalyani had this reverie was when she was very upset about Vishakha getting all the attention and praises during a particular shoot in an indoor location where a luxurious set of a high dressing table and bedroom fittings were ready. The whole interior of the place was done up according to the erotic theme of the scene. A large painting of a nude woman bathing under a cascading spring was hand painted on the wall, "There was a life-sized marble statue of Kamdev, the Indian cupid, standing against a 'chick', a veil of finely split lateral bamboo."

The bed was strewn with white fragrant *mogra* flowers. The curtains, bedspread, aromatic candles and pink cushions every detail worked toward creating a love saturated environment for the lead pair's romantic interludes.

The scene demanded that Kalyani be a simpleton, wearing a cotton sari, with the *pallu* covering both her shoulders while Vishakha's role was a fetching seductress showing off her curvaceous figure in a short, flirty georgette dress spangled with sequins. Vishakha had amplified her sensuality by choosing tomato red for her lips, topping the lipstick with orange gloss. For her eyes, she opted for a shimmery blue liner. Not only her face, but her whole body was made up with bronze foundation. Vishakha was looking a perfect catch for a nouveau rich playboy. It seemed to Kalyani as if the whole unit was slavering over her.

According to the script the character played by Kalyani had to establish her virtuousness, pleading her simplicity before Kabir. On the other side, in her author-backed role, Vishakha had to sweep Kabir off his feet using her flirty charms so naturally along with her already hypnotic looking Kabir, made it sure that the shot was okayed in one take. ···

Their success in doing a passionate scene with a near natural performance was a stab of envy to the till now carefully suppressed ogre of jealousy in Kalyani's heart. She was feeling hopeless and helpless. What could she do in such circumstances, except one thing? She did this one thing. She started weaving a fantasy, by exchanging her role with that of Vishakha. This in how daydream number three – The Dust of Gold – came into existence. In this reverie, Kalyani polished her body with almond oil first and sprayed gold dust all over, along with the bronze liquid foundation as base. For Vishakha she chose a thick, rough khadi sari, draping it around her in such a manner that she was covered from head to toe, not even showing her toenails. In this vengeful reverie, Kalyani left enormous scope for her to play with Kabir. As in reality, she did not permit Kabir's shot to be completed in one take. Here he required numerous takes in various poses till the unit packed up; rather, her reverie was never ending.

• • • • • • •

Seven

"WERE YOU BETRAYED by your lover or did you fall into a trap laid by someone?" Janki asked Maria Videnia. Maria laughed a nervous laugh, containing a bit of remorse, some lament and self-mockery. "Neither betrayed nor trapped, it was me rather, who was trying to lay the snare for a golden catch. My mother worked in a state-run factory. There, she had to slave for a pittance with no rest; even after she reached home, there were domestic duties waiting for her. My father too was a commoner. Once he left for a government duty on war-front and never came back. I did not want my life to be like that of my parents.

I wanted to make it big. This was the time when Russia was changing. You know now there are many in Russia, who are super rich. My dream was to get married to a man who owned a private plane, a yacht and ··· oil wells."

"A private plane!" cried out Janki in bewilderment. "How did this ambitious idea cross your mind? You said your parents were commoners ··· ."

"For two or three years, I had served as a nanny for an eleven-year old daughter of a super rich, self-styled aristocrat," Maria recounted. "The girl's father had appointed three bodyguards for her. I fell in love with one of them, not exactly in love; I was having a fleeting affair with Andrei. This time around the super rich divorced his wife and married a bar-dancer, Vera."

"What is so special about Vera, why did the moneybag marry her?" "I had asked Andrei. He replied in a gargling, vulgar laugh saying, 'Maria you should also learn the craft she is adept in and that way, I will become as lucky as your old cash bag." "Andrei had not just suggested that I learn the craft, he got me the address of Alina's 'become an expert in three months' class," said Maria.

"Expert ··· !" Janki questioned Maria in the hope of getting details. Speaking to Janki's hope, Maria answered, "yeah, Alina taught women the art and craft of making themselves more desirable in her workshops. There we learnt to command our vaginal muscles in a way that we could please our man enormously. We were even taught different poses of lovemaking on dummies so that we know how to draw maximum pleasure from the act and relay it to our partner."

"Poor Andrei, he did not know I was not using his money for him but for an ulterior motive that of catching a big bird. ···"

"But instead of a bird, you yourself got entrapped ··· by Alina! Right!" said Janki completing the sentence.

"That's right," Maria replied meekly and asked Janki whether she, too, was trapped and sold by somebody.

Janki wanted to answer, but before she could open her mouth Mac broke in. They had to close the chapter abruptly, but the topic of catching the birds remained with Janki, reminding her of her childhood.

Janki remembered that her father Ghunghru used to call

owls a golden catch.

He knew that in the market of greed and fear, how precious were these death-portending banshees! At the same time, they were the vehicle of Goddess Lakshmi. At the time of Diwali, Ghunghru used to sell owls to *tantrik*s, who forked out thousands of rupees for a single bird. On regular days, Ghunghru would sell the owls snared by himself or purchased from tribal owl trappers of village *haat*s (small town bazaars). Once he went to the hill station Panchamarhi and brought back a burlap bag full of dead owls. He sold them at a high price to Ganpat, a bird bazaar merchant.

Though Ghunghru had set his greedy eyes on the two beautiful owls that were sitting on a Bengal quince tree in the Lord's estate farmland, little Janki loved those two brown, feathery birds, capable of twisting their head around. Whenever she would stand under this tree and look up at the owls, they would reciprocate by seemingly beckoning back to her.

Parrots, sparrows, bulbuls, mynas and many other birds used to visit the farm they lived in. For Janki, every bird was a *chidia*, she couldn't distinguish between them, but she loved them all, and knew the different *chidia*s by their colours and their chirps and whistles, not by their names. Sometimes she would ask Hariyaliram dada. "Dada, what is this *chidia* talking about?"

Hariyaliram knew the language of birds. So he would immediately translate birds' talk into human parlance for Janki. Like what two mynas were conversing about, the lyrics of a bulbul's singing, what the sparrow community's gossip mill was churning out today, the fortune-teller owl, perching in the neem tree-hollow, had declared somebody's fate tonight and what did he exactly say.

Hariyaliram would very happily decipher bird tongues for

Janki, on one condition.

Janki had to stop her barrage of questions for a while, so that he could close his eyes and concentrate on the birds chirping.

In the evenings, lying under any big tree, with his eyes closed and listening to the birds' choir, was Hariyaliram's cherished avocation. He would even encourage others to sit on the concrete ledge of the farm as well and listen to the musical concert the birds held every morning.

Hariyaliram would say birds' songs are so melodious that Mama's band – an orchestral ensemble – stood nowhere near them. "These are God's own bandsmen," he would say. "Look at their colourful feathers, how splendid they are! Which band could afford to dress up their members in such flamboyant finery?" Hariyaliram would ask, addressing Janki by her nickname "Munia," if she knew what the bird on the branch was saying about her. "The red myna is praising your innocence," said Hariyaliram. "What is innocence, dada?" Janki would ask back innocently.

Like Ghunghru, Hariyaliram was also a regular to village *haat*s, but his purpose was different. He would not go there to sell owls or other birds but to set them free from the clutches of bird trappers. He would buy the caged birds put up for sale in the bazaar. After owning them he would open the doors of the cages to set the birds skyward. "The birds were imploring their freedom," he would clarify his reason for setting them on the wing again.

One day, Janki and Laxmi also visited the *haat*, along with their father Ghunghru.

Their mother Saoo did not want to send the daughters to the *haat* with Ghunghru. But he coaxed the girls into going by dangling a favourite carrot for each of them. He promised Janki that he would buy her a musical balloon with a reed pipe. A balloon which would be blown through the pipe attached to it.

Removed from the mouth, the balloon begins to dip with a little musical sound of *pin* ··· *pin* ··· as the wind gets released from it! To Laxmi he promised an *odhni* with floral patterns in block printing.

Ghunghru knew it well, looking at their mother's reluctance that the girls may refuse the offer. He therefore had fooled them into coming along by promising them their favourite gifts. His actual motive was that he wanted to sell fresh cucumbers in the *haat*. His girls could carry the baskets on their heads as "free" porters.

In fact, the girls didn't mind. They did the job happily. Ghunghru had also put a few possessions in a cloth bag hanging from his shoulder.

All the cucumbers were sold off as soon as they had reached the *haat*. Maybe, within ten minutes. Now the girls were not required to sit in a corner with the baskets. They were free to roam, along with their father.

Though it was a "Wednesday *haat*," not a Sunday one, the place was throbbing with life, there was a medley of vendors shouting and selling regular ware and some other curiosities. Buyers walked, scurried and bumped into one other in their gushing enthusiasm.

A few strides away from the entrance, there placed a Ganpati idol by a private owner of the god! Villagers were offering *laddoo*s and coconuts to Ganpati. Just near the idol was a stall where a man was selling flowers, coconuts, *laddoo*s, *chironji* and other offerings. Possibly the owner of this shop was the same person who had placed the idol nearly. Why "possibly?" For sure, the same person had put up the idol and the shop nearby. The shop owner was a superb showman, it seemed. He was playing a Ganesha *vandana* cassette on an ordinary tape recorder running on batteries, as there was no electricity connection in the *haat*. In front of the shop one of the salesmen was dancing to the tune of *vandana* wearing a Ganesha mask and *motichoor laddoo*s in his hands. He was wearing a saffron *dhoti* which was identical to the one worn by Ganesha.

The devotees, caught up in the festive spirit, were typically circling currency notes around the head of the man before offering them to the idol.

There were many makeshift shops in the market – push carts, bullock carts, wooden planks, small mud huts, tents – all were serving as shops. A toy seller had a unique way of putting up the toys for sale. He had a bamboo pole as the shop.

Many trinkets, puppets, colourful masks and models of real guns and cars were hanging from the bamboo pole and its artificial branches. The owner of this bamboo sales counter was playing a melodious tune on a musical contraption he had made out of spliced bamboo strips.

Next to him was a vendor selling a hot mix of grams and onions with a dash of lemon. He had hung a round basket with a rope around his neck, as a container for his *chana jor garam*. The vendor was selling this spicy fare with a readymade punch line from a famous Hindi film song, *chana jor garam, laya mai babu majedar, chana jor garam*. He was handing over the delicacies to customers in the paper cones, rolling them on the spot.

Juxtaposed to this was a *pani-puri* stall. In the same line was a sweet shop. Here, in a big round vessel was a heap of red syrupy *imarti*s. Like human beings, it seemed, flies too were greatly attracted to this mouth-watering dessert, so the *halwai* had covered the vessel with a netted hood.

He would swiftly and briefly remove the hood from the vessel whenever a customer would come; after executing an order, he would close the lid quickly. But the flies were quicker than the moving hand of the *halwai*. Plagues of flies would swarm in within a second in the opening and closing of the hood. So the *halwai* was constantly making a sound of *hurrr*··· *hurrr*··· along with the waving of his hands. Never disheartened by this insult, flies would quickly settle on other delicacies as there was no dearth of them in the *haat*. Very close to the *imarti* shop was a jaggery stall. The salesman was guarding the round jaggery bars piled up in rows. He was kind of surrounded by walls of the jaggery. But this high, hard and sweet wall was not protecting him from the flies; rather the flies were swarming to get to the compelling taste of the jaggery fort.

The salesman was Ramairam. He was balancing a bar of jaggery on an old, manual, balancing instrument, when the girls and Ghunghru stopped there.

Ghunghru was acquainted with Ramairam, so when he said *ram-ram* to him, Ramairam replied not only with a *ram-ram*, but also gave a small piece of jaggery to each of his girls, who were very happy with this largesse.

This had mitigated their disappointment of not being able to have any of the *imarti*.

Rolling the piece of jaggery in their mouths, they went along with Ghunghru to see some more interesting things in the *haat*.

There was a push cart on which hung frilled frocks and baby suits, looking like colourful streamers. A nearby sari shop displayed fluorescent saris with loud floral prints. Close to the sari shop in a small, rectangular box-like place was sitting a seamstress with her hand run sewing machine. She claimed that if a client gave her measurement that day, then she would definitely get her blouse ready by next Wednesday *haat*. Despite this claim, instead of letting her take their measurement, the women in the *haat* would not stop there, passing by smiling at the tailor. The reason for this was that these were mostly adivasi women who traditionally did not wear any blouse, but just covered their busts with their sari.

These women were actually interested in buying *kajal-tikuli* and nickle trinkets and the shop carrying these gewgaws was thronged by them. The shopkeeper perturbed by their noisiness shouted them into forming a line. The ladies merely laughed this off by saying that they are not ants, why should they queue up?

On the other side of the lane, there was another row of shops. A city returned young man, wearing Western clothes, was sitting cross-legged on a small mat.

Though his clothes were a constraint in this position, there was no other way. This man was selling spectacles. There was no eyesight checking. The salesman had laid out a piece of cloth in front of him and put a few spectacles and a hand mirror on it. Villagers would come and try on these eye pieces lying on the cloth and would choose the one which gave them the "most" clear vision. Some would look in the hand mirror to make sure that the spectacles suited their personality.

"Wow! Jiji look! There is an elephant," Janki pointed toward an image appearing from a short distance. Laxmi looked up and really there was an elephant in the *haat*. A mahout was sitting on its back. "The mahout looks familiar," the sisters thought, the one they had seen before. The ambling elephant was producing a *chrrr choo, chrrr choo* sound. The girls heard one more kind of *chrrr choo* coming from another direction. A wooden swing, with a circular moving handle and four box-like wooden seats, was going up and down. It was not running on electricity; its operator was rotating it with this handle. As the swing would move up and down full circle, the adivasi women riding on it would burst into uncontrollable giggles. Shrieking with laughter, some would hold their stomachs to control the wrench they felt, brought on by the hysterical laughter.

The swing and its excited riders attracted Janki immensely. She expressed her longing to Laxmi, who in turn conveyed it to Ghunghru, who promptly refused. "Get lost, what do you think? Do you think that whatever I had earned from selling cucumbers, will I squander it right here on your silly demands?"

Laxmi accepted her father's rude reply silently, with her head down, but Janki started throwing tantrums. She sat on the road with her legs stretched out and hands down touching the ground. There were no tears her eyes, but she made a lot of sound as if she was crying. Ghunghru was really annoyed for his daughter creating such a scene. He raised his hand to give her a whack, but stopped midway, staring at her. But it was not a father's melted heart that prevented him from hitting her. It was something else.

It was one of the silver rings she wore on her ears. Ghunghru knew well that it would not be that easy for him to remove the silver rings from his girls' ears. Their mother Saoo had acquired this gift for her daughters with much difficulty. The girls were not ready to get their earlobes pierced in the first place. She had lured them with the promise of getting silver rings for their ears instead of the thin leaf stem of the neem. Saoo worked really hard to execute her promise. She had made an endless number of garlands for a flower shop, until her thumb and index finger were sore, because of constantly holding the thin needle. There was one more source from where she got money but naturally after much toiling. This tedious job required her to remove kernels from dates.

Ghunghru observed Saoo silently until the work was done. As soon as she finished it, he started searching frantically for the money she must have earned. Inside the tea-leaves container in the kitchen, under the mattress, below the chutney-stone, she could have hidden the money anywhere. In his frenzy, he had even ripped apart the seams of pillows in the desperate hope that Saoo might have sewed currency into them. But despite all these efforts he could not get his hands on the money. A few days later he realized that the money had been used in buying silver earrings for the daughters. From that day onwards, he was eying these rings bought from his wife's grinding labour. And here the opportunity came knocking. In order to exploit this opportunity Ghunghru made an offer to the guileless girls. It was an opportune offer, the girls were to give him their silver rings and Ghunghru would buy them *imarti*s and would get them on the wooden swing. But it was on one condition that they would convince their mother Saoo that the deal was done out of their own wish, Ghunghru had never asked for the rings. Janki said a big "yes" to the offer and was looking happy. Laxmi, on the other hand, was now mature enough to understand the ruse, though she, too, agreed just for the sake of Janki. Now the two were on the swing, eating *imarti*s and the rings in Ghunghru's pocket.

After enjoying this venture the trio went ahead to see some more colours of the *haat*. Now they were in a section where peasants were buying seeds and fertilizers and selling their produce. There was no platform, neither was any stall. They were sitting on the ground cross-legged or squatting, each one with a heap of grain he had produced. Wheat, maize, *moong* and even heaps of cotton seeds were there, so also some irrigation equipment.

A life-sized weighing machine was placed here for the evaluation of sacks full of grain. The peasants called it a *dharamkanta.* When Janki came near it, she saw a large sack of rice placed on one of its pans and a man was putting and removing weights on the other. Janki found the big weighting machine and the act of balancing very amazing. Standing stationary she stared at the moving pans and the moving hands of the shopkeeper. At which the shopkeeper made an offer rather nonchalantly, "*Eey*, *chokri*, would you like to be weighed like this rice sack?"

Janki was delighted with the idea and said "yes," in a chortle. The shopkeeper had the grain sack removed from the pan, laying it on to the floor; he gestured to Janki to come over and ride the emptied pan, which she did. Now he started putting and removing the metal weights from the parallel pan, to get the right balance. And lo! In a trice the pans got equipoised, with the pointer, stopping exactly in the middle. "Oh, lord! this girl is just 24 kg," the shopkeeper cried out in astonishment. Janki giggled at his astonishment, though she never knew what 24 kg was equal to.

"Over!" said Ghunghru and shepherded the girls further, toward the other parts of the market. Now, in this part, there were not only villagers, but city dwellers also, roaming around. The question arose naturally – what were they doing in a village *haat* when they get everything in modern city markets.

But actually, there were some things which they really didn't get in city malls; rather they didn't even refer to them in polished cosmopolitan places.

Here, on a cemented platform, a chalk circle was drawn.

The circle was divided into checkers. Outside the circle, a man was sitting with a falcon perched on his left shoulder. At the man's command, the falcon would come down, pick up a dice with its beak and throw it randomly into a section of the circle. The owner of the falcon was telling customers their fortunes, according to the number of the square the dice fell and settled onto.

Behind this high platform was a sort of hidden market. Here, shopkeepers and customers were talking to each other in low voices, low enough to be called whispers.

Sitting on the ground, the shopkeepers were selling some small, mysterious items, in varied bundles, spread out on cloth. Some reed thatch-roofed mud huts were there; near them was a big neem tree.

A luxurious Mercedes crept toward this section and halted below the tree. A solitary passenger who seemed to be a rich man got down from his chariot. He was wearing a branded three-piece suit; a heavy gold chain adorned his thick neck and all his fingers had gem-studded rings on them. His gunboat like shoes shone brightly, almost like his diamond cufflinks. The man walked toward the cemented platform, before ascending its stairs, he spat out some of the betel leaf juice he was chewing, onto the wall of the platform. He knew that the force with which the red drizzle fell could sprinkle on and spoil his expensive shoes. So he looked down at them and heaved a sigh of relief seeing that his boots were not besmirched. He took the stairs and reached the platform.

The man with falcon offered the moneybag a high stool to sit. After a while the falcon was throwing a dice into the circle for an answer to the question the rich man was awaiting.

Laxmi and Janki again saw the ambling elephant and heard

its bell.

As the elephant drew closer, it was becoming evident to the sisters that this was the same elephant and the same mahout they had encountered near the cremation ground.

Ghunghru was watching Mr Moneybag with a keen eye and the minute the rich man began ascending the platform Ghunghru followed him and began talking to him, as if explaining something very important.

Meantime, the elephant neared the platform and stopped at its rim waving its trunk. Seeing this, Ghunghru now almost darted toward the animal, drew a paper packet from the bag hanging from his shoulder and put it on the elephant's extended trunk, which in turn gave it to his mahout. The mahout accepted the paper pouch gleefully but there still remained a question mark in his red eyes.

In response to this unspoken question, Ghunghru opened his bag little, just enough for the mahout to see what was in it. Getting a glimpse of dead owls inside, Ghunghru's bag made the mahout's eyes glint with greed. He gestured to Ghunghru to come along and to bring the rich man with him toward the mysterious market behind. Ghunghru informed the mahout in a low voice that old moneybags had already been informed by him to join them at Lachchhuram's hut.

After a few minutes, the father and his daughters were there in the rear end of the market. This was the owl market. Here aboriginal women wearing colourful skirts and glass-work blouses and men in *dhoti*s and turbans were selling owl's body parts. Amulets of owl's bones to ward off evil spirits, ash acquired by burning the owl wings to be applied over the whole body as a tantric ritual, dried owl meat – about which the aboriginal salesgirl claimed is for bewitching a person or over whom one wants to cast a spell. She was explaining to a gullible customer the efficacy of the dried flesh of the owl: "This is for the bewitchment of the opposite sex. If you want to control somebody, then mix this ingredient in his tea or may be in a sweet without his knowledge. Once the person eats this, he or she will become your slave. That much I can assure you," said the salesgirl.

"Hundred per cent, hundred per cent!" shouting this, an aboriginal was trying to woo the passing-by people. "Brother, sister, babuji," addressing the curious public thus, he was attracting their attention. "Want to take somebody into submission, make him wear this locket made from owl's claws! I myself have prepared this, especially for you babuji, for you! Take this – hundred per cent guarantee, hundred per cent! Your child is unwell, your mother ailing ··· your wife suffering from a long-term disease; whatever it is, take this concoction prepared by me and the patient will be all right, hundred per cent!, hundred per cent!"

"I have the recipe to make every desire come true and the remedy to overcome your every sorrow. I can guarantee you this. ···"

"Want to mould somebody's mind to think on your lines," then take this *mayajal*, a man claimed loudly.

The hubbub was making it increasingly difficult to hear anything clear, still one could catch pieces of phrases. "Look at this untended wild garlic, it will save your child from the evil eye ··· buy this *hathajoda*, put it in your safe along with your money and the money will be multiplied. ··· Babu, brother, sister look here, take this if you have a rival at work ··· this is going to finish him without him even knowing. An enemy always ready to sour your desire to get something ··· your wife neglects you ··· look,

Mr! I know your wife doesn't even look at you ··· eat this real Shialsing. I have gleaned it from deep woods ··· just have two or three doses and your work will be done. ··· She herself will come to you, no need for wooing her anymore."

"Bhaiya, my mother has poor night vision, is there any remedy?" an obvious urbanite, dressed in suit, asked a tribal salesman. The salesman immediately gave him an ingredient. "This is owl's eye powdered. Give this to your mother mixed in desi ghee made from cow's milk only, not buffalo's milk."

"I have many more things which are very-very special and exclusive," the travelling doctor claimed. "though they are a little costly, their results are marvellous," saying this, the persistent salesman started showing some of his mother-cure-alls." "This is owl's brain. If anyone has a seizure, give it to him. ··· Now I have this concoction of owl eyes, brain and ears. Guile must be used to put some in regular food that is to be given to the person you want to bring into your thrall. So the person who eats this will be your slave forever. That is my guarantee. If this does not happen then I will become your slave. ···!! You see, no lies. I am at stake. Trust me."

In this market of deception, guile and bewitchery everybody was swearing on trust.

But this was very small a thing in comparison to what was coming next.

The salesmen in the hovels behind this owl market were not ingenuous aboriginals like here, but were cunning *tantrik*s. In the owl market there were many customers from simple villagers to some what sophisticated citizens. The visitors to these huts were sporadic, entering them in a sly manner. They were not here to control mortals but were here to enslave Lakshmi, the goddess of wealth. Naturally, they were rich and greedy enough to attempt making more money for their already bursting pockets. So if any of them was able to pay 3 to 5 lakh rupees, he would be entitled to bathe in rare golden grey owl's blood!

The *tantrik*'s middleman would convince him that Goddess Lakshmi would be at his command and after this rite; there would also be a special offer for Diwali night. According to the *tantrik*, after an exclusive ritual performed on this night, the owl begins to talk in a human voice, and becomes omniscient to give clues to hidden treasures! The offer is, "Spend a few lakh and Lakshmi will be at your feet, along with her vehicle, the owl."

The corpulent rich man present in the market was to be brought to the *tantrik*'s hut and made to participate in one of the *tantrik* rites.

The mahout was the *tantrik*'s middleman, while Ghunghru served as an agent to the mahout. So it was left to Ghunghru to persuade, even lure the rich man to the hut. At this point his daughters, he felt, were turning out to be the obstacle in the scheme. He repented over his own decision to bring the girls along to the market, though his resentment did not last for long. Soon he was to realize that his elder daughter was actually an asset not a liability.

The mahout was ogling at Laxmi right from the beginning. Acutely aware of this ugly leer, as girls of her age always are, she tried to avoid his gaze by drawing her sari *pallu* over the vertical half of her face, like a curtain. As soon as they entered the hut, they detected a peculiar smell of *dhooni* smoke. In a big brass chalice filled with chips of cowdung cake, a small fire was burning, emitting grey, aromatic, pungent fumes.

Sitting near the chalice was the *tantrik*, Lachchhuram alias Akbar, attired in a black *lungi* and black *kurta* with a green stole around his neck. Showing up now and then from under the stole was a string of cowries.

A woman, supine on a thin mattress nearby, was looking at the roof blankly. Her legs were covered with a checked blanket.

Meantime, the mahout also came in, leaving the elephant outside; the mahout and the *tantrik* exchanged shifty smiles as they came face to face. The *tantrik*'s *surma*-lined eyes glinted with cupidity as he looked at the mahout.

"I have caught a golden goose," said the mahout.

"Then where is it?" asked Lachchhuram pointing a finger at Ghunghru, "he doesn't look like one."

"No, no! Not that pitiful blackfaced loser! The moneybag I have found is on his way, he might be reaching here anytime now," said the mahout quickly to reassure the *tantrik*.

"What does he look like? Someone going to offer a high-priced puja or the one who is able to spare only a few hundred?" asked the *tantrik*.

"In a mood to expend a few lakh, the desperate man seems to be very low on luck these days, otherwise he would not have wandered into a village *haat* like this wearing a heavy gold chain," the mahout presented his quick analysis and looked at Ghunghru for an affirmation.

"Am I right Ghunghru? What do you say?"

"Hee ··· Hee ···" Ghunghru simpered in reply.

Now it was Lachchhuram's turn to say something. "But my Bhairavi is down with fever. Without her, vital rites are not possible."

"Would any other girl do?" asked the mahout. While he hurled his question at Lachchhuram, his head was turned slightly toward Laxmi.

"My Bhairavi is a highly-trained person, stupid! No ordinary girl can endure going to the cremation ground with me on a black moonless night," said Lachchhuram.

"But we cannot let go of this rich man, we need to bind him … !"

"Yes, of course, don't let him to go, keep him engaged somehow till Diwali night. Otherwise also the Diwali rite is the most efficacious of all we do …," said the *tantrik* and then abruptly declared … "now, all of you go … leave the place. …"

"Come, come, we should go home now," said Ghunghru almost pushing his girls out of the hut.

• • •

"Come, come, Mac is calling us girls, the van is ready." Maria's voice drew Janki out of her reverie.

• • •

For Laxmi, the chapter did not close that night with the *tantrik* saying, "No other girl will do. Only my Bhairavi is capable enough."

Meanwhile, Bhairavi's condition had worsened and she subsequently died before Diwali. So now, the *tantrik* was perforce to take Laxmi (or any other girl) as his Bhairavi.

"Now the *tantrik* needs a new Bhairavi" was a great pretext for the mahout, who would now, with this excuse, drop in more often at Ghunghru's place, though the ulterior motive was to possess the lass for himself, he was fooling Ghunghru in the name of the *tantrik*. It is a different matter altogether, though, that Ghunghru was not the ultimate authority when it came to giving permission to his girls. Saoo would sit on them like a snake on a treasure, guarding them. True, the girls had to work outside their home, but then they always had to be home before it got dark. Saoo was a strict disciplinarian in this matter; she would check their records from time to time. In these circumstances it was difficult, almost impossible, for Ghunghru to "loan" her girl for a *tantrik* puja on a dark Diwali night, in the cremation ground. So touching his own ears and sticking his tongue out, he said a resounding "no!" to the mahout, who nevertheless did not stop pursuing him. It rained very hard that night, with the thunder accompanying the downpour. It was quite dark outside, except for the occasional flashes of lightning across the sky. The power, too, went off with the rain and the storm.

A single low-powered bulb, emitting a weak light in the hut, also went off. Now the flickering flame of the logs burning in the *chulha*, over which Saoo was cooking the dinner, was the only light to see by.

In the yellow glow of this flame, she was watching with immense satisfaction the innocent faces of her girls, eating the simple meal happily. This was a moment of great fulfilment for Saoo. Her daughters' very existence gave meaning to her life. She lived for them, definitely not for Ghunghru.

"But think of the devil and the devil appears." A dripping Ghunghru entered the hut.

Saoo immediately got up and handing him a towel returned to the *chulha*. After drying himself Ghunghru also sat down near his daughters and asked for dinner. Although there were not enough bowls to serve soups or curries with the food, Saoo would handle this situation in a practised manner. She would put a small piece of wood below the plate to keep it slightly inclined and serve the curry for the person to eat without inconvenience. It was a handy piece of wood. In the same manner, she served dal in Ghunghru's plate along with eight rotis and some garlic chutney.

Ghunghru began to eat the serving with relish by closing his eyes in ecstasy! While doing so, he asked for more dal, which Saoo had forgotten to serve immediately. Janki meantime requested Saoo to feed her a morsel with her own hands, a great gesture of love for Janki.

But Ghunghru felt neglected by this and not being served immediately was considered by him an interruption in his pleasure of eating. Vexed, he hurled the plate toward Saoo. Angered, she retaliated by tearing off his shirt. Ghunghru lunged and pulled her hair. Not to be outdone, Saoo struck back by digging her nails into his arms.

Scared by the escalating fight, the girls started crying. This was reason enough for Saoo to surrender first.

Now Ghunghru was thrashing her and she was taking it without fighting back. At this very instant, the lights came back. The little yellow bulb, began to shine again. With this, Ghunghru came back to his place and Saoo to hers, resuming her serving Ghunghru – chutney and rotis on a fresh plate.

Seeing things coming back to normal, Ghunghru decided it was definitely the right time to broach the topic of sending Laxmi for the *tantrik* puja.

He addressed Saoo, "Listen to me oh, dumb woman! What is the harm in making a few extra rupees. We have nothing to lose in this; on the contrary we will gain something Lachchhuram is not asking to sleep with your daughter. He will send her back after the puja. It is just that they need a woman for the *tantrik* rites."

"Dumb, you! and your forefathers ···, not me." Retorted Saoo, "don't you understand, if a couple is required to attend a rite, the man and the woman need to be married. Then what is it here? Only a lecherous man would ask for a virgin to sit through a rite."

Ghunghru had tried to hide the fact from Saoo that it is a black tantra not a simple puja; but she sensed it. Anyway, now it was time for them to go to bed. The need that drives a man to assert his authority welled up inside Ghunghru. He had to go soft on Saoo, maybe, for a while.

He was waiting for the girls to fall asleep, so that he can take Saoo to the cot kept behind a curtain.

After a while, Janki was swimming in a deep slumber. But Laxmi, laying still, pretended to sleep, hearing the *chrr ··· chrr ···* coming from the cot behind the screen. Then, she did not know when she was lost in her own world of sleep.

The weather was bad outside and there could be more power cuts during the night so Saoo had kept a paraffin lamp handy, ready with oil and wick and a match box, beside her cot. "But that night the lights did not go and the lamp remained unlit."

After every dark night comes a morning, it happened that day too. But the morning was not bright, rather it was foreboding.

Since it had rained all night, everything around was damp and slushy, so much so that the compost, collected in a pit had turned marshy. From a group of red-faced monkeys, jumping and vaulting on the trees, one fell right into the compost pit. The monkey was desperately thrashing its limbs in an effort to escape from the muck, but only sank deeper. "*Cree ··· cree ··· cree ···*" the monkey shrieked helplessly.

Its companions meanwhile gathered around the pit and were whooping collectively, a jeering audience. Even the birds had begun to sound an alarm instead of singing full throatedly. In the mansion, Kalyani's Tauji was in a state of deep concern. A monkey symbolizes the Hindu deity Hanuman, so if one dies within the estate it would bring bad luck to the owner. Also it would be considered a desecration of the place. In that case the deity would have to be appeased by performing a havan.

The monkey was to be saved at any cost, so Tauji sent for Hariyaliram who knew the language of nature.

Hariyaliram in fact had told Saoo that in the morning he had overheard two owls chatting with each other. "the owls, which could foresee the future, seemed anxious about some imminent death in the estate," said Hariyaliram.

The owls were right, despite the numerous efforts to save it, the monkey had eventually died. Tauji became very perturbed by this development. So when Hariyaliram suggested that it was now time to call in the municipality to dispose of the carcase, Tauji refused the suggestion outright. He said he was willing to cremate the monkey with all the sacred rites. A popular brass band should accompany the funeral procession, he decided.

According to the ritual the monkey was bathed and ghee smeared all over its body. All this was done by Hariyaliram whose role was up to this point. Thereafter a brahmin was called to perform the main rituals.

A *dhoti* with a golden border was bought to dress the monkey. The *dhoti*, probably, was designed for children to wear on festivals like Diwali and had an elastic band to hold it up. This was just right for the monkey.

A sacred thread had been put across the monkey's chest; a red *kumkum* mark was put on its forehead with a few grains of rice stuck onto it.

Janki was very keen to watch the last rites of the monkey. But Saoo explained to her that at the moment only the preparations were going on and the funeral would be performed in the evening when all of Tauj's relatives had gathered there. With this excuse Saoo had managed to bring Janki back to their hut.

Tauji had no children of his own. His mentally challenged, younger brother had just one descendant – Kalyani. A compulsory sterilization programme had been instituted by the government. Government officials, in a bid to fill their ledgers, forced people into vasectomy. Not only the married men with two or more children but also old men long past their prime, young boys who had not even reached puberty, unmarried young men and others were coerced, forced or cheated into being sterilized.

But, of all, the easiest target was the patients from the psychiatric hospital. There was no fear of them ever going to the police to lodge a complaint. True, that a little physical force would be required to bring in a kicking and screaming patient to the doctor's table. But once he was there the macabre work was done. This is what had happened to Kalyani's papa. That day he had been to the psychiatric hospital; while he was under the effect of some medicine given to him there, the government doctor on duty, dragged him to the operation table and sterilized him, against his will. Knowing this, Tauji was devastated.

The only hope of sometime getting a male heir for the family was destroyed.

Being an orthodox ritualist, Tauji believed not only in religious traditions but also in tradition embedded old wives tales. He had a great fixation for making offerings and celebrating festivals replete with religious fervour. He would invoke the small gods and supplicate different dieties from time to time! There was no male heir in the family who could be the centre of all this. So animals became the focal point of his religious obsessions. He would continue his traditional activities with anything except dogs among animals and lower-caste people among human beings. So he had created many occasions to celebrate traditional observances.

Once, the status of a cow with a calf was solemnized with great ostentation. When a new pair of oxen was bought for the ploughing season, that occasion too was celebrated with much fanfare.

When there was no reason to celebrate; occasions were created.

Tauji had once organized marriage function in honour of Mrs and Mr Frog! It was supposed to be the rainy season, but there were no rains.

Desperate eyes looked skyward for clouds. A clairvoyant suggested that there would be rains if the rain gods were propitiated by tying the nuptial knot between two frogs, male and female!

The betrothed pair had been kept in a small basket with the male frog's right hind leg tied to the female's left hind leg with a sacred cord known as *mauli*; The *mauli*-tied pair was circled seven times around a small fire, like the seven *fera*s in a marriage. And this frog-wedding function was celebrated with a feast. As it happened, rains followed the feast and Tauji's beliefs were further validated. So when it came to the monkey's last rites, Tauji was convinced that after the *sanskar* the monkey would get easy entry to Vaikunth Dham (the kingdom of God). And since it was going there it would take along a good impression about Tauji in person.

It was a Saturday and on that day Laxmi and Janki were to go on a bizarre, but serious errand. Saoo had taken on rent two small iron containers, with one black idol of Saturn (the Shanidev deity) placed in each. The small containers had handles so that the girls could carry them. Saoo had already placed a few marigold flowers in each container. What Laxmi and Janki had to do was to go door to door with the rented diety, asking for oil and money, shouting. "Hey, it's Saturday, pour some oil on Shanidev and wither away all your storms!"

Those who are plagued by misfortunes, students preparing for their exams, a father searching for a suitable boy for his daughter, all would pour oil over the idol and drop a few coins into the container. In the evening, when the girls would return home, Saoo had to collect the oil in bottles and wipe the coins with a clear cloth. The collected oil and the coins would be given to the owner along with his basins and idols. The girls would be paid a few rupees for their day-long job, by the idol owner.

In the evening when the girls returned home, they saw a crowd gathered right at the entrance of the estate. None of them was related to Tauji; rather, most were the urchins from the nearby slum.

On one side of the passage, leading inside the estate, lay red and white winding sheets, garlands, flowers and *gulal.* The *dhoti*-clad monkey reclined neglected, on a ladder, as nobody was interested in readying the bier.

As soon as the girls set their feet within the estate, the onlookers began to retreat, leaving a passage for them, in a manner as if they were queens! A hush had fallen over the crowd. As the girls moved in further, they saw an elephant standing under the big *maulshree* tree. A little distance away, its mahout was seated on a stone for want of a bench.

The girls thought, Tauji has called so many people for the monkey's funeral. So it seems he has organized it grandly;

definitely, he would have called a brass band too and along with that Mama Bajaram might also have come. But he had not, neither was the brass band.

Instead, two or three policeman could be seen from afar toward the hut. As the girls reached near the well, they found that the policemen were questioning Ghunghru who, with a long face, was nodding gravely.

Nearby, Hariyaliram was pacing anxiously up and down, while Lantarani had thrown herself on the floor and was ululating.

• • •

One of the four Russian girls was putting liquid mascara on her eye lashes, a fleck of which by mistake went into her eye. As a result, black tears began to roll down her cheek. This had smudged her make-up.

Irritated, she was cleaning her cheeks with cotton dabbed in cleansing milk, mumbling and fretting all the while.

The other one was painting her nails, leisurely. The third was shaping her lips with lip liner, to fill it with crimson red lip gloss. Just then, the fourth one let out a shrill cry, because she had by mistake burnt the toast she was making. This charring smell of something burning was what Janki could never put out of her mind. The stink of Saoo's charred skin was embedded deep in her mind. When the incident was still recent, the typical stink of charred skin almost always haunted Janki. She even hated eating hot, fresh rotis because she used to get the same malodour from them. With time, the force of the feeling reduced. The anguish subsided gradually. She grew up and her world had changed completely. Still, even now, if something burns, its smell rings the disturbing memory of Saoo's charred skin in Janki's mind.

She had forgotten Saoo's face, but not the smell of the burnt human flesh.

Janki could never, in her heart, exonerate Ghunghru, though Saoo had declared him innocent in her dying statement. The reason she had cited for her burns was this: while lighting the paraffin lamp, unknowingly her sari *pallu* caught fire.

Though the statement was legally registered by the police, still people related to Saoo did not believe it. They theorized that Saoo had spared Ghunghru for the sake of her daughters. The daughters themselves were suspicious and were not ready to buy the theory of the sari *pallu* catching fire accidentally.

People had many persisting doubts why had she been lighting a lamp at noon when the sun was high in the sky. Saoo and Ghunghru had a quarrel the previous night, so this possibility also remained that they had picked it up again in the afternoon which could have culminated in the misery. Right, Ghunghru would not have dared to set Saoo alight, but perhaps out of anger she had herself transformed into a human torch and Ghunghru, being a coward, did not come forward to save her! He may have been scared after seeing the flames engulfing Saoo and fled for his own life, leaving Saoo alone!

Whatever may be the case, the truth that the seeds of doubt that their father could be a murderer would always be in the mind of Laxmi and Janki.

Ghunghru himself never clarified anything about the fatal incident; Saoo's statement was there to shield him.

But something else was there which he was trying to clarify, without being asked. He was telling everyone that Saoo had consented to give Laxmi's hand in marriage to the mahout.

And very soon this happened, but not without any monetary

exchange. The mahout had sold his elephant and gave this money to Ghunghru in exchange of his daughter who had barely begun her entry into womanhood.

• • •

Tears rolled down Janki's cheeks. The Russian girl's eyes had shed black tears, because of the mascara, but Janki's tears were blackened by the sadness in her heart. How wrong she was! When in Bombay, she used to think she had forever buried the memory of Saoo and Laxmi in the dungeons of the past.

But the truth was something else. Her sister and mother had always been there deep-seated in her heart. "Hurry up girls. Come out quickly! Time to leave for the show," Lara came calling.

Eight

IT WAS A DARK, moonless night. They all wore black saris. Their unbraided, long, black hair left flowing down their backs. All were barefoot, except for one who had roller skates to her feet.Though every one was barefoot, their footwear was suspended to a string, tied around the waist.

One was holding a shovel across her shoulder, the other one bore an axe. The third one had a box of sharp nails, a hammer and also a few thin, wooden planks with her. The one who was carrying the shovel wore a string around her neck, to which was hooked a round basket. The basket was full of some round, thorny fruit. They were all alive, except for one. The small group was "walking" the corpse on skates, toward a cemetery. The hundred-year old hijara guru had died and was taken to be buried in a secret manner, according to their custom. They did not want anyone to know that it was a funeral procession.

It was a winter night and people were nestled under quilts in the warmth of their homes. There were few people on the road and even the street dogs were lying curled up on sidewalks. So they reached the cemetery almost uninterrupted.

At a designated place in the cemetery, they started digging

the grave.

The wooden planks they had brought with them were fashioned into a coffin. After lowering the coffin into the grave, they sent down the body into the coffin. But, contrary to convention, they laid it face down. Then they brought out their footwear fastened to the string around their waist and begun to beat the dead body with the assertion "Don't be born again as a eunuch. It is a curse which has to be removed."

Now one of them came forward and clipped the guru's finger nails along with a piece of her silver locks and wrapped them in a piece of green cloth. The intention was that the guru's body would be buried there in the cemetery but the tomb would be made, with all reverence, in their home. And with this, they covered the grave with soil and put a simple stone slab on it.

The night was getting darker and the cold unbearable, still, instead of returning home they stayed on in the cemetery. To fight the cold they built a small bonfire and sat around it in a circle. It was time for them to choose a new guru here and now, from amongst themselves. They were perpetually living under a guru, their sheet anchor. It was a sheer psychological dependence for them and a tradition too. They would feel directionless without their compass. One more issue was raising its monstrous head, which could not be crushed without the commander. The evil eunuch Lallan's gang was ready to play havoc with the plans being laid.

• • •

Though the singing-dancing and tip-raising territories were already being divided amongst various hijara groups, Lallan's prying eyes were set on the huge amount of cash, priceless gems and precious jewellery possessed by this group. Everybody knows how difficult it is for a eunuch to open a bank account in India. So it is quite natural that they tend to keep their wealth hidden somewhere in their homes.

These may be buried beneath their house or may be hidden in a secret vault behind the walls of the guru's personal room. This also may be above in the attic, locked in strongbox; the treasure could be anywhere. As the legend goes the late guru was very close to the last king of the Sugandhi dynasty. Once the king was so pleased with her that he gave her a precious *naulakha haar*. On some other occasion the guru was given a true pearl waistband and a golden headband was given some other time, with many more gifts. The belief about the great, hidden treasure had tempted many a thief to break into the house in the middle of the night. But nobody ever succeeded. Now there is a way presented itself. If somebody ascended the throne, she would automatically be given the authority to gain access to all their wealth. Lallan also had his evil eye on two beautiful eunuchs in this group. Rekha and Rani, both were young and pretty. Once, when the late guru was alive, Lallan the conniver had come to her with the exhortation that they should begin using them as money-minting machines. The guru, at that moment, was reciting her rosary; without even putting it down she had replied curtly, "My daughters are capable of earning their bread through respectable means."

"Respectable means? You mean begging?" Lallan had begun to throw taunts, "Whom are you fooling, chachi, everybody knows. The king was so fond of young lads! And let me know." Further he continued wryly, "Why on earth did your guru's guru visit the king's palace so often, heavily made up, dressed to the hilt, bejewelled and trailing a fog of attar? And why did the Raja gift her such priceless items?"

The guru did not react to any of his provocations. And

Lallan had left angrily.

The late guru was a strong person, almost invincible. She had never surrendered to Lallan's muscle. She was well aware of Lallan's criminal activities. He had recruited a few impersonators in his gang passing them off as eunuchs, while in fact they were fully men.

The guru's party had tried to lodge complaints with the police several times about how Lallan was using these impostors to loot people and was extorting money in the name of eunuchs. "This is going to ruin the image of the eunuchs in general," was their accusation. The police dismissed their charge on the plea that inquiring about someone's gender is illegal. "Legalities, my foot! We all know how fair and democratic our police is," the guru had commented acidly. What the guru had said was absolutely right. The hijaras of the group were very often thrashed by the police. They extracted money from the public but most of the times it was grabbed by the police.

Today, they had brought with them a gold chain with a tiger claw pendant to adorn the neck of the new guru. Before this, the late guru wore this chain and the guru's guru before that. It's difficult to trace how old the traditional chain was, but it was fabled to have its origin even before the British Raj.

According to a legend, the chain and pendant belonged to an era when kings ruled India. They would recruit eunuchs into their armies because of their bravery and fighting skills. Since the eunuchs could have been presented as either sex according to circumstances, their ability to metamorphose had given them opportunities to work in royal detective agencies, too. Here they had often held respected posts.

There were many more opportunities for them to work and intermingle in society of that period. Eunuchs were esteemed performers who would present classical dance performances in the royal courts and in temples, winning accolades in turn. Eunuchs were the best choice when it came to assigning them the duty of guarding the harems – the royal *janankhana*s. Their inability to have sex with women was not mocked at; rather it was taken as a virtue. And this is how a eunuch received the chain with the tiger pendant. He had saved the king's daughter from the clutches of a minister who had a lecherous eye on her! The chain given to the eunuch was a sign of gratitude from the king for saving the princess. Actually eternal contempt toward eunuchs had begun during the British Raj.

The collar was preserved by the group of eunuchs who had received it, as the token of their once respectable position in society, and was being transferred from generation to generation since then.

• • •

Coming to the present here in the cemetery the eunuch group was readying itself for the coronation of Hamida who was selected as their leader. They were going to put the collar around her neck, but not before the completion of an essential ritual which was rather lengthy but would include each and every member of the group. Each one was required to recount her life story. It was left to the narrator whether she wanted to finish it in a few lines or to stretch it to an hour, whatever.

But while recounting the tragic incidents of the past the narrator could break down. Anticipating such repercussions, Hamida had handed to each person a thorn-apple along with a sharp stone. Using the pointed stone as a knife, each one broke open the fruit given to her and ate at least two-three seeds from it. They don't eat seeds from each others fruit, but only from the one given specially to her. Why this is so is difficult to understand, but that's the tradition and they all followed it.

After eating some seeds, Anarkali began to speak first. She finished her story in a few lines. "I was a few days old when somebody found me lying on a garbage heap. Who was the one who had picked me up from there – this I will never know, but one thing I know for sure is that I had opened my eyes under the care of Vrinda guru."

"*Arre-o-naspeeti*," open your mouth a little more. Basically we all know each others' story, but here we are following a ritual, by this short-cut you are spoiling the mandatory catharsis, my dear. Have you devoured and digested the seeds of *dhatura* like chana-kurmura!' asked Anguri to Anarkali.

At which Anarkali got really irritated, "So you want to hear it from my own mouth again and again, that my own mother would have dumped me in a garbage bin, out of disgust, horror and shame when she found that I had only a wretched hole instead of genitals."

Hamida broke in, "Okay, don't fight. Stop arguing now. Anarkali has successfully passed the test. Now let the next one tell her story." At which Anguri smiled and Anarkali came up to Hamida, touched her feet and went back to her place.

Now only a few seconds had passed and Anguri erupted again. "*Arre* Anarkali, what I was saying was for your good. After eating *dhatura*, you could have easily gone cathartic and purged all the toxins churning inside you, throwing your inhibitions aside. ··· *Arre haramjadi*, let it come out now that if Vrinda guru would not have saved you, pigs and dogs would have had torn you into pieces. Your mother had already offered you to them."

"Now keep quiet, you bitch. I will kill you, if you are going to curse my dear mother!" said Anarkali in quite a melodramatic manner but rather fondly. Saying this, she went up to Anguri hugged her and started crying ··· as if a chain reaction, all of them began to cry in unison ··· their sorrowful chorus reverberating in the silence of the cemetery.

"Stop it!" roared Hamida, and they all stopped crying, as if on cue. "If you will elaborate each hearing this long, the night will be over without the completion of the ritual," said Hamida, at the same time gesturing at Ramila to start narrating her story.

"My mother was not like that," she loved me. Ramila began to tell her tale with this phrase. "Since I was like this, my mother used to keep me behind closed doors, hidden from the outside would. She was afraid that once my status was known, the eunuchs will snatch me from her and take me along with them. I was delivered at home with the help of a dai, who had cut my umbilical cord. If I had been born at a hospital, the *toli* would have got the hint from the hospital records."

"But as I was born within the four walls of my home, my mother told the world that she had given birth to a boy. She had been careful enough, not to unfasten my diaper before anyone, ever. But once the dai had a fight with my mother over some trivial matter and she had spilt the beans ···! This had happened at an age when I was about to go to school. And you know, my mother suddenly died around that period. Not even twelve days had passed after her death and Vrinda guru's disciples had come over to take me from my home. And you know I had protested and cried so much. ···"

Before Ramila could finish the last sentence, Hamida interrupted, "Yes, we know you are a crybaby! You cry over every small thing! Don't you think, you should instead be happy that Vrinda guru had taken you under her wings at the right time?"

Then turning toward the others, Hamida said, "Look at what

she says. She was at a school-going age. Someone should ask her whether she had been admitted to any school. First, they would have asked male or female? Don't you remember the plight of Sharmila. Her father had admitted her to a school as a boy. The teacher and others were suspicious; rather, they were sure of her gender or no gender! And one fine day the teacher had publicly pulled off her undies and kicked her out of the school. Umrav guru's group had given her shelter, otherwise she would have died of hunger," said Hamida.

This was seconded by Anguri. "Yes, very true. We are always looked at with scorn. People do not spurn the crippled. Nobody hates the deaf and dumb because of their disability. Almighty God has created us disabled the way we are. Then why do people discriminate against us? Let's ask them?"

"Ask them," "ask them" others chimed in. Suddenly, Anguri stood up and started clapping her hands. Others, too, rose to their feet and began to clap in tune with Anguri, all of them together to the same beat and they used the words "ask them" as if these were the words of a lyric. Now clapping and singing "ask them, ask them" they were revolving around the bonfire they had lit to fight the cold. This singing and dancing went about just for a while and Hamida, again in her authoritative voice, ordered them to sit down. Though Hamida knew well that her companions were acting in such a melodramatic manner to lighten the atmosphere and make it more bearable. After all, they were giving vent to their sorrows and anguish and here, in a cemetery on a moonless night, so it was essential for them to subdue the vulnerable situation by acting loud and coarse.

"*Arre*, Anguri! You are so curious about others and instigating every body else to reveal their history, then why don't you come forward and recount your own story now. We know

Rani is also waiting her turn but we will put her last, when the morning star appears in the sky. As you know, Rani has certain phobias. So it will be difficult for her to go back to her past, while it is still dark," said Ramila.

"Before blaming Rani, look into your own heart, Ramila. It is not only Rani who is fearful. You also get scared. How frightened were you, do you remember, on the day of *nirvan* when the dai was preparing to do *khacha? ... k.k.* ...! We were feeling like virgin brides who were full of fright on the eve of her first night," said Anguri. "Oh yes, Anguri! I was really, really scared, I was screaming out of fright and pain. Then Vrinda guru's disciples had begun clapping, singing and dancing around me in a circle, so as to drown my shrieks. They wanted to save me from the terror of my own screams!" said Ramila. After a pause she continued, "But when I look back to the incident, I realize it was for my own good. They had weeded out what was not required by me. With that, from a powerless man I had become a powerful eunuch. *Nirvan* had endowed me with the power of benediction. Now I could sing, dance and earn my living."

"Rani dear, now you tell us your story," said Hamida very softly, putting her hand on Rani's back in a caring gesture. The sympathetic touch made Rani break into tears. After a while, wiping them she said, "I know all of you are describing your painful nirvanic moments just to give me strength. But *nirvan* is a rite of passage. When it was performed, you were there for each other. After the *khachak*, a turmeric emollient was applied on your wound. After forty days of care and recuperation you were decked out like a bride and the occasion was celebrated. I was not so lucky. On the contrary, I was deceived."

Now the bonfire began dying out and seeing this, Anarkali left for the backyard of the cemetery to collect some firewood.

Khat! Khat! The rattle of knots and pieces of wood could be heard by the group as Anarkali collected a few from the heap. Suddenly, Anarkali's sharp, frightened scream reached their ears, followed by the footfall of an unknown animal running away and then voice of a baby crying.

"What's wrong," everybody asked in unison.

Amid the confusion and apprehension, Anguri and Ramila ran toward the backyard in case Anarkali needed some help. Rani began to yell and cry and Hamida's attention was drawn to pacify her. But very soon they saw smiling Anarkali returning. After her were Anguri and Ramila walking at a steady pace, with no sign of alarm. All the three were carrying firewood.

The bonfire was raked with a stick and the faggots put into it. Again, they formed a circle around the fire as the embers ignited.

"What had happened?," asked Hamida of Anarkali.

"Nothing. It was a civet. It might have come to filch the corpse of a child buried in there. When I removed a plank from the pile, the civet, hiding under it, jumped out and ran away," replied Anarkali with a smile on her face.

"A civet?" Rani's eyes grew big in wonder!

"But then where is the child who was crying?"

"There was no child," laughed Anarkali, "Rani is an educated person, which is why she doesn't know that a civet cries almost like a human baby."

"Oye, Anarkali! You are teasing the girl," said Hamida feigning anger. Then she turned toward Rani, "So Rani it is now your turn. Just remember that you have been brought here to clean the debris from your heart. Try and cleanse yourself of all the fears and all the sorrows of the past."

"But it is Anguri *mausi*'s turn, *na*!" Rani procrastinated. She was buying time. Her past was so tragic that she preferred to keep herself in constant denial, instead of facing the monster and finishing it with a single hammer blow, forever. She tried to suppress the melancholic memories, which went against the hijara tradition; their motto was, "open the lid; let the toxicity be dissipated."

Anguri wanted to motivate Rani to a catharsis. So she made up her mind to lead by example. She said, "Okay, then, first I will recount my story, but in a nutshell. I had been a dejected person right from the beginning because I was like "this". My mother had tuberculosis. And my father got hitched to another woman while my mother was still alive. We were six siblings in all. Except me, all were complete physically. When I was growing into an adult, I showed no signs of masculinity. ··· Neither facial hair, nor a change of voice at puberty. My siblings would mock, harass and ridicule me. Even beat me. They detested me thoroughly. Even my father used to thrash me from time to time. Then one day I ran away from home. But only to begin starving for the lack of a job! I went from door to door. I had knocked on many doors, but was knocked aside myself. Nobody was ready to give me some work. Like once I asked a family to give me a job of dishwashing. Instead of giving me the job the owner taunted me, 'Is a hijara going to clean our utensils?' 'Have we come to such a pass?' I retorted with same bitterness. I also said one needs hands for dishwashing, not what you are suggesting. ··· The owner was so scandalized that he called the police, reporting falsely that a hijara was harassing the women of his home and talking vulgarly.

The police took me into custody. There they not only beat me mercilessly and you know ··· they even sodomized me.

Somebody should ask these animals in uniform why do the guardians of law take us to male police stations, why not to a female police station? And if that is not possible then make a third *thana*!"

Don't you think so?

"Yes, yes, you are right, they should have some provision for a third *thana*."

"Then, one day, while I was sleeping in a pipe lying empty along the road, a stray dog while eating, left half of a roti there. Famished, I ate it, my self-respect now long deadened. Vrinda guru's disciples saw me there and immediately I was taken in and given shelter. ··· That's enough for today. This is my story."

The morning star had appeared in the sky, which was turning from black to mauve to blue, gradually. This hint of light could give Rani some courage to narrate her story. Definitely, it was better than the complete dark. So this was just the right time for Rani to begin her story. Actually there was no excuse left now. So slowly, fumbling and stuttering, Rani began to recount her story.

"My name was Raja not Rani." As Rani began with this sentence, the eunuchs laughed for a while perhaps at the irony of the situation. But Rani did not stop and the tale continued.

"It was not merely a name. I was in fact a *raja-beta* (a lovely child). A little boy who went to school, without throwing tantrums. An obedient son, complying with his parents' wishes, except for one thing, sometimes I would be adamant to wear a frock. This was negligible, because otherwise I was an outstanding student. When I reached the seventh and eighth standards, I began getting drawn toward girlie things, like lipstick and *bindi*s. I loved to gaze into the mirror for hours and used to do make-up. One day, my papa found me doing my 'gorgeous' act and he gave me a tight slap, which was the first of a number of smacks to come."

"I had begun to grow my hair long and one fine day I went to a beautician to get my hair styled like a girl. I had my eyebrows plucked in an arch for that 'feminine' look of surprise. That day, when I came home my brother spat at me in revulsion." He said to me, "You should never be seen with me; for me it will be a disgrace. I don't want my friends to ridicule me."

"I did not want to earn the disgust of my own family," said Rani weeping.

"I didn't want to go against their will but I was helpless. I had the body of a man, but the soul of a woman. My family was unable to understand this, forget about sympathizing or accepting my condition."

"Only my mother, though sad about the turn of events my life had taken, would give me food, bringing it to my room on the sly. Sometimes, she would hand me some cash she had kept hidden away. Crying, she would implore me to get rid of this 'perversion'."

In the school, for the crafts and sports period, when I chose dance as a subject instead of cricket, my papa beat me up and stopped my pocket money, too. But I sailed through this difficult time, because I fell in love with a boy, not a girl. My lover did not belong to my school. My schoolmates were interested only in girls. Rather, as they had just stepped in puberty, the boys were completely obsessed with girls. Their jokes were obscene and revolved around the opposite sex. Clearly, this did not interest me, so while other boys used to roam around the girls' school, I visited a tea stall in front of our school. There I had found him.

That time around he had just joined the tea shop, as the

chief tea maker. And really, what a marvellous tea maker he was! He used to make *ekdam mast* ginger–cardamom tea, which would look literally crimson in colour. Even the boys serving tea yearned for tea prepared by him. It was not given to them; it was strictly for the customers. But their craving for this special tea was so strong that those *chokra*s would collect the left overs from the glasses given to the customers and drink it with great relish.

While working Deepak would remain barechested, neither wearing a vest nor a pyjama, just a red, thin towel wrapped around his waist.

He was tall and muscular with a washboard belly and popping biceps. Bewitched, I would stare at him without even batting an eyelid.

He certainly had sensed my enchantment. One day, he came close to me and caressing my face said, "Oh, Hi! Creamy cheeks, does your father feed you only cream and chocolates?"

"Then one day, he took me to a movie. He had money in his pocket. He belonged to a lower stratum; still he could spend the way he liked to. He earned the money. It was his money. On the other hand, I was from a rich family, but could not spend a single paisa as I liked. Deepak was smart enough to catch this minute but important detail. He had begun to splurge on me. He was a fully grown adolescent while I was just stepping into my adolscence.

One day, Deepak gifted me a shirt. The next time he brought me a tiny bottle of perfume, though it was of a feminine fragrance and next he took me to a hotel ...!"

"Oh Lord! *Ya Khuda*! *Hey Bhagvan*! ... then what happened?" all of them asked in unison. And they got the answer, "What else could have happened? We became true lovers and got physical," replied Rani.

"So Rani, your story is over, by this account. Lovers consummating their love at last should be the end of the story," broke in Anarkali casually.

"No, No!" replied Rani vehemently. "This is not the end of the story; rather the story takes off from here."

"Deepak was a jealous boy. He was very possessive of me. He did not let me talk to other boys. But he used to fulfil all my whims and fancies. My obsession to do girlie things was no doubt aggravating with each passing day. So he would buy me all things I desired. ··· He brought a printed maxi skirt with a frilled top for me. Then brought an evening gown with open shoulders; thereafter a pink frock with a matching pink hairband. He even gifted me a cupped bra and two Chinese balls to keep into it.

"As he met all my demands I, too, reciprocated by fulfilling all his carnal desires. I would act like a girl before him. So it was he who had changed my name from Raja to Rani." One afternoon, while we were in a hotel room, I danced for him to a loud bollywood number *aaja ··· aaja ··· aaja.* He liked it so much that he asked for more and then more and more. I had spent the afternoon dancing to various bollywood melodies. He was so pleased that he promised to give me whatever I would ask for. And I expressed my desire to learn dancing.

Years back, I had expressed my desire to learn dancing to my father too, but he got so angry that he thrashed me. He had beaten my mother, too, on the pretext of making me girlish.

"You have tied him to your apron strings. So why just dance? Go ahead and teach him some cake baking and roti rolling too," he had taunted my mother.

Ma did not reply. She took the beating silently and kept

crying. I was really shaken by mother's tears. So I stopped voicing my desire to learn dancing. And this time, encouraged by Deepak, I again approached my father. This time he was so enraged that he told me to quit home that instant, saying I should never again show him my face. "Your face is a caricature of distorted humanity, stay away from this house ···" he screamed. With this, I had come to live with Deepak. I had to stop going to the school, but joined dance classes, though it was not any classical dance. They taught folk dance and salsa.

Salsa required a dance partner and I was paired with a girl named Shalu. There was something bizarre about Shalu. Her father accompanied her to the class and would keep his eyes on her all the time. Shalu did not want to be paired with me. She wanted to dance with Rohit. Her father was against her desire. That was why he escorted her everyday – to keep a watch on her.

Shalu was a Jain and Rohit a Sindhi. This difference of caste was a big issue with her father. So Shalu could not dance with Rohit, but while dancing with me, she would keep looking over her shoulder toward Rohit. It was quite natural then that my attention was also drawn repeatedly toward Rohit. And you know what, this merely looking in his direction was turning into a strong attraction. O God! I was falling for him obviously. But Rohit was not a homosexual, so there was no way he could or would reciprocate. I was not a girl either. I repented over this truth even more than at any other time in my life.

Then one day, as I was flipping over a magazine lying in the dance institute book shelf, I stopped at a page where the title of an article said that people with a gender ambiguity can change their sex through an operation. I went through the article and realized that all the years, I had been cursing the creator in vain for making me a male, when it was possible to become a girl if

I wished. I required money, a huge amount. Not just for surgery, but even for consulting a specialist.

But I had neither the means nor a father who would pay for it. The hefty sum could be paid only by Deepak.

I was so engulfed by my joy at discovering a desired truth that I overlooked this fact, I should not have put this demand to Deepak. After all he was my lover. So, naïvely, I asked for the money and tried to explain the purpose as to why I required it.

Listening to this he became so angry and bitter that he replied harshly, "I want you to remain a boy. Who needs a girl? I can get a hundred, if I ask for one. What do you think; I have a dearth for girls? So never again raise this foolish demand," he warned sternly. But I was so obsessed with the idea of becoming a girl that, from time to time, I would express my wish to him, despite his anger over the matter.

Now Deepak had begun to give me a white powder before sex, to heighten the experience. Gradually, I became deeply addicted to this substance and I would beg for it, if he cut back on my "quota". I became a slave, literally.

Then one afternoon after taking this powder, while I was presenting a sinuous cabaret item for him and he was watching me with obvious relish, a photograph slipped out from my blouse. It was Rohit's snap, which I had stolen from Shalu's purse, with the intention of constantly keeping it close to my chest.

I had dared to betray a man like Deepak, who was mighty. Now I had to pay dearly. Filled with anger, Deepak gave me a dreadful punishment, said Rani.

• • •

Now she started crying so loudly as if an amplifier had been fitted in her throat. Her heart-wrenching cries made the hijaras very sad. They were dumbstruck. Soon, a civet cat matched its cries with Rani's, though this *jugalbandi* lasted only for a few seconds. Dawn was breaking. It was time for the group to leave the place immediately.

• • •

After that incident, Deepak and his drug peddler friends fed Raja with enormous amounts of heroine. One day, instead of force feeding him, they brought in a medic, who gave him an injection to make him unconscious. When he came to his senses, he realized to his (her) horror that he was being emasculated. His penis had been removed.

After a month or so, Deepak sold Rani to a eunuch named Chameli just for seventy thousand rupees. Chameli too wanted to sell Rani; but not before a month of prostitution. But, somehow Rani managed to escape from her clutches, and was given refuge by Vrinda guru. This was Rani's story. Amid all these horrible happenings Rani had lost her appetite for life, except for one thing, she still harboured the desire to become a "girl" undergoing the sex surgery. The new guru Hamida very fondly promised Rani that she would definitely help her to fulfil this desire. All the others endorsed this by clapping vigorously and with this everyone left for home.

• • •

Kalyani was lying down on a high table, her eyes blindfolded. Still she could sense the tiny sparks on her face. Doctor Chopra placed his finger on Kalyani's face indicating a point to his assistant, "here." And the assistant immediately moved the laser beam to that spot, *chatak* ··· *tar* ·· *tar* ··· the laser beam dwelt on that spot for a second, giving a burning sensation. Now the doctor moved to a second spot ··· within ten minutes, first sitting of laser treatment was over. The blinders were removed from Kalayni's eyes and she got down from the table.

The first thing she did after getting down from the table was to take out a hand mirror from her purse and to look into it. Watching her, the doctor and the nurse smiled at each other meaningfully. Kalyani was embarrassed a bit by this. Her cheeks reddened even more deepening the colour left by the laser. Sensing the discomfort in the air, the assistant tried to change the subject, "It will take a few more sittings, may be two or three," she said.

"So will my skin regain its original texture after the whole treatment, I mean, as clear as before?" asked Kalyani.

This time the doctor tried to be tactful, "Look Kalyaniji, to explain it in simple words, the form and texture of ones skin is different in different ages. The skin changes as we age. This treatment will make your skin better in relation to your age. Though the freckles will fade they may not vanish completely. But you should not worry," the doctor added, "your freckles are already very light and there are not many," he comforted Kalyani.

Meantime, the assistant was preparing the bill which she handed over to Kalyani with the advice that she should not go for the crystalline treatment immediately. "There should be a gap between two treatments," she suggested. Kalyani nodded and came out of the clinic.

Observing Kalyani's habit of keeping a hand mirror in her handbag, Rani Lantarani also commented once. In fact, she narrated similar anecdotes about Kalyani's grandmother who was also very conscious about her beauty. "Do you know Kalyani? Your grandmother was as beautiful as a celestial nymph. When I used to massage almond oil on her legs, her skin felt like royal velvet to me," Lantarani would say.

"Lantarani, have you ever seen a celestial nymph? You have neither seen the paradise nor the royal velvet. You are only spinning yarns," said Kalyani.

"Ya, true, very true," said Lantarani, drawing a pinch of snuff. Though, this time instead of gossiping she was presenting a real scenario. Kalyani's dadi was exceptionally beautiful, with an exquisite complexion and was aware of her beauty. Every seventh day she would shape her eyebrows with ash and thread. Every fourth day she would rub turmeric and gram flour paste on her body. She would make a ball out of whole wheat dough and roll it on her figure, so as to get rid of her body hair, if there was any. She would constantly chew betel to keep her lips glowing red.

She used home-made kohl, to outline her doe-like eyes. Every fortnight, she would call a local henna artist home to get a mehndi tattoo on her hands. But her greatest passion was the mirror; she loved to look into it often. After the demise of her husband, the compulsions of widowhood made her stop adorning herself. She abandoned mehndi-kajal, stopped wearing bangles but could not stop rolling dough on her body. Then after a few years, the black lusture left her hair, but the mirror did not leave her side. Even when she was ailing and bedridden she would keep a mirror handy to look into it interminably.

The ailing grandmother would constantly measure her own pulse rate, with her fingertips. There were many more rituals to perform in the day. Like she would stick her tongue out and check it in the mirror, for further signs of good health. She would pull the lower lid of her eye and look into the mirror, just to see if her eyes were as clear as they used to be.

"Oh Kalyani, isn't it amazing how our ancestor's traits percolate down to us! Their virtues and flaws continue with us," said Lantarani. Kalyani knew the comment was directed at her. Call it vanity or whatever, like her grandmother she was also very conscious about her beauty. The big turn of events in Kalyani's life was somewhere related to her narcissism. Kalyani had accepted Gautam's proposal because he was smitten by her charm. But she herself is attracted to Kabir because he is an exception.

Kalyani was a beauty queen of a small town, she was always welcomed by boys whistling for her and men gave her red roses and scented envelopes. But no features of her could entice Kabir and he neglected her *in toto*. Naturally, Kalyani felt rebuffed and tried to address the challenge of winning his heart throughout her youthhood.

The next turning point, in the form of Janki, also came into Kalyani's life because of her acute consciousness of her own beauty.

It was the time when Gautam had completed his fellowship on "the effect of antioxidants on ageing" and he and Kalyani had come back from Bombay, as Gautam got a job in the life science research centre in their own town. Everything was fine between Gautam and Kalyani. His love for her was deep and sincere. But Kalyani was not in mad love with Gautam though she liked him. It was his blind love for her that made her marrying him five years back. But in the smooth flow of their married life, there developed a small rift. Gautam wanted a child. But Kalyani was afraid of child bearing and rearing as it would have destroyed her beauty, her physique. She couldn't think of the wrinkled belly skin, postpartum.

She wanted to convince Gautam citing her own grandmother's example, who never breastfed her children. Her husband, Kalyani's grandfather, understood her feelings and always arranged for a wet nurse to feed her babies. But she would stop herself from giving this example because it could open the subject of her hereditary genes; Gautam could link her quirks with the mental illness of her father. And the truth is that sometimes she herself would suspect whether she was getting paranoid. She knew she had this weak link, so she would keep quiet.

Progeny versus beauty was often the matter of argument between Gautam and Kalyani. Generally, Gautam would have to accept defeat because Kalyani would silence him by saying he was in love with her, not she; he had chosen to live with her. Another time, she would not be that harsh and try to explain to Gautam that youth and beauty are important, otherwise why was he doing research on the role of antioxidants on ageing? "The whole world was running after the imaginary fountain of youth so how could I be singled out as paranoid?" asked Kalyani.

The same Kalyani, on another day, would happily play a guinea pig for Gautam when he was carrying out some experiment, "The effect of food on our skin." On such occasions she would be ready to gulp down any potion prepared by him or chew up pieces of cucumber or peach without making faces. So, despite the on-again-off-again arguments they gradually developed a bond. And ultimately, Gautam consented to adopt a child from some orphanage.

Before returning to their town, Gautam and Kalyani had visited many orphanages in Bombay, but nothing seemed to materialize. Sometimes, the child would be too small to handle for Kalyani, or a legal complexity would be there, because the pair was from a different state. At other times, Gautam would want to know the family history of the child, at which Kalyani would imagine the barb was thrown at her!

But ultimately Gautam accepted the theory of them not begetting a child, not because it had to do something with Kalyani's figure, but because within his heart he was concerned about her family history, though he didn't mention this to her openly.

The day Kalyani and Gautam arrived at the Lord's bungalow; the estate had already witnessed two deaths. Even the funeral rites had been completed before their arrival. There was a great disparity in the manner in which the rites had been performed. While the adieu bade to the monkey was a gala affair, Saoo's body was sent off without even a goodbye. Ghunghru and Hariyaliram had taken her to the nearest cremation ground loading her body on a pushcart. They had to use one of the white petticoats Saoo owned, as the *kafan*. Before making this compromise during the last rites of Saoo, Hariyaliram asked Tauji if he could get a fresh, white cloth to wrap Saoo's body in and a marigold garland to put over her body. But Tauji flatly denied her this last show of respect. He said there was no such provisions in a brahmin's last rites for a lower-caste person, that too, a woman.

"Then why such elaborate rites for a monkey?" asked Hariyaliram. Tauji replied, "A monkey is a brahmin in itself, he is the earthly manifestation of Lord Hanuman. So whatever rites we are performing in its honour are less than what we should actually do. Even if we had offered a golden monkey to god it would not have been enough."

Hariyaliram was a bohemian. He did not like to spend time in one place for long. Once he made up his mind, he would immediately set off for wherever he had set his heart on. He would go to faraway places; sometimes to a Himalayan village; at times, down south to Kanyakumari. He chose to remain unmarried. So footloose and a free bird, he was at liberty to go anywhere the four winds blew him at any time. After the monkey and Saoo's death, Hariyaliram left the place as usual for an unknown destination. Generally, when this happened, Lantarani also set off for her husband's home. Hariyaliram was more than a friend to her and this, even her husband Bholaram knew well.

But, this time, Lantarani stayed over. She was concerned about her nieces and for two nights she was with the girls at Ghunghru's hut. She had cooked food for the three. But on the third day, the police suddenly arrived at the hut and carried Ghunghru away with them. Because of Saoo's deathbed statement, the police had spared Ghunghru that day. Why then, did they all of a sudden take him today! Lantarani could only wonder.

Anyway, she waited a day for him to return. But when he didn't turn up, Lantarani took some money from Tauji with the intention of getting Ghunghru out on bail.

The mahout was probably keeping an eye on these developments. So, as soon as he found the girls alone at home, he crept in. Using the opportunity at hand, he took away the crying Laxmi with him.

Janki ran after the car for quite a distance, but could not catch up with the speeding vehicle. Tired, she stopped running and returned to sit on the veranda of the Lord's bungalow. It was a little dark there. Alone, she felt scared, and called for Raju, the mongoose. For Janki, right now, the mongoose was the only one she knew and trusted.

Kalyani and Gautam had returned just one day before. That night, they had gone to see the last show of a movie. Tauji was tired; the monkey's death celebration had exhausted him. So, he too went to sleep early. Taeeji was in the prayer room deeply engrossed in reading Sundarkand from the *Ramayana.* These days, Kalyani's father was getting frequent attacks, so her mother had taken him to the psychiatric ward that day. When she returned, she saw Janki weeping and sitting with the mongoose in their veranda. She went in, settled her husband in their room, went into the kitchen and, without the knowledge of her sister-in-law, came to the veranda with two rotis and potato *bhaji* for Janki.

Taeeji might not have objected to this, but somehow Kalyani's mother was afraid of her authority, because she was the wife of a powerless husband and, after remaining for a long time under Taeeji's thumb, meekness had become her second nature. So after feeding Janki she asked her to come in but it was a feeble offer, she was not sure whether she should let the mongoose in along with Janki. For the latter, for now, the mongoose was her guardian and she was seeing a protector in it. Janki was but a child and she preferred to remain in the veranda. Putting her thin arm around the pet's neck, she curled up on the floor and went into a slumber after a while.

The rain was gradually getting heavy, accompanied by hailstorms. Powerful torrents began to fall obliquely into the veranda, soaking Janki. Flashes of lightning were etched across the sky, and as thunders rolled, there was a power-cut. Some electric poles were knocked down, no doubt.

This was quite common here, whenever it rained hard; at times even with a small downpour! When people called the electricity board, the phone lines were invariably engaged. Babus would keep the receiver off. Today was no exception.

Janki was completely soaked now. Sitting propped up against the wall, she was staring into the dark. Her hut was a little away from the veranda. Then there was the fear of snakes and scorpions coming out unhindered. Though Janki had many a time in the past seen snakes creeping into their hut, nobody in her family was scared of this. It was a normal thing for them. Ghunghru, Hariyaliram and even Lantarani knew how to catch a snake. A cloth would be thrown over the creeping reptile. The disoriented creature would then easily be captured and transferred to some container. After a lid was put on the container the snake would then be taken to the outskirts of the town and would be freed there. Normally, the snake would not be killed because it is associated with Lord Shiva.

Even scorpions would normally appear in and around the hut.Once a scorpion had stung Lantarani on her palm. It was not a shocking incident for the family or Lantarani for that matter. Saoo had simply put some lime on Lantarani's palm. Though she had to endure severe pain for a few hours, it was soon forgotten.

But just now, for Janki, it was not such a small matter. Everything around her was scary. She did not know how to trap a reptile and handle it without being bitten. She was afraid that taking advantage of the dark a snake may easily bite her if she tried to go toward the hut. Anyway, on this dark, rainy night she could not stay alone in the hut which had been her cosy home until a few hours back. At this moment, Janki pined for Saoo, her mother. But Lantarani had told her that Saoo would never come back. Yamaraj – the god of death – had taken Saoo with him. Lantarani had explained to Janki that her mother's body was charred because the dark-skinned Yamraj's shadow had fallen over it. Now this explanation was causing a new fear in Janki. The mahout was also a dark-skinned man with burning red eyes. Was he too a Yamraj or a man? And the mere thought gave her shudders. Because if it was so, it meant Laxmi too was dead and would never return. But just now there was nobody who could answer the questions propping up her perturbed mind.

She would get answers only when Lantarani *bua* came back. For now, Janki was here alone with her fear. With her head on her knees she cried her heart out.

Suddenly, intense beams of light fell on Janki. She raised her head to look. It was a vehicle's headlights; honking along, it threw its twin probing fingers at the house. This was Gautam and Kalyani's car. They were back home from the movie. Alighting, they saw a figure on the veranda and moved quickly toward it. "Who could this be, at this hour, on this rainy night?" Kalyani thought apprehensively. This could be her father, who might have come out in a state of confusion. She knew that these days her father's condition had worsened.

No, but this was not her father, but Janki, Ghunghru's little daughter. The girl was all wet and crying. Gautam lifted her in his arms, and with Kalyani took her inside the house.

After laying Janki on a bed, Gautam immediately left to bring medical help. Since Kalyani had brought Janki in, Kalyani's mother felt more confident and she went into the kitchen with her head up now, to cook some fresh *khichadi* for the girl. Tauji was still asleep. When Janki was brought in, Taeeji, too, had gone to sleep after finishing her Sundarkand recitation.

Before the doctor arrived, Kalyani had changed Janki's clothes. She was made to wear Gautam's old shirt and shorts, because there was no alternative. Meanwhile, Kalyani kept Janki warm by rubbing mustard oil on the soles of her feet. Next morning, Janki appeared to have recovered. But Lantarani's mongoose was found dead in the veranda. In the morning when Tauji and his wife came to know that Gautam and Kalyani had saved Janki's life, they were very happy and proud, except for one thing. Taeeji complained about fresh *khichadi* being made when there were many extra rotis left from the afternoon meal. And Tauji agreed that it was necessary to give Janki a quilt and dry clothes to save her life. But it was weird that she was made to sleep on their bed.

"Kalyani, *beta*, we have enough mattresses and beddings in our house. Some of them are especially meant for the servants, you could have given the girl any of them. Alright, if you did not know about this, your mother certainly did. She could have shown you the place."

Kalyani, often wondered how the couple thought along similar lines, though she had never seen them sharing the same room like husband and wife. Maybe their thoughts ran together because they had grown up together. Tauji was fourteen and Taeeji merely twelve when they got married.

Tauji was not bad, Kalyani thought. It was just that ritualism ran deep in him, and made him behave in a certain manner. Whatever it was, this also was true that he doted on Kalyani. And he really and deeply loved his younger brother, too, despite the latter's mental ill health.

Tauji did not have children of his own, so he wrapped all his love around Kalyani. All his concerns were related to Kalyani, the chief among them was that even after a few years of marriage Kalyani remained childless. She had never mentioned to her family that it was she who did not want to have any children. Typically, Tauji inferred that Gautam was to blame because he was unable.

Tauji had his own orthodox views and solutions for the problem. According to him, Gautam had best performed certain religious rituals to lift this obstacle from their lives. He was sure divine powers could help Kalyani. He had suggested that Gautam go to Mother River Narmada and immerse the urn holding monkey's bones, accompanied by all the rituals. But Gautam had point blank refused to entertain this suggestion. He said he did not believe in all this hocus-pocus. Tauji then decided to send Kalyani's mother and father on this "important" mission.

While seeing them off, Tauji instructed Kalyani's mother, "Bahu, you need to ask the gods for a son for Kalyani and good health for your husband. We understand that Maruti Hanuman himself is a celibate, but so what, he can always bless married couples. You should do this much for Kalyani."

Kalyani's naïve mother did not know the ways to life. She feared her husband might get an attack while they were on tour. So without even consulting Kalyani or Tauji, she gave her husband an extra dose of medicine. The one which was to be given at twelve was given at seven in the morning too. She thought her husband would not get violent if he remained a little drowsy. Lethargy would keep him in control.

The driver Kanhaiya reported at 7:30 sharp, and the couple left for the river district in their trusty Ambassador. In the meantime, Kalyani and Gautam went to visit the local orphanage. When the couple was assiduously searching for a child in Mumbai, people had suggested that they try in the orphanages of their own state. This would make the legal processes of adaptation a bit easier.

Kalyani and Gautam wanted to adopt a toddler so that they could watch the child growing and enjoy the frolics of the moppet. This was not so easy, they were informed. Another couple, who wished to adopt such a child, told them that they had chosen one child two years back but still could not take him home because of bureaucratic delays, and the child in the meanwhile had crossed the age at which they wanted to take him home.

There were many children in the orphanage that Kalyani and Gautam visited. This boy, who was six to eight months old, had six digits on each of his hands and feet, besides, he was very dark. That was why nobody had ever shown any interest in adopting him.

Maybe this was the same reason for which his own parents had abandoned him. They might have feared the child as an ominous sign.

Then there were identical twin girls who were found on the floor of an empty train bogie. Two girls meant a double burden of dowry, and the family might have considered getting rid of the twin girls by "forgetting" them on the "last train." A frail, prematurely born girl child was laid on a burlap mat. A nurse was trying to feed her milk, by slowly pressing a milk-soaked cotton piece into her tiny mouth, much in the same manner one would feed a helpless baby squirrel.

Kalyani and Gautam submitted the application to adopt this girl. Government officials responsible for the orphanage were to visit Kalyani and Gautam's house; so that they were assured everything was fitting for the baby to be looked after by her new parents. These bureaucrats had already interviewed Gautam and Kalyani about their financial standing, other commitments and source of income. The couple had satisfied them with their answer. Kalyani deliberately held back the information about her as the heir to the vast empire of the Lord's estate. Actually, there was no need to say all this now. She knew the orphanage people would keep track for at least two to three years after giving the baby in adoption and everything would be cleared up automatically. But, for now, the couple thought it might complicate the process of adoption. Because the officials would in that case come to the Lord's estate and possibly there they would encounter Tauji, who would definitely fuss over the obscurity of the religion and the caste of the baby, and maybe the whole need to adopt one. This would result in the rejection of their application. So why not declare these details after the process was completed, the couple thought. They went ahead to find a home on rent, to which the orphanage administration could visit.

Otherwise also, Gautam had a deep difference of opinion with Tauji, and living with him as a resident son-in-law was against Gautam's self-esteem. They went on a searching spree for a house of their own.

Despite spending the whole day meeting property brokers and visiting prospective houses, they didn't find anything satisfactory. When they returned home in the evening, Taeeji was cooking a meal for herself, which was rare. There used to be a regular brahmin cook who would prepare meals according to the methods approved by religious Hindu traditions. When the cook was absent, Kalyani's mother would bathe and enter the sanctum sanctorum. But today Kalyani's mother was not there and the cook had resigned from the job merely a week ago. Taeeji needed a new cook, who had to be a brahmin, no other caste would do. This specific need was rather difficult to meet. It could take some time.

The rain had stopped and had washed the sky clear and Tauji could be seen sitting on a cot, puffing a hookah in badshah style. Lantarani was also there, near the cot, sitting on the floor at Tauji's feet. Near her was Janki, sitting so close that their arms rubbed against each other. "Tell me Lantarani, where have you been? Thank God, at last you have returned," said Kalyani. "But why is Janki sitting on the bare floor, she should get on to the bed or she will catch fever again."

The reply came from Tauji, not from Lantarani, "Why should she go to your bedroom now Kalyani? Her aunt has come and the girl will go to her own home and sleep whatever arrangement has been made there. Why should we bother, our responsibility is over now. ..."

"... and above that I have given her a considerable sum of money," added Tauji superciliously.

To which Lantarani waved two five rupee bills – the considerable sum provided by Tauji – as if in corroboration with what Tauji had said.

With that, Lantarani went to the shanty taking Janki along. Now Kalyani did not ask Janki to stay over. It was quite natural that Janki would go home with her *bua.*

It started raining hard again during the night. This time, the lights did not go, but phone lines went dead. Not dead exactly, rather stopped working smoothly.

Someone was trying to call but the line would disconnect, once the receiver was picked up. The caller tried again. This time, the desperation in his voice could be sensed but his words were incoherent. It must have beem something very urgent because the caller tried several times but his voice would drown in the buzz of sound from the receiver. At last, the phone really went dead. And throughout the night it remained mute.

By the morning though, crying and beating his chest, the caller himself appeared at the Lord's bungalow. This was Kanhaiya, the driver of the Ambassador. It took him a few minutes to summon up the courage to narrate what had happened.

What came out of his mouth was no less than a huge,

devastating tornado. Kalyani's parents had drowned in the Narmada. Her father was under the influence of a heavy dose of medication. He and his wife were standing on the riverbank, from where he was to immerse the urn of monkey's bones. But suddenly without warning he got down into the water and started moving toward the deeper side. His wife called after him, but he didn't care, so she gathered up her sari and jumped into the water. Walking into the shallows she reached up to her husband, who was now in the deep where his feet did not touch the ground, and he had begun to drown. As soon as his wife reached him and extended her hand to save him he held her tight in his arms. They both drowned, screaming. His voice was weak and her's loud, because he was not in his complete senses.

After hearing the tragic news, the bereaving Tauji and Taeeji immediately left for the river district, to bring home the dead bodies that were recovered by the guards. As if death had spotted the Lord's bungalow, the next day, a man came from the orphanage to give the news that the girl child, Kalyani and Gautam had booked for adoption, was no more.

Kalyani wept and mourned within herself. But Tauji wailed loudly, banging his head against the wall, howling and beating his chest with his fists. His naïve, dependent brother meant everything to him. So after performing the rituals, he left for Haridwar, along with his wife, not just to immerse the urn of his brother and sister-in-law's ashes in the Ganges, but actually to live there for a few months, and spend time with ascetics and fakirs, disenchanted as he was with life.

Along with her grief, Kalyani felt a sharp pang of remorse. "Why didn't she ever sit with her mother and share her sorrows and concerns," she thought with contrition. She should have seen things through her mother's perspective. On the contrary, she had always blamed the mother for attending to her father all the time, attending to his needs. He was her single focus. Her life revolved around him. Kalyani would feel neglected and unattended by her mother. It was Taeeji who would fix meals for Kalyani or oil her long hair and put covers on her notebooks. Tauji had always attended her parent–teacher meetings; he took her to the general physician whenever she was sick or bought gifts when she had to attend a friend's birthday party. He had always done his duty on behalf of her father. So actually, it was Kalyani who had forgotten the presence for her parents when they were alive, because Taeeji and Tauji had met all her needs. But, today, when they were no more, she realized their existence.

• • •

In these five days, Janki had recovered but she could not regain her sprightliness. She had forgotten to run after cavorting butterflies and singing with birds.

The dark shadow of grief had covered her innocent face, her big eyes filled with a barren look. In this state, one day Lantarani, holding Janki's small hand, in a strong grip, took her to the Lord's bunglow.

"How are you Lantarani, was that money enough, that Tauji gave you, you must have got the girl treated?" asked Kalyani in a blank voice as if she were just doing a duty by asking about the well-being of the little girl. Her personal grief had soaked up all life from her heart, so also any trace of emotion from her voice.

"I did not come here to ask for money only," replied Lantarani, "I mean that you will give me some anyway and whatever you give will be gracious on your part and help the child. I will oil her hair and get her something to eat. But the question is: what next? How is she going to survive all alone, once I go back home?"

"Why don't you take her along, Lantarani?" suggested Kalyani.

"But, in that case, Janki will not be able to shape up her life. My mother-in-law and sister-in-law would exploit her for domestic chores. She may face taunts, and bad behaviour from my family members ..." said Lantarani.

To this, Kalyani did not say anything. There was silence in the air for a few seconds. Lantarani broke it saying, "Kalyani, that day you said if we send Janki to school, you will give the money for her education."

"I still say that; you send her to school, I will give the fees. I had always wanted to support this girl, it was you who said the money given by me will not be utilized for the cause," said Kalyani.

"That is what I want to explain. If I take Janki to my home, the money given by you will be sucked into our big family's domestic needs. The scenario will be the same, if the girl continues to live with her father Ghunghru. This would have happened even if her mother were alive, but…."

"But what Lantarani?"

"But then the things would have been different. In that case, even if Janki could not get education, under the loving care of her mother and sister she would have led a meaningful, and a little more, respectable life. ··· And now you see, Kalyani ··· you can understand how it feels when one loses her mother," said Lantarani coming to the point. Whether or not Lantarani intentionally directed the arrow at a weak spot, this was not easy to make out for anybody, but that much was sure that the arrow struck the target. The sentence affected Kalyani immediately and deeply. After all, both were bereaved and grief-stricken in the same manner.

Seeing the effect of the point she had made, Lantarani took the matter to another level with more confidence. And she raised the issue for which she had been preparing the base.

"Yesterday I saw a staffer from the orphanage visiting the estate," said Lantarani in a low and unsteady voice.

"So you want to send Janki to the orphanage though her father is alive," asked Kalyani sharply.

"No ··· No ··· *tauba-tauba* ···; Lantarani held her ears with her hands simultaneously drawing Janki close to herself, as if somebody was taking her away. With this gesture, Lantarani begun to further explain what she meant. Though Gautam was not involved in the conversation he was having a shave, sitting nearby, yet he guessed what was coming, which Kalyani could not. So he stopped moving his brush and began to stare into the mirror. He could see images of Kalyani and Lantarani, along with his own face. So again, as Lantarani in a low voice said, "I mean when you are bringing a child from the orphanage, then why don't you keep this unfortunate girl with you ··· and uplift her life ··· ?"

As soon as Lantarani threw this hint, Gautam left his place, with shaving cream on to his face and came near both of them. But Kalyani exploded, "Have you gone mad, Lantarani? Do you think I am going to adopt Ghunghru's daughter? Tauji is never going to accept this," the answer silenced Lantarani but spurred Gautam to speak, "Kalyani anyway Tauji is not going to accept this proposition lying down, any child we bring from an orphanage is going to face the music···."

At this Kalyani now looked at Janki with a steady gaze. She recalled her mother saying, "I would have taken and kept the unfortunate girl here, if it was my own home."

With this, Kalyani's heart begun to weep again for her late mother, who was her mother but never behaved like one, she was a mother to her husband only, not to her daughter. This had always enraged Kalyani, but not now. Now her rage for her mother had turned into compassion; compassion for a woman who had to sacrifice everything in her life, in order to serve her dependent man. "Would adopting Janki be a tribute to my mother?" she asked herself. But the moment of overwhelming emotions passed unhindered and the confusion obfuscated her thinking, "The girl has become old enough to understand her own history and knows where she comes from. And everybody else knows whose daughter she is and which background she belongs to," these were the thoughts which plagued Kalyani's mind.

Feeling the tenderness of the situation and Kalyani's dilemma, Gautam again pressed his demand, "Think again Kalyani, why should we adopt a child? Why can't we have our own?"

Sensing Gautam's changing mood, Kalyani's dilemma vapourized, and emotions began to overpower her again. Maybe at the back of her mind she had this thought that she had to decide about Janki now or the whole attempt at adopting any child would be wasted. So Kalyani, now looked at Janki again more keenly and she could clearly read the plea in the mist of Janki's eyes. Then Kalyani shifted her gaze toward Gautam. In his eyes, too, there was this request as if he was saying, "We should take the decision now, so that we don't have to live in a constant dilemma and can realize our own future plans." Lantarani's eyes also implored, "Please consider the life of this hapless girl." One more person made this request, which only Kalyani could hear; that was Kalyni's late mother. Kalyani imagined her mother saying, "You are not incapable like me, you have power and resources to help someone like Janki, then why do you want to live a futile and empty life like me?"

Kalyani's grief over her own parents' death was still so fresh and moist that Janki's sorrow could easily leave its impressions on Kalyani's consciousness. If Kalyani's parents had not died at the same time as Janki's, then it would have been a normal sympathetic vent, to be forgotten in two days after a superficial "*tch* ··· *tch* ···" condolence for the girl. But ultimately coming out of their quandary the couple decided to adopt Janki. The father of the girl, Ghunghru gave his consent with his thumb print on the adoption papers.

In turn, Gautam had bought him a motorcycle and some cash. Ghunghru was feeling happy and truly liberated that he was able to shrug off the responsibility of bringing up a daughter in such an easy and beneficial manner. He was freed by police also because of Saoo's deathbed testimony.

• • ● ● ● • •

Nine

MOHAN HAD LEARNED to play the flute from his mother. "Learned" is not the appropriate wordE here. Mohan had mastered the technique and was proficient in using this splendid, yet simple, wind instrument. Its popularity notwithstanding, the flute in Mohan's hand became akin to the phrase *om mani padme hum* (behold the jewel in the heart of the lotus). His mother was the daughter of an elephant owner; rather, he was a man who knew the ways of animals. Her name was Kaplia. Kapila's home was at the edge of a forest in south India. Her father reared elephants which had been injured or orphaned in the wild. In fact, he was an elephant *kaviraj* (a doctor for elephants). Reading Sanskrit books like *Hastyayurved* (Ayurveda for elephants), *Matanglila* and *Meghdoot* was his favourite pastime. Often he was found sitting in his tree-house, reading thick volumes of Sanskrit texts. Since *kaviraj* had so much knowledge about elephants, their diseases and remedies, he was almost always on a call in that area where there were many elephants. Sometimes, a person from a sanctuary would come to take him to treat an ailing elephant or a man from a temple would ask for *kaviraj* because they were preparing for a festival and their elephants' heads were required to be decorated;

only *kaviraj* knew how to do this quickly and creatively without torturing any of the tuskers. Sometimes he was called to train baby elephants for Lord Shiva's *abhishek*, teaching them to play football or raining flowers on gods or guests with their trunks. He knew everything about elephants from helping a domestic female elephant in labour to deliver the "child" to teaching elephants how to come in queue when they were required to perform in a festival. Since *kaviraj*'s life revolved around elephants, so his five daughters, too, were very involved in matters concerning these pachyderms.

Kapila and her sisters would take their elephants every day for a bath in a nearby pond. Elephants from the wild would often join their domesticated cousin's. They would come in herds and cross the pond together. Across the pond was a bamboo thicket. The elephants would go there and eat soft bamboo leaves and shoots. Sometimes a baby elephant would not want to get into the water. Then the mother would push it in and leave it to enjoy the water sport. Now he would learn to cover himself all over again in mud, after bathing in the pond and spraying dirt over himself like all other elephants in the herd.

When Mohan was young his mother Kapila had thousands of stories to recount about elephants. Mohan would hear them in rapt attention. Kapila loved to tell these tales to Mohan but at the same time she missed the company of the elephants around her. At the time she was far off from the woods where the animals were plenty. Her father was no more and sisters were married off.

• • •

In Kapila's home place where elephants were in abundance, there was the Jagatnarayan Mandir, about twelve kilometers from her residence. It was a common belief there that donating an elephant to the temple would liberate the donor from the shackles of karma, earning him divine blessings. According to this custom, a female elephant was donated to the temple, her name was Meera. The temple priest, Gorakhnath, had migrated from Uttar Pradesh to this southern land. He knew nothing about the care of elephants. Also he would be busy performing numerous religious rites and rituals of the temple and he did not get time to take care of several small chores. On Gorakhnath's request, *kaviraj* had sent, one of his five daughters, Kapila to the Jagatnarayan Mandir to take care of Meera. Though *kaviraj* promised to come himself in case Meera took ill, he could not meet this promise. One day, *kaviraj* died suddenly and seventeen-year old Kapila remained in the temple. Kapila had a certain routine here and everything was going well. Then, one day, Bherulal, a man from pujari's village reached the temple to live there with his uncle Gorakhnath.

Thirty-year-old Bherulal was a man of doubtful character but attractive with a sturdy physique. He would smoke in style like a grand film hero and would wink and whistle at Kapila. In the evenings, he would distribute *bhang-ghota*, (the marijuana paste), prepared by rubbing marijuana between the stones8i. This *bhang-ghota* business was a new and rather shocking thing for the south Indian temple. Bherulal would dispel their hesitation by convincing them that it was nothing but God's *prasad.* If they did not believe this, then they should go to Benares and see for themselves. Who would go so far, up to Benares, to check on these facts? So people would believe what Bherulal said. As a result, many lungi-wearers had begun to enjoy the evening *bhang-ghota*, while Bherulal began to wear a lungi to become one of them.

• • •

Kapila had many duties at the temple. Taking care of a female elephant, collecting flowers and making garlands for the deity, preparing sandalwood paste and other small but important chores. Now one more task was added to her list. She would help Bherulal in preparing *bhang-ghota*. Very soon, Bherulal began bantering with her, something which she too enjoyed. The fire got to her. Soon she was sucked entirely into his charms. Sensing her blind love for him Bherulal began to plan elopment. He would paint an alluring picture of life in Benares, with her. Clever Bherulal had his eye not only on Kapila but also on Meera, the female elephant, which Kapila used to look after. Bherulal knew that Meera was a prized possession. But he, till that time, knew nothing about rearing elephants. So Kapila was the solution to all his problems.

Finally one day the elephant, Kapila and Bherulal boarded a freight train and migrated toward north India. How did Bherulal manage this grand feat, Kapila did not know. But instead of getting more impressed by Bherulal, she was disenchanted. He had promised Kapila that they would exchange flower-garlands at the Vishvanath Temple in Benares. He would put bright red vermillion on her head. A true gold *mangalsutra* around her neck, and then they would celebrate the golden night of their marriage.

But Bherulal did not keep any of his promises. He raped a resisting Kapila right in the freight train compartment. He didn't even take her to Benares. They got down from the train, in a small town of central India and there he became a mahout. Riding on Meera's back he would roam in the city all day long, he would take the animal from door to door to collect alms. He could do this because of people's belief that an elephant was an incarnation of Ganesha, and would not let it go from their door without an offering. This was not the only duty Meera had to perform for the mahout. The female elephant had to work hard in order to earn money. She would carry children around on her back and the mahout would charge them for this. Meera would thus be rented to marriage celebrations, fetes, processions and parades.

Kapila, meanwhile, clad a barren life. She had forgotten to smile. But her smile returned to her lips as Mohan was born. Her child was her god. She began to recount stories about elephants to him even before he had reached the age where he could comprehend what was being narrated.

While reciting an anecdote to Mohan, Kapila would often ask Meera, present nearby, "Right Meera! It happened this way?" In response, Meera used to sway her head, flutter her ears and raise her trunk in a way as if agreeing, "Yes, yes, you are correct."

In fact, the boy was christened Mohan, because of one such anecdote, which Kapila repeatedly recounted. That was the love saga of elephants Mohan and Radha. The story dates back to the time when Kapila was only thirteen years old.

It was the fag end of the rainy season. That day it was just drizzling. A very thin veil was there, through which one could roam around in the jungle without even having the cover of a large banana leaf. Every grass and leaf had turned lush. Tips of long grass blades held sparkling drops of water. Whether hillock, plain or field everything was covered in a glistening green. Freshly washed leaves were shining. Bamboo, teak and other trees, it seemed, were swaying in abundance. As the drizzle stopped, a kind of heavenly aroma filled the atmosphere. It was difficult to perceive the source of the fragrance. It could have arisen from the moist earth, sandlewood trees, wild flowers or grass. Maybe, it was from the lotuses in the pond or by a mixture of aromas from all these sources. A very subtle and sweet scent wafted through the air, which could only be sensed either by the female elephants or by the bumblebees.

It was time for bull elephants to go into *musth*. Mohan, the tusker, was also in *musth*. The elixir of passion was streaming down his head. He was trumpeting and swaying restlessly. That day Kapila and her sisters witnessed a majestic science. Bumble bees and their cousins, honeybees which usually hovered over blue lotuses were swarming around Mohan's head. The sisters knew at once that today Mohan would wander crazily in the forest in search of his beloved Radha. Radha belonged to a herd of elephants which lived in the jungle across the pond. This herd was often seen bathing and splashing in and around the pond. The sisters had heard that elephants dance in the wild, a kind of group dance performed in unison.

Today, luckily it was a brilliant full moon night. The sisters fancied seeing the grandeur of the elephants in a tango, and they immediately left for the jungle across the pond in a coracle. Kapila did not forget to carry a flute with her. Eventually, they wanted to play it to the steps of the dancing elephants. There, whatever the sisters saw from behind a hillock was much more than what they had imagined.

The valley was surrounded by mountains. In the middle there was this vast open space covered with green grass. Some elephants could be seen there. Some were males and some were females. All were facing the big moon, but they were not standing in a queue, rather they had dispersed in a loosely rectangular fashion. They were swaying their heads and trunks as if listening to some music, moving their right front legs in unison.

Actually, they were feeding on grass together. Each would uproot some grass, by kicking tufts loose. All would then bend their right front feet and extend the trunk to pick the grass they had uprooted and lift it to their mouths. This had a tempo. Their bodies, shuffling feet, swaying heads and swinging trunks worked rhythmically.

"This is so ordinary, we have come here to see the elephants in *rasa*," whispered the sisters, a little disappointed. Kapila then brought out the flute, fastened to her waist. Since Mohan had so many times swayed his trunk to the melody of the flute when she played it in her courtyard, she thought here, too, the elephants would begin dancing.

But Kapila's sisters dissuaded her from doing so, suggesting this was going to agitate the beasts and they might leave the place altogether. The eldest sister as if found an opportunity to display her know-how remarked, "They don't need this music. Elephants have their own inner rhythm like they talk to each other in a voice which is below our hearing range. Similarly, they make their music, and dance to it." She was right. As the moon rose higher in the sky and its sparkling whiteness brightened the valley, it seemed the animals were singing with the whispering gentle breeze. Viewers could sense the music from the rhythm of the elephant's undulating bodies and vibrations in the air.

While singing, the elephants formed a rough circle and a pair came into the centre. This was Mohan with Radha. They butted their heads delightfully and entwined trunks. Elephants encircling them, too, followed their movements. Spellbound at the splendour of this *rasa*, the sisters were frozen in the moment.

There were many such anecdotes regarding Mohan and Radha which Kapila recounted to her son, to the extent that the boy Mohan began fantasizing about a Radha for himself. Radha, who would be unadulterated like a dewdrop on a blade of grass and she, bewitched by the sweet melody of his flute, would begin to dance.

Even when Mohan's mother Kapila was no more, he still had a treasure trove of elephant stories which she had left him. As whiskers of manhood began to appear on his face, he started to dip and dye the tendrils of his fantasy into brighter colours of romance. And one day, he came face to face with the girl who was just like the Radha of his dreams. But her name was not Radha, it was Laxmi. She was older than him. He was fourteen and she was sixteen.

But alas, the girl of his dreams had come into his life as his stepmother, his father Bherulal mahout's new wife.

Mohan was in the eighth standard in a government school. This was the year of the board examination and his class teacher Masterji was expecting Mohan to score good marks. He was very fond of this sharp student, so much that he gave him private tution for free. One day, Masterji had left a little earlier and Mohan was arranging his notebooks, when his father Bherulal arrived at the door of Mohan's makeshift room. He had Laxmi with him. Her head was covered with her sari. Standing there with her head down, she was digging the mud floor with her toe. Though pale with fear, the reflection of her yellow sari seemed to light up her face. To Mohan she looked more like a lantern winking at midnight. Spellbound, he looked at her without batting his eyelids. But very soon, his father's thundering voice, broke through, "Touch her feet, she is your new mother."

Mohan already hated his father Bherulal because he had often seen him thrashing Kapila without provocation.

Then Bherulal sold Meera. Now he had brought a new wife. Mohan felt disgusted. Sullen, he turned back and immediately went inside, without touching Laxmi's feet. This time, Laxmi raised her head a little and looked at Mohan silently as if asking him, "What is my fault?"

That night the mahout stopped Mohan from coming to his *kholi* and ordered him to remain in the makeshift room, Mohan had risen for himself with planks. Deep in the night, a disturbed Mohan through his fitful sleep heard the subdued screams of a woman. Half-conscious he could not make out whether he was dreaming or it was for real.

The next morning, he saw Laxmi outside the *kothri*. She was rubbing a vessel clean with ash and coconut fibres. With her red, empty eyes she looked at Mohan and asked him whether he would like to have tea. Her voice was heavy and hollow.

Mohan replied, saying he would make tea for himself. To which Laxmi said nothing and went away to fill the vessel with water. The mahout was still sleeping, his loud snoring could be heard outside.

Mohan drank the tea he had made and left for the examination. Though there was no verbal communication, a kind of rapport began to develop between Mohan and Laxmi. Now Mohan would eat food made by her. After Laxmi had cleaned the vessel, he would go to the municipality tap to fill it. Slowly, they began to talk to each other and sometimes they would laugh at something they both found funny. Bherulal abhorred this. One day, he raised his hand on Laxmi, she cried a lot but then quickly resumed normalcy. After this incident, Mohan and Laxmi, never spoke to each other when Bherulal was there. In his absence, they laughed and talked and Mohan would regale her by playing the flute. She once told him that because of this talent he could always find a job with any local brass band. She suggested that he meet Mama Bajaram, sometime. And this opened the chapter about who Mama Bajaram was. Further, she told Mohan about Lantarani, her late mother Saoo, sister Janki, Hariyaliram and her father Ghunghru. She even spoke about the owners of Lord's estate Taeeji, Tauji, Kalyani Didi, her father and mother. With this, Mohan got to know about Laxmi's people and the world she had left behind.

Poor Laxmi did not know that meantime, the world she knew had changed completely. She did not know that chachaji and chachiji (Kalyani's parents) had died in an accident. She was unaware that Kalyani had adopted her little sister Janki. This was so, because Bherulal never let Laxmi leave his *kholi*. Neither was Laxmi ever sent to her father's home nor did Bherulal go to meet Ghunghru after he had obtained Laxmi. He never informed Ghunghru that the *tantrik* did not take Laxmi as his *Bhairavi*, because she was no longer a virgin. Bherulal had violated her before giving her to the *tantrik*. He was happy, when the former had rejected Laxmi, because this was what he had been angling for, right from the beginning. The greedy father Ghunghru could never fathom this.

Some day Mohan was planning to take Laxmi to the Lord's estate to meet her people, especially Janki. He knew stealing this opportunity was very difficult. Meanwhile, another opportinuty came knocking. Bherulal was not at home. That day Meera unexpectedly arrived at their place. How and from where she came was difficult to say. But Mohan was very happy to see her again, after Bherulal had sold her to somebody else.

In fact, it was Laxmi who had first seen Meera ambling down to their home. As she reached nearer, her size seemed more and more intimidating to Laxmi. Laxmi was so scared when the big beast actually arrived at their *kholi*, that she threw away the vessel and began to scream.

Mohan was sitting in his cabin, reading and hearing Laxmi's shrieks, he ran out immediately, apprehending some trouble. But, instead, he found Meera standing by the door. He was so glad that he began to clap. He turned to Laxmi and explained that she should not be afraid of the elephant. "She is Meera, our own Meera!" he said enthusiastically. Meera, too, seemingly shook her head in agreement, as if saying, "Don't be afraid of me, I am your Meera, I am not going to harm you!"

As Laxmi looked a little resourced, Mohan took the next step. He gently and fondly stroked Meera's trunk. When she reciprocated by flapping her ears Mohan held her trunk firmly and climbed up to her neck. He called down to Laxmi for a joy ride but she refused. She was not afraid of Meera now, but still a bit hesitant to mount the beast's back.

Sitting there, Mohan fondly patted Meera's neck, but not for long. He took back his hand in shock. Meera was wounded; there was a gash on her neck. He realized at once why Meera had come here. He came down and told Laxmi prepare a fine meal for Meera.

"A fine meal for Meera?" asked Laxmi in amazement. "Shall I prepare *kheer*, *puri* and *halwa* for Meera?"

Mohan laughed fondly at Laxmi's simplicity. He said, "Do you know what my mother used to cook for Meera? Bajarah or wheat roti from at least ten kilos flour a day."

"Ten kilos of wheat flour! From where are we going to get it? Just now we have only one kilo wheat flour," Laxmi expressed her concern.

"Alright, don't worry; we will take Meera to feed. Meera is injured; so anyway we have to go to the Vankhandi Mandir where they have some medicinal plants in their courtyard."

'No, I am not going to ride. I am afraid of tumbling down her back," Laxmi said apprehensively.

"We have a way of handling that, too. I will fix a howdah on her back; you will be able to sit in it very comfortably. Just do one thing. Whatever small amount of flour we have at home, knead it for Meera. Then we will move out of here. And please don't say no. You will realize later how good the world around you looks when you peer at it from Meera's back."

Mohan was right. That day Laxmi had seen the world like never before. Sitting on her neck Mohan directed Meera, while Laxmi enjoyed the ride. First they went to the Vankhandi Mandir, which had rolling acres for its courtyard. The priest of this temple considered an elephant a good portent. Any mahout who takes his elephant to the Vankhandi Mandir would be met by the priest. He would stand before the elephant, with his hands folded in *namskaram* and waiting for the elephant to bless him by putting its trunk on his head. The priest did exactly this when Mohan and Laxmi reached there with Meera.

After Meera's blessings, the priest offered her an entire bunch of bananas. He also fed her dry coconuts from the offerings to the deity. Meantime Mohan collected some medicinal herbs from the nursery at the back of the temple; Laxmi accompanied him with a chutney stone in her hand. By rubbing the herbs with water Mohan prepared a thick paste. Taking the paste in a cup made from a leaf, Mohan climbed onto Meera's neck and softly rubbed the soothing paste on her wound. Then they mounted Meera again and left the place, wending their way toward the woods nearby.

Meera enjoyed this expedition very much. She ate from the trees and shrubs, not only leaves but also flowers. She especially liked the aromatic flowers like *champa*, chameli and *mogra*. But actually she began the eating spree with oranges; succulent, aromatic oranges from the garden behind Vankhandi Mandir. She would pluck one, then throw it up, only to catch it by letting it fall directly into her open mouth.

On their way they came across a settlement with narrow lanes and small one-storey houses. There, a group of children was playing *sitoliya* on the road. As they saw Meera coming, they left their game and the whole group began walking behind her whistling, shouting and dancing happily. All of them were jumping around like crickets to the sound of the bell which hung around Meera's neck. They left following Meera at the point where the road took a turn.

Now the three reached a comparatively open space where there was a pond named Devi Talab hemmed by greenery. A thicket of old and big trees could be seen across it. Mahouts used to visit this copse with their elephants to let them feed on figs, other fruits and leaves from the banyan and peepal trees. There were some flowering trees, too. Even the pond was full of blue lotus. Meera was so enchanted to be there that she began frolicking. She filled her trunk with water and then raised the trunk up and sprayed all of it on her own body. But she was not alone. She was carrying Mohan and Laxmi. The sprinkle fell over them drenching and tickling the two. Laxmi enjoyed it so much that she began to giggle non-stop. This, as if, set out a current setting off a light mood and Mohan too started giggling. This was contagious enough for Meera also, who in turn began to spray them with more water and greater enthusiasm. A wave of sheer ecstasy took hold of them. Meera went a step ahead and poured some water on the idol of Lord Shiva, placed under a banyan tree nearby, as if performing an *abhishek* of the deity. Meera then astounded Mohan and Laxmi, by pulling out two blue lotuses with their long tube like stems, from the pond and, instead of eating them, offered the flowers to Lord Shiva.

Now rocking, Meera set out toward the copse behind the

pond. There she ate leaves and flowers from the trees, to her heart's content. Here, in an open space, Mohan and Laxmi got down and began to walk. At a point Laxmi stopped and spread out her sari *pallu*. Meera comprehended the gesture and promptly began to toss flowers into the outstretched *pallu*: *palash*, *gulmohar*, pink *kaner* and other blossoms. When the *pallu* got full, Laxmi threw them around creating a kind of flower carpet. Then they saw Meera trying to lie down, in gradual movements. Finally she was lying on the flower bed! Laxmi was overwhelmed to see this. This was beyond her imagination. But Mohan explained to her that this was nothing compared to the romantic anecdotes his mother used to recount about the elephant country. He promised Laxmi that one day he would definitely share with her all those interesting stories his mother used to tell him. Happy and satisfied they returned from the expedition. After coming home, Mohan drew a vivid sketch of Laxmi sitting on Meera's back, with a charcoal pencil gifted by Masterji. After this, Meera went back probably to her present paddock.

• • •

Charcoal pencil, yes, this was what Janki wanted, too. Or rather she wanted crayons, colourful wax crayons and a drawing book. Kalyani had got her admitted to a recognized English-medium school, where there was a special period for drawing and painting. She took Janki to a high street beauty parlour to get her hair styled. Apart from the regular school uniform, Kalyani also bought some designer clothes for Janki.

In the beginning Janki was very happy to go to school wearing a uniform and shoes. But very soon it became a dreaded task for her. She was mortally afraid of going to school. She knew no English. She could not comprehend what was going on. Her classmates were younger than her, yet they could understand the instructions and lessons. Janki did not know the English names for birds and animals or the colours. So when she said *hathi baba* instead of the elephant, the other children began to laugh. They also mocked her by calling her *hathi baba* though Janki was thin to the extent of looking almost malnourished.

In fact, Kalyani should have informed the teachers about Janki's adoption and her background. Then naturally, the teachers would have helped her in sailing through these difficult times. Instead, little Janki was left to fight all alone. Instead of revealing the truth Kalyani tried to suppress it by changing the girl's attire and hairstyle.

Though Gautam had begun to coach Janki regularly, besides basic things related to her courseware, he also taught her to call Kalyani mummy and him papa. Kalyani was very happy with this. But her focus was more on severing the girl's ties from her past than teaching her new skills of a new world. She stopped Ghunghru from meeting Janki. Tauji and Taeeji were for it, though Gautam didn't like prohibition of this kind, but he accepted it because he knew Ghunghru's character. But Kalyani distanced herself from Lantarani too, as a result she stopped coming to the Lord's bungalow. Janki missed her; she missed Laxmi even more, perhaps the most. This complete isolation from the world she knew made her sick at heart.

As if this was not enough, a new affliction knocked on her door. As pocket money for the day, Gautam had given her two coins of 25 paisa each. Janki now began to go to school by school bus with other children. Near the bus stop was a shop from which she used to bring bundles of bidis for Lantarani. So Janki knew this well that the shopkeeper kept various kinds of colourful sugar candies. In the past, she had always wanted to buy those candies, but never had money. Having coins in her hands today she has the power to buy her long cherished sweets, which she did.

When sophisticated kids saw her buying cheap stuff from a rundown shop, they started calling her *chavanni*. After this day it had become almost a routine for them to call her *chavanni*, in a melodious chorus. As soon as Janki boarded the bus, the children would start singing *chavanni*, *chavanni*, as if Janki was an alien, a specimen from another planet.

"A specimen from another planet," this title was true for her, here at home too. Taeeji was an orthodox person who observed the four *varna* casteism suggested by the religious texts. According to the tradition followed by her, she would eat food cooked by herself and her family members. Outsiders could enter her kitchen only if they were brahmins. Lower-caste individuals like Ghunghru and his bloodline were a complete no, no. Taeeji had a long list of clean and unclean food. Onion and garlic were unclean. "Egg," this word could not be uttered in her home. Non-vegetarians were monsters in her opinion.

Since the time Kalyani adopted Janki, Taeeji was living in fear that the *chokri* might sometime touch her food. In that case, Taeeji would have to discard the food, or maybe even to go without a meal. Actually it happened one day. In a bid to help Gautam in serving, Janki had brought a small container of rice, from the kitchen to the dining table, saying, "May I help you papa?"

That day Taeeji ate no food. She believed firmly that people of a lower caste have a different kind of blood, so marrying such people would mean contamination of the pure blood of a higher caste. This was also her belief that the people of a lower caste were dim-witted. "There is no point in sending them to schools, nothing is going to trickle down their head, because

Ramji had made them this way, it's God's will, you cannot change it, however hard you try. Lesser human beings have been sent to earth for the purpose of serving others."

It was useless to ask Taeeji where and when she met Ramji and why in the world he had chosen her to reveal this noble truth about the so-called lower caste.

Initially, when Janki was new to this home, it was a regular complaint from Taeeji that she stinks of garlic and onions. When this was said, Kalyani would always request Taeeji to remember never to say such things while Gautam was within earshot. Taeeji accordingly fell in line because she knew only Kalyani was family to her, and she could not afford to lose her and Gautam.

Kalyani also knew that Taeeji was hardwired for such things; her religious beliefs did not allow her to accept certain foods and their odour. Despite her conditioning she was mum for Kalyani's sake. On the other side, Kalyani did not want to hurt Janki and Gautam; so she settled for a middle path. She began to give Janki real Kashmiri saffron in milk which Kalyani herself used in her teens for a fragrant body.

• • •

That day was not the end of the tale. Meera returned to her new owner, Mohan and Laxmi to their home after the ride. Incidentally the present owner came across Bherulal somewhere. He was furious, blaming Bherulal for kidnapping Meera. His charge was that Bherulal had lured Meera with a bunch of bananas. Dangling before Meera he had taken her to his place, and after earning money from rides Meera was sent back. In his petty calculation he thought the new owner would not come to know. The present owner asked for the money which Bherulal might have earned from the supposed rides.

Furious at this baseless accusation, Bherulal was returning home in a bad mood when the people in the settlement complained against his wife about how shamelessly she, with Mohan wandered around sitting on Meera's back, without even covering her head.

This angered Bherulal even more. He thrashed Mohan and locked Laxmi in the bathroom. After this incident he had begun to keep his wife under house arrest. Whenever he had to go out, he would lock Laxmi inside the house.

Laxmi would shout, cry and beat the doors and walls from inside. Calling from outside Mohan would offer help saying it was not difficult for him to break open the door and set her free. But Laxmi never knew where she could head in the event she was released from this jail. So she persistently denied Mohan's help. There was this fear too, that if she was caught running away, her life would become worse. But she did not remain locked inside for long. One day Bherulal opened the lock and, taking Laxmi with him, went off to an unknown destination.

Mohan was left alone. He had to evacuate the *kholi* just in fifteen days after his father went away. He had no money to pay the rent, there was no roof above his head and he had nowhere to go. So he took his clothes, a small hand mirror, a few books, his flute and the sketches of Meera and Laxmi, and came to Masterji's place.

Masterji accepted him without a word, probably because he knew the circumstances Mohan was in or maybe he was just reluctant. Though his wife was not happy with the addition of a non-earning member to the family, she too said nothing but her irritation was clear with the way she banged around the utensils. She would even slap her children for no reason. It was clear that Mohan's weight was creating discordance in Masterji's already shaky household. So during the day Mohan would spend his time wandering like a lost soul; the nights spent sleeping on the stairs of a temple nearby.

Masterji lived in just one room, divided by a curtain, the kitchen and bedroom on either side. At night, the children would sleep in what was otherwise the kitchen.

The solution to this, Mohan thought, would be to earn some money to put it in Mrs Masterji's hand. He recalled once when he was playing the flute that Laxmi had told him he played so well he could very well get a job in a brass band. She had assured him that if required she would put in a word with her uncle Bajaram.

This was a situation that demanded urgency but Laxmi was not present to follow it up. That day Mohan had promised Laxmi that sometime he was going to take her to the Lord's estate to meet her dear little sister Janki. Laxmi was quite happy to hear this and had suggested cheerfully that Mohan should definitely take along the sketches of Meera and Laxmi. She had said "Janki will be very happy to see the drawing of an elephant. Actually you should teach her how to draw."

• • •

Janki had to go to the bus stop on her own. Kalyani would not go to drop her there because she was conscious of the sun ruining her complexion. Gautam would be taking classes in his college at this time. As for Tauji or Taeeji there was no question of them minding that Janki goes unaccompanied. Their considered opinion was that Janki was in the habit of wandering about all alone, even barefoot, so her going to the bus stop unescorted was not an issue.

For Ghunghru the opportunity to talk to Janki came when she would go to and fro the bus stop. He would sit on a culvert nearby, and smoking bidis keep an eye on the girl. He saw that gold rings had replaced the neem stalks in her ears. Here was a chance to use his sleight of hand skills. Ghunghru bought some metal trash earrings and when Janki passed him one day he called out to her. Pretending concern he said, "Oh, Janki it seems to me that your earrings are hanging loose, let me fasten them before they fall off somewhere!"

Naturally the girl brought her face towards him. Ghunghru suggested it would be better if the rings were removed and were worn again more carefully. He took off Janki's earrings and pretended to fix them back in place. Finally he said he couldn't and that it would be better if she carried them with her in a *pudia*. She came home with the rings wrapped inside the paper.

When Janki reached home in the evening she found herself alone. Only Gautam was there, ready to teach her as usual. Looking at her he suddenly realized that her earrings were missing. He asked her about them so she handed the *pudia* over to him. He laughed fondly telling Janki that those beautiful golden rings were for her to wear, not to be kept in a *pudia*. Then Janki said that Ghunghru had wrapped them up because they were loosened and about to fall!

Hearing this Gautam was alarmed. He picked up the rings and watched them closely. Suspicious, he left the place, instructing Janki, not to mention the incident to anybody. He took the rings to the goldsmith who confirmed the apprehension. The rings were not made of gold. So Gautam bought a new pair of gold rings, of the same size and design as the previous one and put them on Janki's ears. Nobody ever realized what had happened. Forget about Tauji and Taeeji, even Kalyani was not told about it. This incident regarding Janki was Gautam's first mistake. But why would he have done this? After all he was an intelligent man, a rationalist above any kind of orthodoxy. When did he acquire the feet of clay?

Gautam was the only child from his father's second wife. She had died when Gautam was just one and a half; he had step brothers and sisters from his father's other marriages. Since he had lost his mother, the father also sort of alienated him leaving him with no support system.

Gautam had no memory of his mother. There was no photograph available of her. She had never been photographed. So Gautam did not know how she looked like. He pined for her, darting his arrows in dark. He would always ask ladies in his village about the looks of his mother so that he could form an image of her. Everyone would describe in her own way making the resultant images so apart from each other that it was really difficult for Gautam to form a clear picture of his mother. Once he found his father in great mood, so he dared to ask him about his second wife.

In answer to his son's queries, the father began to describe her in detail. Her nose, her eyes, her complexion ··· Gautam stopped him midway saying he had always been hearing this description from people around. Making a concrete image of his mother was difficult. Something unique about her was missing.

The father paused over what was typical of his wife. It was a battle to recall a special feature of her. When he put his finger on it he realized it was something he could not share with his son. So he rummaged through his mind again. Just then his present wife appeared at the door. "Papa," the son said in an urgent undertone and the father blurted out what he was holding back. Gautam's mother had a mole on her right breast, he said.

The father's good mood did not last long. He was not a happy-go-lucky man and that he owed money to almost everyone in the village did not make it easier. When a creditor came to his door, he would send a family member to say that he was out. The deception was transparent and seeing how family members were lying, the creditor would throw a barrage of bitter choice expletives at the door. Who would come out to face this wrathful person? Everybody in the house would cover their faces and push Gautam out to confront these brickbats.

Gautam had to live in continuous embarrassment. Keeping the head down in shame and taking barbs had become the teenage boy's destiny. Gautam was good at studies; still teachers mocked him. Gautam's father had taken money from the Sanskrit teacher too, who worked as a priest in his extra time. So the priest's wife would call Gautam at any time to send him on errands. Sometime he would be sent to the grinding mill with a sack full of wheat grains, some other time he would be sent to the bazaar to buy provisions for Panditji's home. Father's debt had caused Gautam to become a servant without salary.

Gautam's plight reached its nadir when, one day, the village *mahajan* ordered him to do sit-ups while holding onto his ears, as punishment. Once when Gautam had done this because of fear, it became an obsession with the *mahajan* to order a repeat performance wherever he saw the lad.

The biology teacher was sympathetic toward Gautam. But having mere sympathy was not enough. Could he give Gautam place in his home? No. But the teacher found a way to help him. Once he brought an admission form from the science college in a nearby town and suggested that Gautam fill this form to try and get admission there. Gautam not only got admission, but also a scholarship, because of the high marks in the board exam despite upheavals in his family. Gautam finally got out of this cesspool but the slate was not yet clear. Something remained deeply rooted within him. He was not rid of the shame, guilt and meekness he had been drowned in during childhood. So who could know better than Gautam how a father's behaviour can shame his children. This was what he wanted to save Janki from. Though Janki was now his daughter her past was known to people who saw her through the lens of who Ghunghru was. This was the reason why Gautam had hidden the saga of the rings from everyone. If not their DNA, they shared the same depth of grief. There was this solid bond of a common experience of suffering between them.

It was winter. Days were short. Gautam had come home early. Actually, everybody was home. The brahmin cook, Radhelal, had ignited a coal *sigri* to cook the evening meal. He did not like a gas stove. And soon the aroma of *bajra khichadi*, cow's ghee and *kesar kadhi* began to waft through the air in the Lord's bungalow.

A few steps away from the bungalow, in the open, Lantarani was readying a make-shift *chulha* with some bricks. A few scraps of paper, twigs and the hard shells of wood apple made for her fuel. She used a piece of cloth dipped in kerosene to start the fire. In this open-air kitchen below a tree, Lantarani sat down on a brick and began to brew tea.

Like any other evening, Ghunghru was not present, but Hariyaliram was on a long visit to the Lord's estate. He had returned after spending a long time in the Tarai and brought with him a treasure of stories. And she was also there who loved gossiping and bantering with him. Yes, Lantarani would come to the estate every day till Hariyaliram was there. They were having an affair, but Lantarani never thought of eloping with him because her husband was a bedridden paralytic. She would have run away (perhaps not) because Hariyaliram was a bohemian and would never stay at one place for a long time. They had to find a way out of this situation. Whenever he was in the city they sat somewhere, generally in a tavern, drinking desi liquor, talking and laughing loudly. Even the regulars were so much in awe of Lantarani's bold guffaws that they would never try to stop her. But today, Lantarani and Hariyaliram were sitting in the Lord's estate, below this tree, brewing tea and warming their hands.

• • •

The previous night when Mohan curled up asleep on the temple platform under his only warm jacket, someone stole it. Mohan was already thinking of finding a part-time job, but this incident had made it all the more necessary. Right now even a cheap sweater from the Tibet market was out of his reach.

The first job he looked for was at the temple outside of which he slept. The temple trust ran a free-food service for the poor and they always needed people to serve it. This had been suggested to Mohan by Masterji's wife. But Mohan knew that before giving him the job they would want to know more about his caste. If he told the truth, they would certainly kick him out. They could even stop him from using their courtyard to sleep and his occasional meals in the temple *bhandara*s. It was not wise for him to let even Masterji's wife know about his caste. One could imagine a brahmin lady's wrath after coming to know the truth. So Mohan thought it best to keep quiet and maintain the status quo.

He thought of working in a bidi factory or driving an auto-rickshaw; but everywhere, either there were unions or a licence was required. It was difficult for a person without connections to get a decent part-time job. Mohan landed a few freelance jobs for a single day but the little money he got from them was not enough to sustain him. This little amount would go into paying Masterji's wife. Then he recalled what Laxmi had suggested. She had told him that since he plays the flute very well, he can learn another instrument and land a job with a brass band. "I will introduce you to Mama Bajaram Bandwala," she had told.

But now Laxmi was not there to introduce him to Bajaram. So Mohan left for the Lord's estate.

It was getting colder outside. Mohan did not have warm clothes to wear. So he decided to wear an extra shirt over the shirt he was already wearing. On asking for it, Masterji's wife had loaned him a tattered muffler. He wrapped it around his head to muffle his ears, slung a cloth bag on his shoulder and left. He did not forget to put his flute and all the sketches he had made into his bag.

When Mohan reached the estate everyone had gone inside the bungalow because of the cold. But a few steps away Hariyaliram and Lantarani were sitting, chatting and sipping tea. They asked Mohan to sit and offered him tea. Only then he was asked who he was and why he had come there. When Mohan told them all he knew about Laxmi and also about her sudden disappearance, Lantarani *bua* began to cry, holding Mohan's hand. After a while, when they had settled down, Hariyaliram began to recount anecdotes from his long sojourns to far-off lands, to guide the conversation to lighter subjects. And again, gossiping took wings. Hariyaliram brought up the subject of elephants; he swore that he had seen a unique kind of elephant. Lantarani, who herself was the queen of spinning yarns, naturally disbelieved him and teased him by saying that he was talking as if he had seen Indra's white elephant, Eravat!

Hariyaliram swore harder this time, which Lantarani dismissed by mocking him saying it seems he had seen elephants with wings, "what could be more unique than winged elephants," she chirped.

But Hariyaliram was no less than her. He mocked her by saying that she was the one who could grow wings on elephants, not he. What he had seen were pygmy elephants.

This time Lantarani believed him but didn't stop her banter. She commented with a smile, "So you mean to say you have seen nanny goat-sized elephants!"

"No not nanny goats, but the size of cows . . ." replied Hariyaliram.

And the conversation went on. Hariyaliram recounted interesting stories from the country of pigmy elephants. Mohan, enchanted, listened to these tales. After a long time he had begun to feel good. Fond memories of his mother came back. He felt as if Kapila was around, asking him softly, Mohan, why did you not wear a sweater, you are going to catch a cold."

Mohan instinctively reached for his shirt. This reminded him why he had come to the Lord's estate. He briefed Lantarani about the situation and told her to introduce him to Mama Bajaram Bandwala. She promised to do so soon but suggested she would first acquaint him with Kalyani.

Lantarani said Mohan should find some pretext to meet Kalyani, rather than Janki. Mohan was puzzled, what could be the pretext? But he didn't have to think hard; Lantarani was ready with the answer. She told him, "Show her the sketches you have brought along, and suggest she sit for her portrait. She won't refuse, I know." Lantarani was right, she knew Kalyani's weakness. Before sending Mohan in, she made him leave behind the tattered muffler and the extra shirt.

Kalyani became sad when she heard about Laxmi, but was

pleased to see her sketches with an elephant. Impressed, when she came to know that Mohan was the artist, Kalyani patted his back enthusiastically. It was a pleasant surprise for her that the artist was self-taught, a naturally gifted person; he had never been to art school. Lantarani was right; Kalyani had readily accepted the idea of posing for a portrait. She even fixed an appointment for the coming Sunday.

While Kalyani and Mohan were conversing, Gautam entered the room, followed by Janki. Gautam had just finished an hour-long session tutoring Janki.

As he saw little Janki coming in, Mohan got up from his place. Bewitched, he was rooted to the spot, not even fluttering his eyelids. For a second he forgot where he was and the people present, except Janki. Soon he regained his senses and as he realized who Janki was, he smiled to himself, "pigmy elephant, indeed," he thought. He had just an hour back heard about the elephants that were a smaller avatar of the normal-sized beasts. Now here was this miniature Laxmi. Janki was just like Laxmi, only a smaller version.

"So, was she the Janki for whom I have been looking but have got infatuated with Laxmi seeing the image of my dream girl in her," Mohan asked himself. "It is a case of mistaken identity," Mohan consoled himself. After all, he wanted to rid himself of the guilt of being attracted toward his own step-mother.

"Oh, so Janki is my Radha, not Laxmi!!" he thought with a big sigh of relief.

Janki was glad to see Laxmi in the sketches. To keep her happiness intact Mohan promised her he would make arrangements for her to meet Laxmi. He also promised her, some day, a joy ride on Meera.

Kalyani routinely asked Gautam about how Janki was doing. Today, also, she threw the question at him.

Janki was present there and Gautam did not want to demoralize her by mentioning her weakness in mathematics and she required to work hard on her English, too. So he evaded the answer by bringing in the optional subject. Drawing was there in her course but it was not necessary to have passing marks in it to go to the next class. It made his reply easy. Gautam said, "To answer your question Kalyani, Janki does not even know how to draw a flag, her drawing is poor. I, myself, cannot draw a simple line so I am unable to improve her drawing skills."

"You do not believe in God, Gautam, but today you will have to accept his existence," said Kalyani.

"Do you mean to say drawing a simple flag needs God's blessing," asked Gautam still smiling.

In reply, Kalyani extended Mohan's sketches toward Gautam, who was surprised at the exquisite work done by the boy. Awed, he looked at Mohan who was standing there, head down. Again, it was Kalyani who broke the silence. "I was speaking about him; he is the one who has come here as if through God's will. He is going to teach our Janki drawing." Then turning to Mohan she asked, "Do you have any problem with that, Mohan? Will you come to teach her drawing?"

Actually, Mohan couldn't ask for more. This was what he wanted; Kalyani also fixed a salary for him. A regular income would be a great support for him. Though what Gautam had said turned out to be true. Even after six months of coaching, Janki couldn't draw a simple flag. Whatever she doodled or scrawled Mohan corrected, giving it shape and rubbing off the extra lines and curves. He never mentioned to Gautam or Kalyani that Janki did not have a flair for drawing. He did not want to lose the tuition and the opportunity to meet Janki.

Meantime, he was introduced to Mama Bajaram by Lantarani. He had already begun to practise the clarinet, though he could get a job only in the season of marriages. But, overall, everything was going well. Playing a musical instrument in the brass band and working on popular Bollywood numbers was fun. There was music in the atmosphere. And here Mohan had an opportunity to befriend Hariyaliram. Though the age difference between the two was of a father and son, they liked and understood each other. The rapport between the two turned out to be marvellous. If Hariyaliram could understand bird language, how could he not understand an artist's heart? Though he was not formally educated, he could cultivate Mohan on various other disciplines. He could take him on long trips to far off places and help him learn to decipher bird and animal language or plant kingdom's behaviour. But for now Mohan did not feel the need to do all this, he was happy and content just teaching Janki. Even Masterji's wife had stopped rattling utensils in irritation; Mohan would regularly put money in her hand. He bought new dresses and biscuits for her children. They had begun to call him chacha instead of "Eyee" or Mohan. Everything went well until events abruptly switched tracks.

The village *mahajan*, who used to force Gautam to do sit-ups, enrolled his son with a donation to the college where the latter was a teacher. Gautam had already seen him in the college at the beginning of the semester. Gautam carried a fear complex of the *mahajan*, but had resolved not to get disturbed by his son's presence there. A mere glimpse of him would fill Gautam with deep shame. Then he would rebuke himself saying he was a respected professor now, so why should he bother?

Things went without the boat being rocked until this

incident occurred. The *mahajan*'s son was caught cheating in the examination. Destiny had it that the case was referred to Gautam. The boy carried a chip on his shoulder because he was a *mahajan*'s son and was aware of Gautam's background. So he had begun to blackmail the young professor, threatening to expose his father's defaulting on the loan he had taken from the *mahajan*. He threatened to spread this message around that Gautam was being vindictive by falsely implicating him.

Already low in self-esteem, Gautam was caught off guard; he let the case pass without a word. That day he returned home head down, deeply ashamed of his own cowardice. This was the first incident.

The second episode had occurred even before Gautam reached home. The tension lingering in the air came in the wake of the storm of a few hours back. Janki had unwittingly touched the idol of Krishna in Taeeji's *pujaghar*, "desecrating" it and creating a tumult.

Earlier that day, Taeeji had come down with a fever; Tauji was waiting for the masseur. It was Kalyani's time of month and for a couple of days she was *persona non grata* in Taeeji's sacred space. Being an atheist Gautam was not interested in puja and otherwise too he had gone to college for the morning shift.

Taeeji had sent Ghunghru for a brahmin who would perform the puja but, even after a long time neither Ghunghru nor the brahmin turned up. It was afternoon, with the sun high in the sky and the deity sitting unwashed. This upset Taeeji. Lying in her bed she fretted while berating everyone she could lay her tongue on. She cursed, Tauji too, for not being able to make proper arrangements. Already, the poor man was afraid of the sin he was committing by keeping the deity waiting. Cancelling the massage, he immediately went in to bathe. This was not enough for Taeeji. She kept moaning and lamenting. She called down heavenly wrath on everyone by name, accusing the brahmin for not reaching in time, despite the offer of a satisfactory honorarium; Gautam, for being an atheist and Kalyani for making it a second nature to sit "aside" whenever there was some emergency at home! Not only this, she was describing all kinds of hell one is likely to go to for keeping the deity on hold.

In an angry tone, Taeeji asked Kalyani, "Why you have not taken pills to defer this continuing nuisance, despite indication that I was not well and might catch a fever soon."

"It's no joke Taeeji, taking pills for stopping menses. I am not a backward, illiterate villager who would do such a thing."

"So you think you have risen above us or attended enlightenment because you are a little educated?" retorted Taeeji.

Janki was watching all this. Her little head made out the root cause of the mayhem, the unwashed deity. "What is so big deal in this?" She thought, "The idol of Krishna is very small. Lying aside is a copper water vessel. One could go and pour some water on the deity and rub it dry with a piece of linen. Then dressing the deity, offering flowers and making sandalwood paste would be taken care of by Tauji later. Thinking this Janki went into the *pujaghar* and washed the deity. Bringing peace was her sole motive, the child forgot she was not allowed to go into the kitchen much less enter the sacred space and even touch the deity. She was too young to fathom the consequences.

Taeeji collapsed when she got to know that Janki had touched the deity. Tauji was slapping himself while repeating Ram-Ram, Krishna-Krishna, vowing to make atonement.

As soon as Taeeji gained consciousness she resumed her moaning and cursing. She railed at Kalyani for finding only an untouchable for adoption.

"Now she is our own child, Taeeji ···," said Kalyani angrily. But Taeeji was not one to accept such an answer; her beliefs were too deep-rooted to take any rational explanation. So she replied in an equally sharp tone, "Our own child? Others are others – they can never become your own. Look at yourself, I had washed your nappies, your mother had always been busy taking care of your father. And you have forgotten all that. Would you have been so cruel to us if we were your own parents?"

"Why are you speaking like that Taeeji, it was never our intention to hurt you," saying this, Kalyani began crying. This confusion scared Janki and as Gautam reached home she burst into tears holding him tight. Meantime, the brahmin who had now come was called in by Tauji for a private conversation. After a while, they emerged with the view that since the deity had been desecrated by an untouchable, a *yajna* was necessary.

The suggestion infuriated Gautam. He became visibly angry. After what had happened in college, he was already ashamed of his own cowardice and went into a paroxysm of violence. Peace at home was greatly disturbed as a result.

The final point of combustion was from Bombay. It was by Jackie Gonzalves of an ad agency. Kalyani's unreleased film which had been canned for six years had been broadcast by the Mumbai centre of the government-owned television station. Jackie had seen the film and liked the simple girl played by Kalyani and invited her to Bombay to do a washing powder commercial.

"How long will the shoot take?" asked Kalyani.

"Look, Kalyani I want to avoid complications in the future, you will be required to sign on dotted lines. The ad will go on air for six months. But it will not be repetitive. We will change the script, location and punch line though not the model, your sari-bindi and the name of the product; of course!

"You mean ···." Before Kalyani could finish her sentence, Jackie interrupted. "Yes, I mean you have to sign a one-year contract with our company, with the clause that prevents you from appearing in any other advertisement during this period."

Holding the phone Kalyani turned her head toward Gautam, who was seated on the edge of the bed, flicking dust off his table lamp. Gautam did not hear what Jackie had said, but he could make out what it was all about. So not even raising his head, he suggested, "I think Kalyani you should say yes to him."

Meantime Jackie, who for a few seconds did not get any answer from the other side, fired the next arrow: "Kalyani, I have a few more names on my list who are ready to do this ad, but since your name was suggested by a star like Kabirji I thought···."

The arrow hit its mark. "Kabirji? Oh, yes I will be doing this ad," answered Kalyani with enthusiasm in her voice.

The fast-moving sequence of events forced them to make a quick decision to move to Bombay. This time Janki was also with them. Kalyani promised a crying Taeeji and Tauji that she would meet them frequently.

Ten

A GLITTERING DROP of blood across the glass surface enchanted Janki so much that she began to clap happily. A white coat-clad uncle, who was passing by, was amused to see the clapping child and smiled at her. Now it was Janki's turn to be surprised because the uncle was carrying a big cage with a few mice in it, not ordinary mice but the ones which had white furry skin and the transparent red eyes of a rabbit.

"Papa, white mice, look there papa"! Janki pointed her finger at the cage, tugging Gautam's arm.

"Yes, this is why I have brought you here, to show you the world of science," said Gautam spreading the drop of blood on a slide with a second slide. Putting it under the microscope, Gautam peered through the lens.

"I, too, want to see through that," said Janki. Just then, one more uncle in a white coat crossed the room. He was holding a big glass container, full of spinach leaves.

"Do white mice eat spinach?" She asked vaguely.

"No, no, I am taking the greens to find how much iron they contain," replied the white coat man with a smile.

"Oh Lord! The spinach is made of iron!" exclaimed Janki,

her eyes widening in amazement.

At this, Gautam smiled at the man with the glass jar and said to him "Shirish, please show Janki our cold room."

There, again, a big surprise was waiting for her. "Oh my God! Such a huge refrigerator, that people can walk into it!" Everything here was a surprise for her and she rained a barrage of questions on Shirish. "Why is everything made of glass here, do they brew tea in that furnace?" or "What is this glass tube for?"

Gautam had brought her here to solve a different question which perhaps lay within her. Janki was a child but this at least she might have guessed that she was the cause of the dispute for which they had to shift to Mumbai, Gautam thought. He knew that Taeeji had explained at length to Janki how her blood was different from theirs. "The colour of the blood you people have is black, you know, that is why it can never match ours. Our blood is of higher quality and sacred in nature; that is what is written in the scriptures. That is why I tell you to keep away from my kitchen; it's not that you are my enemy. I am just following the holy scriptures."

When Taeeji said this Janki looked at her own skin and began to rub it for a while. This might have given her the impression that the colour of her skin was a bit darker. This was what Gautam wanted to remove from her mind. A verbal explanation regarding the universal colour of blood could be difficult for a child to understand properly, so why not put everything before her so she knows the truth, thought Gautam. To show her that the colour of her blood was also red, he had brought her to the laboratory. Here she was shown the slide of her own blood, Gautam's blood, his colleague's blood and even the lab assistant's blood. The colour of all blood was red; Janki was now reassured.

• • • • • • •

Eleven

KALYANI WAS LEAVING for the shooting of her portfolio; and there was one more appointment for the day, a screen test in a private studio in Versova. The make-up she wore was light but she had taken her vanity bag along. Also, some extra clothing, though the outfit she was wearing now was glamorous enough. She was getting the ads where she was required to wear the sari–bindi combination. Now she wanted to get rid of the *bahenji* tag that the sari–bindi might have attached to her. In the film world, actors get typecast once they start doing certain kinds of roles. Kalyani thought she would never get glamorous roles, despite being beautiful, merely because of this image. So why not take the glitzy doll route? The dress she wore to the studio was body hugging. It was a long one-piece dress, reaching to her toes. There was a slit down the left from below the waist, through which her left leg would become visible with the slightest move. Its neckline was deep and back open. The stress of the padded bra underneath the fitting dress was making her cleavage accentuated. She was wearing heeled sandals and had removed the curlers just before leaving home. The brushing and styling would be done later on. This left her hair looking quite messed up.

Janki had never seen Kalyani like this before. She was so amused that she started laughing loudly. Holding her stomach she rolled across the bed. This was contagious enough for Gautam to lose control; unable to hold back he too joined Janki. Kalyani got so irritated with this that she pinched Janki's ears and threw a pillow at Gautam, even as they continued laughing. Sulking, Kalyani took off her sandals and threw them in the corner. Addressing Gautam, she said if both of them wished that she could stoop to continue doing washing powder endorsements then she would haphazardly put on a cotton sari and leave for the studio.

Gautam caught the delicate moment in mid-flight and switched off the laughter button. He suggested to Kalyani that she should not go in a local train wearing what she was and instead take a cab. Kalyani smiled at this and put on her sandals again saying "why are you getting jealous, I will take a cab only."

Kalyani was normal now and seeing this, Gautam began to tease her again. "Kalyani, it's never very cold in Mumbai, otherwise you could have wrapped a shawl around your shoulders, but don't worry I can always buy a nice dupatta for you," Gautam said; Kalyani smiled back at him. And the heaviness evaporated.

From the time they arrived here the family fell into a daily routine. Kalyani was the first to leave, followed by Gautam going off to the university. Janki's school bus picked her up thereafter. Though Kalyani did not have a fixed job, she was getting a lot of work as a freelancer. On some days she dubbed for a vague south Indian heroine and on others she anchored a television show. So there would be days when Kalyani left home after Gautam and she would be the one who made breakfast and got Janki ready for school. On other days it was Gautam's turn.

Janki preferred the days when Gautam was in-charge. With him she somehow felt free to demand her favourite food. The disciplinarian in Kalyani kept her in check. She liked the days when Gautam was present in the morning; he did not stop her from playing with Kundu.

The maid who came to clean their apartment and washed the dishes, brought her son Kundu along with. In school, children spoke fluent English and Janki found it difficult to bond with them. Her broken English prevented her from making friends, further, because they laughed at the way she spoke. With Kundu it was different. Janki spoke pidgin English to scare and impress Kundu and she enjoyed it a lot when he listened to her slack-jawed. Playing with Kundu also lifted the suffocation she felt at school.

Kundu, too, had his reasons to make friends with Janki. His mother did dishwashing and cleaning in several homes but the children there never talked to him in a friendly manner. Rather, the lady of the house would often order Kundu to dust their school bags or to help them put on their shoes. Why would somebody make friends with a person who touched their shoes? But Janki befriended him. She was the one who talked to Kundu first. Kundu also had somebody to borrow a few rupees from when he needed to.

Very soon this happened. That morning Kalyani and Gautam had both left home early. When her time came Janki locked the apartment and made for the bus stop. But before she reached the bus stop she met Kundu in the parking lot.

"Hi Janki, going to school? Your bag seems heavy; may I carry it for you? It is loaded with books and papers, isn't it"? asked Kundu.

"Of course, it is full of books," said Janki with pride, "but

I can carry it myself."

"Alright" said Kundu and kept walking along without a word. Then, after a few seconds, he asked her whether she had two-three rupees. Janki nodded, finding she had five rupees instead.

"I have a five rupee note, papa gave it to me as my pocket money," said Janki.

"I don't understand why you people get this 'fokat money,' but any way give it to me and I will buy you a cup of mind-blowing tea," said he.

"Mind blowing tea?" But Kundu, I am not allowed to have tea. Papa told me to drink milk instead. He says milk will strengthen my bones. Mummy also warned me against having tea. 'You will get darker with tea,' she told me."

"That I understand, your mother herself is very fair ··· but you are not going to turn dark by having tea just once," said Kundu. His chance of drinking that special tea was in danger of evaporating. Janki's mouth watered thinking of that heavenly brew, which she had last tasted when she lived on the Lord's estate. Her taste buds recalled the jaggery tea made by Saoo.

"But Kundu, I shall miss my bus. I will be marked absent. People at home will come to know," Janki said.

"There are so many children in your school, seeing bus loads of them surprises me. With so many of them, already, they will surely not miss one of them for just a day," he replied.

Janki was convinced by Kundu's logic.

"Do you know Janki, Mumbai is a *mast* city?"

"I know Kundu; it is a *mast* city, that is why trains run through the city itself. Not only trains, it seems everyone is running here," said Janki.

"What could be the reason behind it?"

"I have no idea," replied Janki shrugging her shoulders.

Kundu thought this was the right moment to come up with his own theory. "I think the city has some continuously rotating underground wheels that keep it on the move. Come out at midnight and you would not miss the buzz," said Kundu.

A Muslim mendicant was seen going from shop to shop with a smoking bowl in hand, the incense billowing free into every shop as it opened. This was his daily routine. It was a sacred ritual for the shopkeepers too; who believed this would bring them good luck. So they waited for the fakir every day. There were other rituals which were essential for them. To ward off the evil eye from the shop they hung a string of fresh green chillies and lemons at the shop entrance every morning. This created business opportunities for others. Readymade chilly-lemon vendors roamed the streets; by mid-morning their baskets got emptied.

In this city of dreams people always tried to propitiate the gods to favour them. Outside the Kalba Devi Temple in the locality there was a special arrangement. Two-three cows were tethered to a post. Those in search of special favours were feeding them from bundles of green grass kept at hand by a motley group of hopefuls. Temple-goers bought the grass for the cows standing nearby.

In the other lane, just opposite the temple, was a milk and curd shop. They crab-crawled across the road weaving in and out through the push carts loaded with bundles with difficulty since Janki was unused to this frenetic hubbub. Kundu had braved the perils of the road to show Janki not just the shop but something more interesting inside it. Here, a bulky woman was churning curd with a rope attached to a pestle almost her own height. She was making butter milk and not just was the water and curd shaking with the oscillation but body and flaccid biceps, breasts and the tyres of her midriff were quivering. Even her huge fleshy backside seemed to have a life of its own. Kundu found this scene hilarious and wanted to share it with Janki. There was no verbal equivalent to such a show. "Look Janki," he pointed his finger and said "there is our dear *thul-thul kaki*." With this they started laughing. The woman raising her hand glowered at them, scaring them away.

As they stopped laughing Kundu presented their next plan of action, "I can show you many more interesting things but there is a condition, you will speak English with them when I introduce you to my friends," he said.

"Why English?" asked Janki.

"I want to show them I have an English-speaking 'gul fend'."

Janki had no problem with this; rather she was happy that Kundu's friends would look at her with their mouths open.

After crossing interminable roads and lanes they now were near the Chandanwadi electric crematorium. According to their previous plan they were to cross a foot bridge, reach Marine Drive and eat popcorn sitting on the sea wall. But, all of a sudden, Kundu changed his mind and instead made for the local train station nearby. By this time, Janki had begun to feel hungry.

Kundu met his friends outside the station. There were five of them sitting – three girls and two boys. Their clothes were dirty, hair unkempt and sunburned.

Seeing Janki they turned their backs on her. From the corner of her eye she saw them eating *pav* without sauce or butter but they would dig their finger into a bottle and bring out a blackish green cream to spread on their bread.

Kundu nudged one of the boy's back with his knee and said with a possessive air, "How about us?" motioning with his eyes to what they were eating.

"It's not for free, we have bought it with our hard earned money," came the reply.

"We too have money," Kundu turned to Janki, "give me the money you have."

"But Kundu what about the tea and train ticket?" Janki asked fretfully.

"Forget the tea, let's buy what they're eating, you are going to enjoy it," Kundu said.

"Will they exchange it for my lunch box instead of money?" Janki offered.

The offer was happily accepted by Kundu's urchin friends. Now they were all eating *methi paratha*, lemon pickle and chocolate. Kundu and Janki were left with bread, Iodex and some thinner. After finishing this goblin's breakfast, they boarded the first train that halted there.

They got down at Dadar and headed straight for the tea counter. Now there was no money to return home or eating something else. Kundu was tired of toting Janki's bag. The enterprising boy suggested that Janki could sell her compass box or some books and raise a bit of money. She refused saying her father taught her every day; it was impossible for her to sell anything from her school bag. Undeterred, Kundu took off his shirt and both of them collected a few rupees by dusting cars in the parking lot. Kundu went further, by gambling they could double their money was the idea.

With this intention the two went under the bridge behind the station where a few young vagabonds were playing cards.

Forget about letting them join in the game, the boys snatched their money and chased them away.

Disappointed the children came out again onto the road. On the footpath a juggler was playing his hand drum and a monkey on a leash danced to its rhythm. To attract a crowd, the juggler played harder, calling out to the monkey in a loud voice. Still nobody seemed ready to stop and see the show. Here again, Kundu got an idea. "Let us dance along with your monkey. We three can certainly attract a big crowd. While dancing I will sing film songs – this can also be charged for," said Kundu helpfully. The Juggler accepted the offer.

The show was somewhat different this time, drawing in a few more spectators. While dancing the children would extend their palms into which some change would be dropped by viewers. A man among the spectators was watching Janki keenly as if trying to make out where he had seen her before. The minute Janki extended her hand toward him their eyes met and there was this flash of recognition. Janki, too, recognized him. He was Bargle uncle from the second floor of their building.

"Lord! What will happen now?" Janki forgot to breathe for a while, and without thinking she pushed through the circle of spectators, running as if for her life. The neighbour didn't give up. He chased Janki and caught her. Sensing a tight situation Kundu slipped away and ran in the opposite direction while Janki was taken home by uncle Bargle. Kalyani and Gautam had already reached home by that time. She was given to her parents, her "saviour" telling them that he had found their daughter begging on the street.

Kalyani began crying and screaming; very soon, it became a fit of rage as she began to throw objects around the room. First she snatched the bag hanging on Janki's back and threw it aside. The bag fell at Gautam's feet. Then she picked up a pillow from the settee and flung it at the sofa. Nothing happened. So she picked up a vase, targeting the dressing table. This time her aim was true, the object shattered the mirror. Trembling, Janki stood head down in guilt and fear. Gautam also wished Janki had not done what she had. He could have scolded her or given a thought to check whether there was something wrong with her upbringing by them. But Kalyani's uncontrolled rage had washed away that feeling. He was greatly disturbed by her wrath and the manner in which it had been shown.

Tired, after breaking and throwing things, Kalyani sat down at the edge of her bed, crying miserably. Losing control over her tongue she had said something which, like an arrow, went through Janki's heart. Gautam, too, was shocked by what he heard. She said, "For this pauper did I leave my dear Taeeji and Tauji? She has shown who she really is."

"Kalyani, do you know what you are saying!" Gautam shouted.

Kalyani looked at Gautam as if she had been shaken awake from unconsciousness. Her eyes were asking "Did I say something horrible?" But very soon she realized she had. Now she was wiping the tears from her face, while putting things in order. Still she could not gather courage to hug Janki and say sorry. But Gautam picked up the thread and patting Janki's face he said softly, "Go and change your uniform Janki. This happens, people make mistakes, but you can learn not to repeat them, Ok? Wait, I am bringing food for you and your mummy." Saying this Gautam left for the kitchen. Maybe he wanted to leave Janki and Kalyani alone together for a while.

At night, before going to sleep, Kalyani said to Janki, "Come here Janki, your heels need massaging, let me put some cream on them." This was Kalyani's way of mending fences. Janki had gone bare feet most of the time in her childhood so her heels were cracked and calloused. Not like Kalyani who always kept them covered in sleepers. Kalyani wanted to fill this gap in their class so she had made it a point to massage Janki's feet once in a while.

Janki said sorry when Kalyani was massaging her feet, she looked at Gautam and said sorry to him too. Gautam apologized and the patch up between them was complete. But something remained which was difficult for Janki to forget. That night she heard Gautam telling Kalyani, "I was not impotent Kalyani, it was you who insisted upon not having our own child."

Janki could not understand the meaning of the word impotent, but she was shocked to hear the word "our own child" from Gautam. So Gautam also never considered her "their own," she thought. This hurt her more than Kalyani's reminder about her caste; it was an unexpected blow to hear this almost bitter comment from him.

Kalyani had sold a piece of her farmland in her home town and bought an apartment in south Mumbai. After all it was a question of bringing up their child in relative sophistication.

Janki never came across Kundu again.

• • ● ● ● • •

Twelve

As Janki stopped the car at the crossing a girl knocked at her window. She was carrying a basket with flowers and a framed photo of a deity in it, around which some coins were strewn. The girl was giving Janki the jitters, standing there asking for some coins. She didn't want to look at the little child but the wheedling and knocking continued. A strange sense of déjà vu seemed to draw a well in front of Janki's eyes. When it became difficult to avoid her Janki got so perturbed that she drove through the red signal. Before she reached the next stop a traffic police man stopped her and gave her a ticket.

Now Janki prayed that her mother should not come to know about this incident. It's alright if Gautam knew. She could explain why she had run away from the girl at the crossing to her father, not to Kalyani. He was friendly and she found it easy to share things with him. It was not so with her mother, though she was the one who had groomed her. She was temperamentally unlike her husband – she could not bond easily.

She was grateful for this life she had been given and wanted not only to forget her past but to erase it from her life, from her memory. There should remain no trace of it, she thought. That was why she had sped away from the girl at the traffic signal, there was too much of her past in that child. She liked to be called Jane not Janki by her college friends. She spoke English with an American accent. Outside the home if somebody spoke to her in Hindi or Marathi she would act as if she did not understand much. She wanted to dash to the top where there would be stacks of money behind which everything is hidden, where caste, colour of skin and class become immaterial. She was eighteen now. At this point she thought money was the panacea for every hiccup in life. When she was fourteen she used to think eating was the mother cure all for her ills.

Around this time, she had a fight with Akshay, a youngster on the third floor, in the parking lot. Later, Akshay's mother had taunted Kalyani about the difference in their complexions, "From where did you get this *kali ghatan*? Why didn't you get her washed in the same machine as yours?" she asked. Her jibe was two pronged. She was pointing at the washing machine ad Kalyani had appeared in and Janki's accent.

That day Janki stifled her sobs until her parents went to sleep. After that, crying, she came out and raided the dining room cabinet to find solace in cream biscuits. Soon the box was empty. She continued crying; when she stopped she felt empty, and she reached for the box of salty snacks. In no time, she had eaten up all the snacks she could find and was down to just sugar grains.

Such bouts became regular. Whenever there was a fight between Gautam and Kalyani, an unknown fear would grip Janki. Eating was the only palliative which eased her stress. Most of the times, Janki was the root cause of her parents' quarrel. Like when Kalyani told Janki to fold clothes or make tea, Gautam would interrupt saying, "Kalyani, like your Taeeji you want to impose chores on the girl."

The mention of Taeeji in a negative context always annoyed Kalyani, who would reply tersely, "The way you speak about them gives the impression that they are your enemies. I know they made mistakes, but they are not bad, just old fashioned. And as for telling Janki to do domestic chores it is for her good. I would have done so, in case I had a daughter of my own, to make her independent."

"But Kalyani you never applied that to yourself. You always kept your hands away from soap and dust. ..."

"This is what I do not want to happen to her. Learning to be self-reliant does not mean becoming a servant. ..."

The argument would go on with Janki at the centre, filling her with tremendous guilt. After the episode the couple invariably patched up, often with Gautam saying sorry first and both retiring to the cosiness of their bedroom, leaving Janki with her guilt and food. But now the kitchen was not her only shelter, she had begun to store chocolates, biscuits and savouries in her school bag spending a substantial amount of her pocket money. Now, it was not just fear and stress which led her to these ravenous bouts, also boredom, loneliness, even happiness and excitement, were the triggers.

One day a long line of ants gave clue to her treasure, but only to Gautam; Kalyani was not at home. Gautam kept this hidden from Kalyani. They already had a fight over the issue of Janki's compulsive eating. Food was fast disappearing, but this was not Kalyani's concern. Kalyani wanted to stop the girl because she was afraid that Janki would reach the point where it would become difficult for her to control her weight. But Gautam was afraid that giving even subtle indications to Janki that she was overeating would hurt her self-esteem. He never said this directly but thought that the girl may connect this control over her eating to her past when she didn't have access to rare delicacies and that people now thought that she was devouring everything in sight.

That day when Janki came home her parents were busy fighting and didn't know when she had come. As soon as she entered the room, they suddenly went silent. But the fragments of their raucous conversation had already reached her ears. She felt ashamed of herself and guilt made her heart heavy, she needed a remedy. At this point the desire to eat began to overcome her. Soon she was eating muffins. Two pieces later she realized what she had done and slid into guilt. How could she do such a thing? She slapped herself, sprinkled some cold water on her face, but without relief. Before she knew it, she was at the refrigerator eating butter, banana and a slice of pineapple. She was trapped in a cycle of shame, guilt and desire.

• • •

Piyush Kheda. Yes, that was his name. He was an excellent batsman in school cricket team, always hitting sixes and boundaries. The girls called him "mini Sachin." He was tall and lean with a thick mop of curly hair and the face of a Roman god. To watch him play, girls remained on the campus, after school, even those who were not interested in cricket.

Popularity had given him certain arrogance; he ridiculed his classmates and spoke to them in a sarcastic tone. Still, he was applauded and befriended by the others. He was their hero. Whenever a match was won by the school team, the hero was carried aloft by his clapping and whistling fans. He puffed out his chest and clapped for himself along with the others. Girls were in awe of him and everybody hoped he would one day play for Team India.

Like other teenage girls, Janki was also crazy after Piyush. He had many girlfriends and liked to flaunt the numbers as if they were his sixes and boundaries. But he didn't consider Janki good enough to be added to his trophies. Janki had given him a love letter which he pinned on the school noticeboard, highlighting in red ink all the spelling mistakes and grammatical errors. He also ridiculed her English and posted a derogatory comment alongside the letter, "A buffalo's love letter to a king." When they came face to face he told Janki that a dark, fat bumpkin-like she should have looked into the mirror before writing to him.

That day, when the family gathered for dinner, the mother and father noticed that Janki's eyes were red. She was running her tongue over her dry lips and was eating desultorily, not asking for a second helping. Looking lost, Janki answered Gautam's questions with a mere nod.

Her parents had observed this and looked at each other with a meaningful glance silently asking each other "what happened, and you ask first." Ultimately Gautam asked and Janki replied that she had fought with a friend. For a while the subject was diverted and Janki left the dining room saying she had to complete her homework. Gautam and Kalyani also got up to watch TV. It was time for a show to be anchored by Kalyani; following which the couple turned in for the night.

In her room, Janki held a book and tried to read but tears blurred the text. She folded the book and cried with her head over her knees. With a heavy heart she tried to distract herself, painting her nails but her hands trembled and concentration evaded her. She looked around and took out a notebook and tried doodling. Nothing worked. Whatever she scribbled was with such pressure that it tore the pages and broke the nib of her fountain pen. Exhausted, she closed her eyes and hugged the pillows on her bed. She muttered choicest expletives drawn from

Ghunghru's bank for Piyush Kheda. Her disturbed mind refused to be comforted. Now the path treaded before beckoned her. She went straight to the kitchen, took out a dish of *chola* from the refrigerator and began to shovel it back as it was, without even heating it. For a while her attention was diverted and the relaxation encouraged her to go on eating. After polishing off the cold *chola*, she wondered what else was there to eat. This reminded Janki that Piyush had called her a buffalo. Now she was eating only to increase her weight. The guilt had set in. She went to the wash basin put a finger in her throat throwing up and ran the tap.

Gautam and Kalyani were unsatisfied with Janki's explanation about that fight with a friend. They had gone to their room but their ears were trained toward the kitchen. Gautam had reason to believe that Janki had become a compulsive eater. He knew she would go to the dining room if she was really perturbed. And he was right. The couple came out as they heard the tap running in the kitchen sink and over it the retching sound.

It was clear now, that Janki had some serious problem which needed to be addressed. Gautam told Kalyani that just that day he had held a lecture in his class about the link between mental health and eating disorders. "We need the help of a psychiatrist for Janki," he said. Kalyani agreed readily.

That night they kept Janki with them in their bedroom. Gautam chose to sleep on a sofa so that Kalyani and Janki could use the double bed. He remained seated, though, at the head of the bed and patted Janki to sleep as if she was a "six months old" infant. Janki felt secure as never before; the satisfaction she drew from this affection was great enough to be compared with eating *chola*. It was neither as superficial nor transitory as eating. While entering into the presence of goddess of sleep she felt as if Saoo was patting her, perched at the edge of her bed. That night, Janki sank into a deep sleep she had never before.

This was a turning point in Janki's life. Now Kalyani had begun to take her to a gym every day. Sitting with her dietician, Kalyani had also drawn up a regimen for Janki. Every week Gautam took Janki to a psychiatrist, Dr Miraj Modi. On some days, the doctor would call Kalyani along so that they could interact. There were other days when he would talk to the parents alone. Gradually, Janki gained confidence; the emptiness within her was gone and with that the weighty problem of compulsive eating. She had become like any other Mumbai girl, the only child of her doting parents.

The butterfly emerged from her cocoon. The dark, obese girl with a dry skin disappeared, leaving behind a plump, young lady, not very fair but with a healthy youthful skin. There was no super flat tummy and her derrière was somewhat bulky. She was big busted, but overall, the ugly duckling had turned into a swan by regular workouts and intelligent eating. Youthful and charming now, it was the boys who were after her. With school Piyush Kheda was left behind. One day she came across him. She could not believe he was the person she had once been attracted to. Cricket was no more his passion. After leaving school, he entered the big world and rend into real competition, which he could not keep pace with and had said goodbye to the game. Now he was a podgy, frustrated man. He showed interest in Janki but she turned her back on him.

Janki was not an intellectual; reading books was not her passion. Academically also, she was not as sound as both her friends Parizad and Pranita. With good cut-off marks Parizad got admission in mass communication and Pranita in BA English honours. Janki started learning folk dance and yoga.

Parizad wanted to be a journalist like her mother Farida, who was an editor with a film magazine. Parizad's father Homi had a restaurant and wanted her to do a course in hotel management. Her sister Farzana was doing a fine arts degree. She, too, took another direction. But Homi was a soft-hearted man and he loved his daughters dearly. He didn't have the heart to impose anything on them. Parizad was the younger one and was pampered by her father. The excessive fondness could be seen clearly in the father–daughter interaction. Janki liked to see Parizad putting her arm around Homi's neck while saying something but this was with a tinge of envy. Gautam doubtless was a doting father, but there was something missing – the expression of their affection for each other was not so informal. The same way, Janki thought about Kalyani when she saw Pranita putting her head on her mother's lap. Kalyani, on the other hand, had set up a wall of discipline between the two, through which normal bonding could not be brought about. Janki could only imagine putting her head on Kalyani's lap.

Kalyani, Gautam and Janki had grown up similarly distressed, their childhood filled with emotional turmoil. Still they could not share the emptiness of their hearts. Each dealt with the same distress differently. Perhaps this was why they found themselves out of sync with each other.

Kalyani's way of dealing with distress was to follow detachment. "Love and emotional dependence ultimately bring distress," had long been her inclination. Kalyani's mother always wanted to sit with her for a while, but her daughter was forever running away fearful of the ensuing distress. One day when Kalyani's father was in stable health, he had tried to show affection for his daughter by putting his head on her lap. She had responded by pushing him aside, jumping up as if startled by a mouse. Deeply embarrassed, he fled the scene never to repeat what he had done.

Kalyani's mother once asked her whether she felt bad that her father was not a normal person or was she just unhappy for him. A stern "no" was the reply, the girl's face almost emotionless. She had created an icy wall around herself, as it were. "If I do not let emotions in or out, no turmoil would touch and hurt me," she thought.

The same attitude caused problems for Gautam also. This emotionless beauty was difficult to connect with. During the college days Kalyani had won the university beauty queen crown. Boys were after her, crazy fans and hopeful suitors surrounded her, but not for long. Soon the realization dawned that Kalyani's beauty was perpetually in a neutral phase when it came to emotions. One by one, all her cheerleaders slipped away, except Gautam.

But his love for Kalyani was true. He was not a mere whistling fan like the others, in that there was depth in his love. Gautam had tried to attract her attention in many ways; when nothing else worked he used the last ploy. He had written a love letter to Kalyani not in ink, but in blood. To his surprise, it did not work though she was impressed. So the next step he took was to propose marriage to her. This worked. After all, she was required to marry somebody, someday, in an arranged marriage, so why not Gautam?, she thought.

This was why Kalyani had the upper hand always in their relationship. She might have followed the "emotional detachment" path but had realized the joy of living. In the matter of emotions she slipped only once. That was for Kabir. But this, too, was not pure emotion; pride in her beauty was there.

Gautam's way of dealing with a life devoid of the love of

his own people was just the opposite to that of Kalyani. He never tried detachment. He would sail through the desert of lovelessness by finding an oasis in somebody and then, laser-like, focusing all his attention toward that person.

Like when he was in school, he had developed a tremendous attachment for one of his teachers. Gautam's devotion to this teacher was such that he was ready to sweep his room, or press his legs if needed. It made no difference if people called Gautam guruji's *chamcha*. It was enough for him that he had found a person to devote his feelings to. After he migrated to a city from his village, for some time he had stayed at his half-sister's place. A cat crawled around the settlement where the house was. It would frequent their home too, looking for the opportunity to put its head into uncovered vessels of milk or curd. Gautam took to the cat and secretly, saved rotis from his meals to feed it. He saved money from his stipend for packets of milk and would clean the floor or the bed sheets if the cat had left its visiting cards on them. Once, when it had taken ill, Gautam took it to a vet. His brother-in-law got so irritated with Gautam's fondness for the cat, that one day, when he was not home; it was beaten brutally and was thrown out unceremoniously. Otherwise also, Gautam was a thorn in the flesh for the sister and her husband; the "cat drama" gave them a pretext to tell him goodbye.

Gautam was more than good academically. He fared very well and before long had begun to receive a scholarship. With that, he rented a simple, one-room accommodation and took on a few students for tuition. This was when he came across Kalyani in college. Gautam was stricken. His love for Kalyani crossed the boundary of obsession. Maybe, he was not obsessed but thirsty for love and care. Now Kalyani was his, but not his, ironically. This he realized very soon from her predictable, cold response.

Then luckily Janki came drawing all his love and affection.

Janki's childhood was not a lonely one. She had experienced the warmth of love from Saoo and the sense of bonding from Laxmi. But the complication here was that Janki didn't want to pickle those memories; rather, they were barred from her consciousness. She was afraid that her past might mar her new identity. She liked both Kalyani and Gautam. She was emotionally dependent on Gautam, yet she was searching for something to fill the void that persisted. Always in and out of relationships, she kept a study score of her boyfriends. May be peer pressure was also there. She didn't want to be seen living in the past. This was the new Janki.

• • • • • • •

Thirteen

MOHAN HAD BROUGHT some brilliant colour pigments from the Himalayas. The fresh and flamboyant tints had been extracted from a range of blooms spread across the valley. When he put them on the canvas their subtle aroma wafted through the air. As he dipped his brush into the colour drawn from the rare golden *champa* it looked like molten sunshine.

A yogi gave Mohan the iridescent *nagmani* dust, taken from the jewel found in a snake's head. Butterflies fluttered by, their wings sprinkling colours on to the palette, the creatures enamoured as they were by Mohan's canvas. After coming into contact with Hariyaliram and spending lengths of time with yogis and people from the mountain, Mohan had learned the language of birds. The same skill made him understand, to a large extent, what the butterflies, had to say when they fluttered their wings, somersaulting and looping through the air. This was like conversing with butterflies. Whenever Mohan was engrossed in his work and a butterfly seemingly wanted to make a point, it would descend and tickle his palm with its wings. This was their way of sharing the secrets of the mystical Himalayas with Mohan. These flamboyant friends led him to Yogiraj Vatsal.

Mohan painted a stunning portrait on a large canvas; a golden-bearded yogi mounted on a lion. His flowing beard touched the lion's golden mane. The ascetic's head, too, was adorned with thick, golden hair plaited into a braid, reaching his waist. This was not an imaginary portrayal; this was the real Yogiraj Vatsal. The Guru was not an escapist; he was present to reveal new ways for human kind to find eternal bliss.

His ashram, Anand Ashram, was suggestive of his mission. Even the vibrations of pure happiness could be felt throughout the place. The ashram's rolling acres were interspersed by numerous dwelling units of walnut wood. The Guru's disciples had engraved beautiful pictures on their walls. The theme differed in each hut, depending on the nature of the activity within it. If a meditating youth was engraved on the wall of one hut, another was adorned by the image of a mendicant preparing a broth of Himalayan herbs in a cauldron. A woman was milking a musk deer in one of the images. Yes, a musk deer; neither a cow nor a buffalo. Guru Vatsal was against violence of any kind, so there was no question that this animal would be killed for its pod of fragrance. Anand Ashram was a place of infinite pleasure and deep-rooted peace. The deer themselves came here to be milked. After taking the musk in the form of milk, ashram dwellers brewed it into a fine wine. This singular drink did not create an uncontrolled passion but overbrimming euphoria.

Guru Vatsal was not a small-time scientist. He was a rishi. He would extract "bliss" not only from the musk, but from life itself by his continuous experiments.

Rare *brahmakamal* flowers bloomed across the ashram land. On full-moon nights, their presence created an illusion of myriad full moons alighting on earth. Moonlight falling on snow-clad mountains bathed these flowers with the same affection; their heady fragrance producing a dreamy effect on the spectator.

During the day, sky-touching cedars and pines, lush green valleys, rushing waterfalls and boisterously coloured blooms made for a perfect paradise. Blue poppies, red *burunsh* and nature's other floral expressions lured butterflies and song birds. In the language course of the Ashram University, there was a provision for learning the language of birds and animals. For the music class, along with the traditional Indian music and European classics, they taught bird music. Some bulbuls regularly came from Persia to take such classes. The fauna of the region had birds like *mahok* and black-necked cranes, beautiful in every respect.

Like musk deer, other animals too visited the ashram. Black mountain bear from the foothills frequently arrived with pots of fresh honey for Guru Vatsal. These would not be earthen vessels but containers fashioned from pumpkins. He never discarded these empty containers, but would make unique mechanisms from them which had the power to separate colours from sunrays. These colours were then filled in seven crystal decanters. The Guru had given some of these colours to Mohan for painting; they were used on the wooden walls of the ashram cabins. The colours were so brilliant that there was no match to their quality. But the Guru did not create these colours merely to paint the ashram huts. He used the pumpkin vessels and the hues extracted from the sun for medical treatment. Though he had invented a method by which he could harness gold from sunlight, he was against using it. "Greed is the worst enemy of one's happiness," he would say.

Yogiraj Vatsal had worked on many more methods to find true bliss in and around people. In this series, he had created a vibration-control tool, where every atom was charged with pure bliss, simultaneously sorting negative particles and burying them forever. This was not as simple for him as the colour separation. For this he needed the support of each one from the ashram. The bliss could not be created merely through gadgets. It also required the positive vibrations of those in the ashram. Meditation, yoga, knowledge, balanced diet was the way of life toward creating an overarching aura of bliss-particles. The yogi believed that taste, odour, sex or any sensual pleasure was in order, rather, added to the formation of bliss. But, above all was the virtue of compassion. "If a person has no compassion, there is no bliss for him," was his principle. The Guru had made a pair of spectacles from the wings of an outsized dragon fly. After formulaic incantations the spectacles were ready for him to witness a phenomenon hitherto unseen by any other mortal being. Through these spectacles the density of bliss particles in the environment was visible in a concrete form. Not only this, the amount of "misty compassion" present around the ashram could also be seen through these lenses. It was too dense to the extent that if a person was bruised, marks appeared on others' bodies.

Guru Vatsal was not against sensual pleasure of any sort, if it was observed within a spiritual discipline. He had a *kama-kala* centre in the Ashram, which taught acolytes how to reach unmentionable joy through sex, called *brahmananda*. In this instance, he emphasized that virtues like compassion were necessary. "A rapist can never get happiness from the act," was his firm belief.

• • • ● • • •

Fourteen

KALYANI WAS CRYING incessantly. Gautam and Janki were unable to understand what the matter was. After this outpouring of tears, as was her nature, Kalyani began to throw things, in reply to Gautam's question, "What has happened to you?" "Mom, tomorrow you have a shoot, you will have dark circles around your eyes, if you continue crying," Janki reminded her. At this, Kalyani stared at the girl, not in anger, rather with a kind of helplessness. Lowering her eyes soon she left for the washroom. Puzzled, Gautam and Janki looked at each other in silence. Without a word, they began to put the room in order.

After a few minutes, Kalyani peeped out from behind the washroom door and asked for an inch tape. "Inch tape!" Gautam said in surprise. "Shut up" snapped Kalyani. In a few seconds, Gautam handed her an inch tape.

The washroom had a mirror, through which Kalyani could see her upper body. Closing the door she pulled out her blouse. Topless, she could see that her alabaster breasts were as white as before, round enough to deceive the mirror. She was certain it could not make out the difference age had brought in her. But, for a few days Kalyani had been apprehensive that the distance between her collar bone and the nipple had increased. She had been pondering over the matter with the hope that it might be a mere doubt.

After what happened today, she wanted to check the truth so that she could prove to herself that nothing had changed. For the first time, she had measured the length from her collar bone to the nipple when she was twelve. She did this a few more times in the intervening years. And after a long gap, she had held the tape deftly against herself. ··· "Down six centimetres!" she was aghast. Shrieking, she threw the tape away as if it was a snake.

She had met Kabir the previous month. It had become almost a routine that big banner films did not have shootings in Mumbai. Most of the time, Kabir was out of the country, filming from Malaysia to London, anywhere but India. When there was no shooting, he was busy doing shows abroad. He preferred to holiday in Ooty, where he had bought an estate. It was very rare for him to be found in Mumbai. Whenever he was here Kalyani tried, not always successfully, to get in touch with him. But whenever she did get an appointment, Kabir was always cordial to her, not showing over enthusiasm. She never expected more than this, because it was enough for her that he did not avoid her.

On one of such occasions, when Kalyani had a rendezvous with Kabir, she saw that he had gone through a makeover. He styled his hair differently, the crow's feet had suddenly disappeared, but his eyes said it all, he was tired. The Botox had done its work, what else would remove them, she thought. His body was lean and sharp as ever and at a glance he remained handsome. But all this was in a jaded sort of way. Kalyani, using her guile, complimented him on this. He replied that she was also looking fit. But she, not wanting to waste this opportunity, immediately expressed her wish to work with him at least once more. Kabir promised her that his personal assistant would certainly talk to the director of his next film, regarding the matter. He made it clear that these days they had separate casting agents and casting directors.

This was not a hollow promise. Within a month, Kalyani received a call from Golden Eagle Films. She was being given a role alongside Kabir. The role was small but important, she was told. "When shall I come for the story narration?" She asked. But there was no need for her to go to the company's office. A private session had already been held for Kabir. In group narration only those who had major roles were called. Kalyani was to be given her dialogues and scenes ten days before the shooting. After shooting for a month or so, the crew was scheduled to leave for South Africa, but Kalyani's part had to be completed here; she was not required to accompany them abroad.

Kalyani found nothing wrong in the arrangement. She knew her place. Rather, she was happy that though she had a bit role, she was in a big star's film. She was wondering as to how the opportunity had come to her door. She tried to guess. May be it was because Kabir knew her, or perhaps that she had maintained her figure, Kalyani thought glowing inside. She always received compliments in parties, "Don't tell me, you aren't thirty yet, Kalyani!"

Then one day an email brought her the dialogue and scenes – "*Beta* you know very well, I am scared of flying. I won't be able to accompany you to New York." Kalyani scrolled the matter up and down several times and went through the script again and repeatedly. There was no misunderstanding here. It was clear that she would have to play Kabir's mother. Dumbfounded, she stared at the screen.

She was furious and disappointed. Even devastated! Mother to Kabir! The idea left no space even for fantasizing over a romantic connection. She was of the same age as Kabir, rather, younger by three-four years. Wrath boiled in her heart, "A man never ages in this industry. Kabir was still running around trees with seventeen-year old girls in many of his films. But female actors had a short shelf life. Shreelekha had to play *bhabhi* to her one-time heroes as soon as twenty-eight knocked at her door. Their double standards!" Kalyani ground her teeth in muted fury.

She tried to reassure herself that she still looked young. It was the film industry's fault that they treated women with a different yardstick. But in the same breath she put aside her own claim to everlasting beauty. In her heart she knew her true age. The illusion created by good grooming could cover your face with a youthful mask, but the windows of your eyes always revealed your real age. Pondering over the age trap, Kalyani suddenly realized she had become a biddy. She asked herself sarcastically, "Came to know only today that you are no more a young girl?" No, not exactly.

For a few days she had been observing the gradual metamorphosis her body was going through. She was aware that she could not wear shorts any longer. Though her legs were still long and shapely, small tell-tale dips had begun to appear on them. She had discarded her old swimming costume and bought a new knee-length one. She had appointed a regular masseur to deal with the unevenness of her thighs. Her dermatologist had suggested she use an anti-cellulite cream. Her efforts were working well or so she assumed. But today she was trapped by a huge disappointment.

Growing old was Kalyani's biggest fear and she had been unable to accept it until now. "Age is only a number. What actually matters is the way you look. If I pamper myself I will look young." Self-delusion had prevented a reality check. The shock of getting a mother's role had jolted her out of the reverie. But instead of accepting the age with grace she was looking to extend this fantasy. She planned to go to her home town and sell the piece of land from the Lord's estate on which Ghunghru's hut remained. Kalyani wanted money to splurge on cosmetic treatments available. Botox, restylene and other wrinkle erasers and fillers, collagen facials, liposuction, breast augmentation and the rest. Kalyani wanted it all. She had begun to dream of a new body starting with her face.

• • ● ● ● • •

Fifteen

THEY WERE NOT IN a mood to dance. Janki and her two friends had come to Mojo, a club in south Mumbai. They ordered their favourite drinks along with some starters. While they were sipping their drinks they saw a big busted woman entering the club. She wore a light green top which appeared florescent on her dark complexion. It was teamed with a black skirt. As she laughed, her white teeth were a flashing contrast against her skin, reflecting their brightness as if they too were florescent. She passed by waving and smiling at Janki's friends Shagun and Dimpy but did not stop for an introduction or fleeting exchange of words. The girl was now near the swimming pool talking to a man inside it. A little later he came out and headed for a booth to dry up; the two then hands around each other's waist, began laughing over some probably put on intimacy.

"Look at that 'shiddu.' She used to live in a chawl in Virar. See how the blackie is putting on airs cosying up to that tycoon – as if he is going to marry her," said Dimpy to Shagun, voice dripping with spite.

"Let her be happy *yaar*, a fling with that moneybag is not going to change her history. Whatever she does, she will remain a *chalwali ghatan*," replied Shagun scornfully.

"History?" Janki mumbled to herself. Her face turned pale as if she had been caught stealing. "What happened Jane, why this sudden fallen face. Not enjoying the drink," asked Dimpy.

Janki quickly put on a smile to hide her reaction and said, "Curfew hours, *yaar*, I have to reach home before twelve."

"O curfew hours! Middle-class parents?" I have no such problem. My parents themselves must be attending some party somewhere, said Dimpy as a matter of fact.

But Janki was not ready to throw in the towel. She offered a lame explanation. "We are not middle-class. The thing is that my Mom ···"

She could not complete her sentence before Shagun interrupted sarcastically, "so you people have a princely estate."

Janki could sense that Shagun was teasing her; the veiled taunt had hit her. But Janki wanted to press home what she had already said, that she was not middle-class; rather, flaunting the princely estate lie had led her toward the convincing invention about her being *khandani* rich. "There is nothing wrong in lying or cooking up things, as long as you don't hurt anybody," she told herself and was now ready to project the Lord's estate as her ancestral, princely estate. No harm done and there was no risk, either. The friends were not about to go to the small town to check. So Janki had confidently fibbed that they possessed much landed property. She added that her father had a sizeable collection of vintage cars in their home town and her mother had inherited ancestral jewellery of diamonds, pearls, emeralds and sapphires, along with a tiara of solid gold. A producer, after seeing this tiara, had given her mother the role of a princess in one film, claimed Janki, laying it on thick.

This left Shagun staring. She had heard a lot about the lifestyle of rich people in Mumbai, and befriended their children. Dimpy was one of them. But this was new for her, this princely estate and tiara thing seemed like a piece of a fairy tale to her. She didn't want Janki to know that she was in awe of her estate. Shagun kept her mouth shut and tried to sound normal. "So, Janki do you have a boyfriend or not?" she asked.

It was easier for Shagun, not for Janki, to keep up this charade because she was lying and needed to keep her composure. Janki indeed had a boyfriend who was from a humble background. Mohan, Janki really liked him. She had dumped her previous lover, a gym instructor, for the passionate Mohan. Janki was annoyed with her previous boyfriend, a skirt-flirt despite having Janki. He shamelessly wooed wealthy wives attending the gym. With Mohan on the scene the *rangeela* gym instructor was thrown out but not before she learned from him the simple truth about this mega city; to survive here you needed to behave rich and be seen in the company of the rich.

After finishing their drinks the girls left the club before twelve. Shagun, on her way out told Janki that their next venture would be a party; if Janki came along, she would be introduced to Keval Ramani, a casting director in the Hindi film industry.

• • • ● • • •

Sixteen

MOHAN'S QUEST FOR Janki had led him to Mumbai. Otherwise he would have been happy to settle down in a village or a small town after returning from the Himalayas. In fact, he first went to his home town after coming back. There he came to know that Janki had settled in Mumbai with her parents. Only then he had come to the big city and found a job in a fine art college but not Janki. The addresses given to him were incomplete. Four years he had been living in Mumbai with the hope in his heart that he would come across Janki someday. This was madness, sheer madness. How an iota could be found in the vastness of this city without any proper address. But Mohan had confidence in the pull of his love. On pavements, in trains, in movie theatres, wherever he went he looked for Janki. He was sure that even after all these years, he would recognize Janki immediately.

That day Janki had come along with Parizad's sister Farzana to the art college. Farzana and her classmates were on the lookout for a model for a special painting session. The idea was a fusion of East and West. The model needed to wear a Marathi nine-yard sari, a big nose ring and bindi along with a hat and tie.

Farzana did not know Janki's history, but somehow she felt

that Janki was the model who could carry off this look. She saw that Janki had something about her, which was modern and rustic together. Janki, agreed, knowing that this required long hours of sitting still. Actually she loved the idea of such a painting.

This was the day when Mohan found Janki and recognized her immediately. Janki did not talk to him initially, but relented when after a few meetings she realized the intensity of his fondness and that he loved her with her history and everything she had or did not have. His love was unconditional. Janki's condition was that her history should not be exposed to her friends and acquaintances in Mumbai. For Mohan, it was a small thing and he embraced it.

Seventeen

JANKI HAD A LOT to do before the party. She needed branded sandals, a bag, a silk gown and accoutrements. Since she had said that she was from a royal family, she needed to arrange for some old real jewellery. For this she definitely could not possibly drip with antic ornaments. It was enough that she was adorned with just one or two really authentic pieces. Though Kalyani had bought an exquisite gold bracelet and earrings with real Basra pearls, especially for her daughter, Janki wished she could get the large emerald ring which Kalyani wore on some special occasions. She would wear it to the party and return it to Kalyani, thought Janki. But it was not that simple. It was quite likely that Kalyani would willingly loan the ring to Janki who nevertheless did not have the courage to ask for it.

Gautam's Happiness Clinic was going well. He had given twenty thousand rupees to Janki to get her portfolio done; her plans were different, though. She was going to meet a casting director Keval Ramani in person and a formal portfolio could wait, she thought. It would be better to use the money marked for shopping, instead. Even this was not enough for her to buy all the branded things for which she had made a mental list of. So she took some assignments, some of which she could not mention to her parents. One of them was posing nude for Kala Niketan art students, to be completed in twelve days. For this period she needed to sit still, without clothes, each day for many hours. These were afternoon sessions, which was no problem for Janki's schedule. She had signed for a C-grade Bhojpuri film also, with the shooting to be done in Patna in a couple of months and had received the signing amount. A film magazine had announced a makeover contest. Aiming for the Gucci shades as the winning prize, Janki essayed a try even here. One more humble assignment came her way which she lapped up eagerly. She had to model for semi-precious earrings for a Marathi magazine of an almost negligible print run. They were giving her cash for the ad, not the earrings; she would not have done it if there was no cash; she didn't need such semi-precious articles.

That day, Janki had two back-to-back assignments. First the nude painting, later she had to appear for the makeover contest for the film magazine. Crooning, Kalyani was in a great mood that morning. She had an invitation for a Botox-party and had taken out the emerald ring from her vault. The family was in a light mood, laughing and bantering over breakfast. Since she had taken it out, Kalyani casually slipped the ring onto her index finger.

Whenever Kalyani had to attend some special event she would brush her teeth after eating anything, wash her face and then put on make-up, never before eating. It was the same that day.

Suddenly, she shrieked bringing Gautam and Janki running to the wash basin. It turned out that while brushing, a piece from one of Kalyani's molars had fallen into her hand. She was terrified. Gautam tried to soothe her, "Why are you getting so anxious Kalyani. There is nothing much to worry about. A cavity in your molar might have weakened it and dislodged the tooth with your brush. Go to a dentist have it cemented and everything will be alright. Simple! Stop worrying about these trivial issues. Such things will happen as we age, why not learn to live with it for a change?"

Gautam was trying to calm Kalyani but it had the opposite effect. Everything went wrong with the mere mention of age. Her mood became more sombre. She had received the "Miss Pearly White" title during her college days and had once done a toothpaste ad. Was she going to lose her beautiful teeth, one by one, with the inevitable depredation? The question was making her miserable. She remembered well, how conscious was she even in her childhood of her smile? She used to dance before the full-length mirror, enchanted with her own image. But, one day the game was spoiled when she lost her first teeth. She wailed so much as if an earthquake had shattered her. She knew that the loss was not permanent and that she would get a natural new tooth in its place. Here the loss was irreversible. She couldn't wear high-heeled sandals for as long as she could earlier, she thought with a sigh. Whenever she went to a party she was complimented about her appearance, but she could not deceive herself like she had others' perception of her body.

Her knees had begun to ache and, on some days when she wore heeled sandals she needed pain killers. Gautam had suggested that she should stop wearing stilettos; she did not need them. Kalyani was averse to dragging her feet in flats; this would do no good for her sex appeal. Despite the enormous pain she always chose heeled footwear. Something had to snap. One day, she attended a garden party, where the soil was wet and the surface uneven. Kalyani had saved herself from falling several times, finally losing her balance and twisting her leg. This was disaster for her knees with the pain spreading to her lower back. The realization now struck her that her age was bringing limitations with it.

Morosed over these compulsions of ageing she had forgotten the emerald ring on the wash basin as she left home. Even Gautam and Janki had not seen it since they were busy calming Kalyani.

Later, when Janki went to wash her hands she saw the ring lying on the wash basin. She picked it up and gave it to Gautam, asking him haltingly, "Papa may I keep this ring for a few days? I have to attend a party next week and today there is a makeover … please let mummy know about this and also that I had asked your permission to keep the ring for a while."

Gautam was in a dilemma. He wondered how to put it to Janki. There was a story attached to the ring. It related to an intimate moment between him and Kalyani. On their first night when Kalyani took off her clothes and ornaments, Gautam had requested her not to remove the ring. "Complete nudity lacks the aesthetic," he had said. Kalyani had laughed coyly at this.

Looking at Gautam lost in thought, instead of giving her permission, Janki felt perhaps she had asked for more than her rights permitted her to. "Alright papa, let it be, if it is not possible. It's not that important," she said.

But Gautam did not want Janki to feel that she did not have the right to make even a small demand. He didn't want to hurt her, so he told her to keep the ring for the day but to return it to Kalyani in the evening, at the same time asking her to keep it further for the party following week.

In the evening when Kalyani came home she got the news of Tauji's demise. In shock and panic, she began to pack her suitcase, crying incessantly. She was to catch the train that same night; Gautam was not ready to accompany her to the Lord's estate, further spoiling her mood.

When there were about ten to fifteen minutes left for Kalyani to leave for the station, Janki entered home. Though her back was a little stiff due to the long sitting, she was very happy since both her assignments had turned out very well. She carried away the first prize in the makeover contest. The magazine's artist had given her the look of an old time heroine – Vishakha. This suited Janki so well that she almost resembled the star. So she didn't change and came home as she was. She thought Kalyani would be happy to see her like this since the same Vishakha, Janki knew, had once worked with her mother.

When Janki entered, Kalyani was arranging her suitcase. As her eyes fell on Janki she was shocked, a look alike of her arch enemy Vishakha stood before her. This startled her. She shouted aloud, "Are you a joker or what, Janki. What made you put on the guise of a witch?"

Janki's smile vanished. Her expression froze as she apologized in a low voice, "sorry mummy," and began crying. This was totally unexpected; Janki could not understand why her mother had reacted this way. What was her fault?

Gautam too was taken aback by Kalyani's sudden outburst and was feeling bad for Janki. But he thought that because Kalyani was upset at Tauji's demise she was behaving that way. Since Gautam was not going with Kalyani, he was feeling a little guilty also. So instead of saying anything to Kalyani, he gestured to Janki to stay quiet. Then Gautam told her about Tauji's demise.

After a while Kalyani left for the station and the ring remained with Janki. Kalyani's mood was already so bad that Gautam and Janki didn't dare mention about the ring.

• • • • • • •

Eighteen

"KEVAL RAMANI, what an imposing personality he has," thought Janki. This sprawling farmhouse and the adjacent luxurious bungalow were his property. He had a stern countenance; his height and physique were good, there were no wobbly tires around his waist or a paunch in sight. His flat stomach was cinched in a belt with his shirt tucked in. He must be working out a lot, it seemed. He had a receding hairline, a loophole in his personality; he had worn big brands apparel and accessories. But his main characteristic was his self-confidence. He greeted his guests in a lordly manner as if he were a king.

Some emerging models and Bollywood aspirants had also made it to the party. Film star Suraj Kiran's son Sami was the cynosure of all eyes. "He too is going to be a big star one day," people whispered to each other. "His father will definitely launch him one day."

Yet Janki didn't like him much. "He seemed rather dumb, one who could not flick away a fly sitting on his nose," she mused. When Sami opened his mouth, speculation became confirmation. His voice was frail and muffled.

"How is he going to do a film? He would be a certain flop," whispered Janki to Shagun.

"He is a star-son. Even if his films flop he will keep getting films. If he is unable to deliver dialogues properly, a dubbing artist will do the job later. Make-up and technology can create a fake personality on screen," said Shagun.

"Then what is he doing in a casting director's party if he is going to get roles anyway?" asked Janki.

"You will come to know soon," replied Shagun. In the same breath she asked Janki whether she had some cash on her.

"Not much ..., Janki stopped mid-sentence, realizing Keval Ramani was standing near them. Dimpy, too, was there with him. "This is Jane my friend. She is new in our group," Dimpy introduced Janki to him. "And this is Keval Ramani, the host of this party," said Dimpy.

With an ear to ear smile, Keval took her hand and shook it warmly."Welcome," he said.

It seemed that there were sufficient guests now for the celebration to gather pace. The hue of the hall-lights was gradually changing; now cool mild blue light threw its halo. As a counterpoint, ghazals were replaced by loud uptempo music. The centre table, sofa and other furniture were moved to the corner of the hall. The waiters, who till now moved about with their trays full of starters, were now standing behind the food tables. The table cloth was removed from a long table, and a few stools were placed alongside it. On a glass-top table in front of the bar was a range of trays in which pouches of a white powder, coloured pills and cigarettes were neatly arranged in small boxes. As the DJ opened, on the dance floor came many pairs. So this was a rave party thrown by Keval Ramani, and

Sami was here to attend it.

The orange tablets had the letter "R" etched on them. This was Yaba from Thailand, which India's drug pedlars called *bhool-bhulaiya*, LSD (lysergic acid diethylamide), Ecstasy and cocaine were also available there. Some youngsters slouched over the glass-topped table snorted lines of cocaine through rolled-up currency notes. Self-indulgence ruled the evening. Some smoked, others quaffed to their eyeballs. And the dance floor lured everybody.

Suddenly Janki remembered something and she anxiously looked at her wrist watch. It was eleven thirty. "Curfew hours," she thought. But soon she comforted herself, "Mummy is out of the city. Of course papa is there but it's always easier to explain to him." It was not an overnight stay, after all. A few hours could be extended, she consoled herself.

Dimpy came over to her and held out some Ecstasy. "Try it once Janki and you would never forget the experience. It is pure bliss," she told. But Janki couldn't gather courage to do so. Instead she greedily looked at the cigarettes lying in the tray. An unfulfilled longing had always lingered inside her since her childhood when she had collected cigarette butts along a funeral procession but could not enjoy them.

She was about to move when she felt a hand on her shoulder. She turned her head. It was Keval Ramani. "Hello, princess, your father owns an estate, Shagun told me."

"Yee..s," she answered meekly.

"Let's dance," he said holding Janki's hand and soon they were on the dance floor. This was a perfect place to lie, but carefully. Janki told him more about her father's princely estate, while Keval enlightened her about his work as a casting director in the film industry and his other occupations. He explained that he also took dance troupes to abroad and organized Bollywood shows there for NRIs. "Would you like to accompany us sometime, let's say to London or somewhere else," asked Keval.

Janki felt no qualms about this, but how could she say anything without the consent of her parents. They would undoubtedly like to know all the details of the troupe, its organizers and owners before sending her anywhere. But she never told him that she would need her parent's permission before taking any step. "It would sound so middle class, more so when he is calling me princess," thought Janki.

The music stopped for a while. The DJ was filling in with gibberish as Keval Ramani left the floor for a drink. Janki, too, went to the bar and picked up a cigarette from the tray. She took it in her mouth and reached for the lighter. Before she could light up a noise outside diverted everyone's attention. It seemed as if a procession of vehicles had entered the compound and came to a screeching halt. With this Keval's watchman came in huffing and puffing and whispered anxiously in his ear. Keval listened to him, walked quickly toward a staircase and disappeared into the basement. Within a minute the celebration turned into chaos; people scattered in fear and confusion. Apparently officials from the narcotic cell had swept in to raid the premises.

The partying crowd was bundled into two police vans, a vehicle following close behind.

Janki was in the same van as Sami. He was feverishly trying to get one of his connections. The cellphones of policemen were ringing incessantly while the uniformed men remained hunched over their handsets. The youngsters remained frozen in their seats faces drained of blood. Shagun seemed a little less scared than the others; probably this was not the first such experience for her. Dimpy had talked to her father or somebody and had almost certainly got some assurance. With a throbbing heart, Janki called Gautam and briefed him about the whole saga. Now he was coming to the police station. Janki could not guess the level of his anger over the phone. How was he going to react? How would he break the news to his temperamental wife? And how was Kalyani going to take it? Janki was dying with fear.

Shagun spoke softly in Dimpy's ears, "all this has happened because of Sami, he is a celebrity, the police had come for him."

"And yes, the media must be giving us chase already," replied Dimpy.

This was meant for Shagun but was overheard by Janki and Sami too. Listening to this, the future superstar began to weep like a child. Sami was weak and a coward by nature. He knew that his father would free him from the police, but this media thing had scared him tremendously.

Dimpy was right. As they reached the police station and were alighting from the van, shutterbugs from different media groups began capturing their subjects. The girls tried to hide their faces with their dupatta or stole, whatever they had. Janki, too, covered her face with her beige stole and held up her palm to keep the stole from slipping.

Blood samples were taken to check for drugs. Those with a cargo drugs in their blood were slated for court. And from there either to jail or rehabilitation centre. For now family members, friends or acquaintances had arrived to bail out their loved ones. To Gautam's great relief Janki was clean. This respite did not last. Soon trouble began brewing. Local TV channels had put up the sensational story of a film star's son found in a rave party. Journalists and cameramen scrambled around to take bites from Suraj Kiran and other film celebrities. Sami hid from the commotion. Suraj Kiran insisted that his son never touched alcohol, forget taking drugs. "He doesn't take even brandy if he ever catches a cold," said the father.

Along with this statement Suraj Kiran's PR department had released many clippings and photographs showing Sami praying in a temple, performing puja at home or touching his grandfather's feet.

The print media reportage treated the incident like a coup. A plethora of photographs covering the rave party and the melee plastered the pages of most of the papers. Unfortunately, Janki could clearly be seen in some of them. A good number chosen for front pages showed Sami getting down from the police van along with others. Here the girls had their faces covered. Amid the panic and confusion, both Gautam and Janki had missed the fact that a sparkling emerald ring was staring back at spectators from Janki's finger as her palm spread across her face. Two days prior to this, Kalyani had called Gautam to tell him that she had forgotten her emerald ring on the wash basin the day she had left for the small town and Gautam had assured her that it was in his safe keeping. He thought he could later tell her why he had given it to Janki without asking Kalyani. He didn't dare tell her over the phone that he had loaned it to the girl. How could he forget the foul mood Kalyani was in that day?

Newspapers had covered the scandal thoroughly. The story was carried over to the inner pages, with the photographs. An informer had generously parted with photographs of the rave party for a prize. These snaps had been taken before the raid in an unguarded moment when the party was in full swing. In one of the close-ups Sami was seen sniffing cocaine. Other snaps showed dancers on the floor. The guests were drinking, smoking or just chatting; Janki had a cigarette in her mouth, the drug counter had come into the range of the lens.

• • •

Kalyani was back to Mumbai but not alone. This time, she had brought Taeeji along. Tauji's demise had left Taeeji bereft. Kalyani could not leave her behind in this condition. The mere thought of it filled her with guilt. So she had offered to take Taeeji along with her to Mumbai. Taeeji had showed unwillingness to move. "I would rather prefer to spend my remaining years visiting temples in my home town than living in a city of heathens like Mumbai," she had said.

"All right, Taeeji, then come at least for a few months," suggested Kalyani. But Taeeji said she was not supposed to leave home now, "the scriptures say that at least for a year after the demise of her husband, a woman should not cross the threshold of her home. I don't want to burn in hellfire by disobeying the scriptures," she said.

Taeeji was obeying every ritual to be followed by a Hindu widow. She had begun to don white clothes and wear her hair short. She had with her own hands broken her glass bangles. The big coin-sized red bindi she applied every single day had been rubbed away from her forehead. In its place a round white mark remained a residue of years of the practice.

Kalyani persisted and through the mediation of a temple priest she was able to convince Taeeji that if she didn't want to go anywhere it was alright, but she could go to Kalyani's place, because that was her own home, bought from their own money. Taeeji was satisfied with the logic and was ready to go along on the condition that it would be a stay of just ten to fifteen days.

Even after this, everything did not go smoothly. Taeeji had many more conditions. She said she would not take a flight.

So Kalyani had train tickets booked for them. But there still remained things to be sorted out. She said she was not going to eat *kachcha* food while in Mumbai because in her opinion it was a city of non-vegetarians. So she took along lots of *laddoo*, *mathri*, *shakarpara*s and *puri*, enough to last for at least fifteen days. "I am not going to leave the path of religion for anything," she said adamantly. This was not the end of her whims; she had kept a bottle of *gangajal* which she could sprinkle on herself in the event a desecration.

Taeeji had succeeded in avoiding air travel but she was not so lucky with the elevator. Kalyani's apartment was on the eleventh floor and they were compelled to take the lift. There was no escape, so Taeeji vented her anger by calling it a demon. With her eyes closed, desperately calling on Lord Rama for help, she completed her ride inside its suffocating belly.

As soon as she entered Kalyani's home Taeeji unwittingly fired an arrow hitting bull's eye. Taeeji had become a little forgetful and was prone to forget names and places. So when Janki came forward and touched her feet, Taeeji recalled everything about Janki except her name. In an effort to ask her name she saiu, "Oh Lord, this is Ghunghru's daughter *na*! She has become so tall. What's her name ··· please help me recall your name girl, I have become quite forgetful these days."

Though there was no malice in Taeeji's remark, "Ghunghru's daughter," the mere mention of his name had shocked everyone in the room. Red faced, Janki hurriedly left the room. A hardened countenanced Gautam sat down to watch TV. It was a letdown for Kalyani. To come out of the shame she tried to correct Taeeji immediately. "This is our Janki, Taeeji. She is our daughter, not Ghunghru's. Don't even utter his name," she explained in a low voice.

At this Taeeji muttered something inside her mouth and then went silent.

That night, Gautam and Kalyani didn't make much conversation, even sleeping with their backs to each other. There was a subtle strain between them. They exchanged a few formal sentences. As they entered their bedroom, Gautam went straight to his almirah, took out the emerald ring and handed it to Kalyani saying, "Here is your ring. Now safely put it in your locker." Kalyani immediately put the ring in her locker. And they went to sleep, without speaking a word to each other.

Next morning their day began like any other day. They had resumed normalcy and were talking to each other like they did every day. Despite spending the night in the same room, there was no stress visible between Taeeji and Janki. Gautam was relieved. Still, he didn't find the courage to tell Kalyani about the rave party because Taeeji was present. Later, when Taeeji would return he could recount everything to Kalyani, he thought. He had already returned the ring so there was no urgency to say anything about it. This also he planned to share with his wife when the appropriate moment arose. For him, this meant after Taeeji's departure.

Taeeji did not stay even for fifteen days. She had become, "tired of hanging in the sky." She meant the eleventh floor. Even on the day she was leaving she refused to take the lift, preferring the physically painful route down the stairs again chanting Lord Rama's name, this time because of the pain in her knees. At last she was put on the train to her home town.

• • •

Like the layers of make-up during the day, Kalyani's night skin-care rituals were getting crazier. She had bought tubes of anti-ageing creams and lotions, spending hours in front of the mirror pampering her skin. That night, her paranoia hit the sky, when she returned from a Botox party. Somebody had put this idea into her head that she should try breast augmentation.

"You don't need this Kalyani. You have a good physique. And most importantly I like you the way you are. Going under the scalpel is not a good idea; it's worthless and painful too. After having silicon implants you may get an infection and many other complications. I don't think you should go for this," Gautam said.

"Gautam, you are speaking like a typical Indian husband, who thinks his wife's world is not beyond him or else why would you suggest I should not go for surgery just because you like me the way I am," said Kalyani.

"Oh no, dear, don't bring your women's lib here. I mean as long as you try non-invasive methods to maintain your beauty it's alright, but age reversal through surgery would be an extreme step. If you are ready to face surgery then you should first go for the operation on your knees, it would be more worthwhile," replied Gautam.

By talking about her crumbling knees Gautam didn't want to hurt Kalyani but she took it for a taunt at her age. The pain in her knees was getting worse day by day. Initially, it was manageable with pain killers, but now popping pills was of no use. With her knees hurting, Kalyani could not workout in the gym. Since she was incapable of exercising, her weight was on the rise. This brought more pressure on her knees, further increasing the pain. It was a vicious circle, creating a kind of helplessness. Gautam's comment offended her; the hint of truth about her age was not lost on both of them. And Kalyani began to cry. Seeing this, Gautam apologized and suggested she should go along with her idea if she felt that this could give her fresh confidence.

The matter now settled, Kalyani had a peaceful sleep that night; she imagined herself as the seventeen-year old girl now seen with Kabir in a film poster.

• • ● ● ● • •

Nineteen

GAUTAM'S CENTRE FOR Happiness was doing very well. On the third floor of a building in Bandra, he had bought two apartments adjacent to each other forming an impressive Centre. Who does not want happiness in this world? Everybody needs it. So, all sorts of people came there, including fashion models, film stars, other celebrities and their wives. Everyone who was anyone with everything in the world, except happiness, came to Gautam who helped them find this elusive X-factor. "Happiness is like musk, it is hidden inside you, only sometimes you do not recognize it," he would explain to the seekers coming to his centre. Here they taught the science of happiness, the biological methods of achieving happiness inside oneself.

After leaving the School of Life Sciences, it took Gautam ten years to establish the private institute. Ultimately it clicked. Now he had appointed many specialists to work for the Centre like psychiatrists, art therapists, mood managers, nutritionist, yoga gurus and aroma therapists. Gautam himself looked after the matters of life science. At Janki's suggestion he had created one more department – the Shwet Prasannta Department, especially for Mohan, because as a disciple of Vatsal Guru in the Himalayas, he had learned the ways to achieve pure and unblemished happiness.

There was one more person who wanted to join the Happiness Centre, but Gautam was not interested in him. This was Dr Karun Prabhaker who was working on reincarnation, for over twenty-five years. The doctor believed that with the understanding of one's previous birth the person could look at life from a fresh perspective. But Gautam didn't believe in this. According to him reincarnation therapy was nothing more than hypnosis.

Since Gautam was not convinced Dr Prabhaker came over to the Centre. He was a happy-go-lucky man with an eternal smile on his face. Gautam had no way of finding out the truth in this doctor's claims about the theory of reincarnation. But he listened to him because the doctor had a convincing way of presenting his points. The peaceful man did not force his views down the listener's throat; rather he spoke in a tranquil manner, explaining his side step by step. When it came to hearing others' arguments, the doctor listened to them carefully. Naturally, Gautam was ready to at least have a conversation with him.

"Look Dr Prabhaker, the human body is nearly a machine. When it stops, everything ends. There is neither a previous birth nor will there be a next birth. The theory of reincarnation is nothing but a figment of man's imagination." When Gautam said this Dr Prabhaker did not argue, but only smiled. With this, Gautam pressed on, "Dr Prabhaker, our cerebrum is the seat of memory. The brain turns off with the death of our body, then where come the question of retaining memories of a previous birth? This is really weird and this is the reason why it is unapproved by people with a scientific approach," said Gautam.

This time, Dr Prabhaker answered, "Gautam bhai, right at

this moment, we have millions of microbes around us, but you cannot see them with your eyes. Science has long proved their existence; otherwise, it would be beyond the ken of your five senses. ..."

Gautam didn't let him finish his sentence. He interrupted, "You said it doctor, 'science has proved their existence.' The same logic applies here; I reject the theory of reincarnation because it is just that, a theory. It has not been proved scientifically," Gautam argued.

At this, Dr Prabhaker threw a wide smile and came back to the point. "Don't worry Gautam bhai; we have done a lot of research on the subject. Also, we have recorded the case histories of various individuals who claimed to have had experienced rebirth. But above all, parapsychology is an enigma. So much is going on in the cosmos which we cannot understand or prove but that doesn't mean it is not happening."

"But Prabhakerji, I have seen it on television; they send the individual into a trance and ask him a rather fixed set of questions. Whatever disconnected and incongruous fancies then produced by the half conscious mind are shown as previous birth experiences. I don't believe in this humbug," said Gautam.

"Yes, this is nonsense. I, too, do not believe in this." There was a look of surprise on Gautam's face when Dr Prabhaker said this. But the doctor ignored his reaction. "Putting someone to sleep to ask questions is a method which has nothing to do with reincarnation. That's hypnosis, actually, which could be good for psychological reasons. Like getting rid of bottled-up emotions, long-stifled feelings and unshared sorrows. But the work we do to learn more about reincarnation is not done on people lying in bed. Please come over to my centre sometime and I will be able to explain it all to you with examples," said the doctor.

Dr Prabhaker had brought along some material for him to see. For more than two and a half hours he had shared with Gautam the histories of individuals who were reported to have experienced rebirth. In addition to the description of their experiences there were photographs of the individuals and the names of the places they belonged to both in this birth and their so-called previous one. Prabhaker and his researchers had adopted various methods to cross-examine the claims of rebirth. No entry was made without these details. If a child spoke of his previous birth then he would be left, without an escort, at the border of the village he mentioned as being that of his previous birth. From here, he had to reach his "home". The unattended boy would be followed by the researchers who watched him closely. In the registered cases, children had not only found their homes but also knew the names and recognized the relatives from their past birth. Also, they were able to tell family secrets and personal matters from which would be confirmed by the person concerned.

Dr Prabhaker said that he was not the only person doing research on the subject. Many people within and outside India had been working on it and had presented some astonishing theories regarding reincarnation. For instance, he said, if somebody had a mole or a mark on his body then he might have a mole on the same place in the next birth, too. Going a step further along this theory given by some German researcher, Dr Prabhaker added that in his opinion not only the physical signs but an emotion or a relationship left unrequited in one birth would be fulfilled in the next. "Karma *bandhan* will unite them." Citing an example he said, "If a woman dies giving birth to a child, then she might be born later on as the daughter of her own son!"

Gautam was stunned to hear the last example. Speechless, he stared at Dr Prabhaker for a while and then lowered his neck. He sat in this position for some time thinking about his late mother. Then, as if coming back to his senses, he declared, "I don't believe in all this."

At which Dr Prabhaker said nothing but only smiled. Meanwhile Mohan had also come to the Centre. Gautam introduced him to the doctor. Dr Prabhaker and Mohan had a lot to talk about. They shared almost the same interests. Mohan proudly apprised him about a special filter he had made from the bark of a Himalayan tree. "If you put this filter to your ear you can hear elephant talk," said Mohan. The filter was ready but he was yet to learn elephant-language from Vatsal Guru; to begin this, his trip to the Himalayas was planned for the next day.

Gautam had been listening to them silently. Mohan was well aware that Gautam would not accept anything unscientific. So, especially for Gautam's ears, he didn't forget to add this well-known scientific fact that at our level of hearing we cannot hear low frequency elephant-talk. Gautam still made no comment at all, though Dr Prabhaker raised this question, now that we have technology to hear low-frequency sounds, why was such a filter required.

"Elephants are not only brilliant but they are also very sensitive beings; they won't talk at all if they would sense an electronic gadget is being used. Anything in Nature, for that matter, is disturbed, by the presence of electronics," Mohan answered.

At last, Dr Karun Prabhaker took leave from Gautam with the request that he should at least once visit his Reincarnation Centre, whether he believed in it or not. Soon, Mohan too asked permission to leave. "I am going to Himalayas to get familiar with the pachyderm language. My guru has prohibited the use of a cellphone or a laptop since it disrupts the natural vibration of the place," Mohan explained.

Mohan had already said farewell to Janki in the afternoon. After this, he went to the art college to take a class for the figurative session. There a colleague gave him a sealed envelope for Janki which contained replicas of paintings for which she had modelled. Before leaving the Centre, Mohan had given the envelope to Gautam to be handed over to Janki. So Gautam took it along.

Though Gautam was denying it all along, the evening with Prabhaker and later on the doctor's exchanges with Mohan left an impact on him. Discussions on parapsychology were ringing in his head. Even after he reached home Gautam did everything mechanically as if in a trance. Janki and Kalyani were not back yet and Gautam was not in a mood to prepare anything fresh. He heated the leftovers of the morning's meal in the microwave and ate it desultorily. He had put Janki's envelope on the TV so that he remembered to give it to her. Then he sat down to watch the programme "You, Me and Nature." To his dismay it was a repeat telecast, the third time they were showing it. Bored, he switched to a new channel showing a Lavani dance programme. This was not a one bit engaging. Putting off the TV he picked up a book, the biography of M.F. Husain, his favourite. This was close to Gautam's heart because the painter's longing for his mother, whom he had never seen, always found expression in his words and images. In this, Gautam found a reflection of his own feelings.

He was able to read only a few pages before he began to feel sleepy. He looked for a bookmark so that he could come back to the same page after a cat nap. Gautam found no bookmark handy so he took the envelope kept on the TV top and placed it between the pages. Within a few seconds, he was asleep. But for not more than five minutes, he was awake and returned to the book. While opening it, the envelope dropped onto his lap. As he looked closely he found that the envelope was ripped at the corner. Part of some colourful art peered through the split. Probably, a red sari with a golden border, the glimpse suggested. Yes, Janki was talking about a modelling assignment, Gautam recalled affectionately. He remembered it in detail. Janki had said that for this she had to wear a Marathi nouvari sari with a big bindi and nose ring. Very strangely, this was to be teamed with a tie and a bowler hat. The tie she had borrowed from Gautam. The recollection made him curious about the content of the envelope. And he pulled open the envelope along the already torn portion. The replica appeared just as he had expected. Janki in a red, "nine yard sari" with a golden border was seated on a teapoy. She was smiling. The big, round nose ring made her smile even broader. With tie and hat, one more accessory was added – probably on the spot – it was a black baton. A title was given to the image, "The Commander." The signature of the artist and the date of the work appeared at the foot of the picture.

Looking at this picture, Gautam couldn't stop smiling. He decided to show it to Kalyani. There were three more pictures below this one. Gautam came to the second one which was Janki's portrait. It had been done two days after the first, as the date indicated. The third painting showed Janki in jeans and T-shirt. She was sitting on the floor with her head resting on her drawn-up knees. It bore Mohan's name as the artist and had been completed fifteen days after the previous painting. As he came to the fourth painting, he was shocked and threw the lot away, as if it was a snake. The painting carried Janki in the nude.

Resting on her palms, hands stretched behind her, Janki's head was thrown back, her knees pulled up. Her waist was turned slightly toward the viewer bringing her bust into focus. A black dot stared from the right bosom at the viewer – the model's breast was clearly visible. The angle had saved the painting from being vulgar. Gautam couldn't miss this black spot even though he had thrown the pictures on the floor.

The empty envelop danced in his trembling fingers. "What was the compulsion? Why on earth did Janki have to take such an assignment?" Gautam was furious. Guilt and shame took him into its grip. Why did his eyes fall on his own daughter's uncovered body? Strangely, the utter discomfort was gradually being mixed with a peculiar thrill as he realized that what Dr Prabhaker had mentioned regarding the rebirth of a person was probably true. Was Janki his mother born again? His father had said that his mother had a black spot on one of her breasts. And here it was. There was no missing it, even as he had glimpsed it for a fraction of a second. Just to confirm this sudden but pleasant evidence from among the photographs on the floor, he picked up the snap showing the mole. He looked at it closely, his eyes fixed on the object of his attention. That was the reason he missed the emerald ring on one of her fingers which was highlighted by the painter.

He looked at the photograph briefly, deciding to put the lot back in the envelope. But before he could do this he heard the latch turning. "It must be Kalyani," thought Gautam with an alarm. He didn't know what to do with the snap in his hand. In panic, he rushed toward his cupboard and hid it below a newspaper. He locked the cupboard putting the key into his trouser pocket.

Yes, it was Kalyani. As she came in, her eyes fell on the

photographs lying on the carpet. "Wow what is this," she exclaimed, bending to look at them closely. The combination of a Marathi nouvari sari with a hat made her smile.

"You are so reckless Gautam. Can't you open a simple envelope without ripping it up?" Kalyani said, looking at the envelope lying on the carpet.

"It was already torn," was the only reply he could give meekly. And the matter was closed. Flinging the torn envelop into the scrap basket, Kalyani put the photographs into a fresh envelop keeping it on the TV top so as to remember to give it to Janki.

• • • • • • •

Twenty

EYES WILD AND HAIR dishevelled she was standing in the middle of the drawing room. Kalyani's lips were trembling, her sari *pallu* dropped almost to the floor, as if she had lost awareness of what was going on. She had thrown and broken almost every object in the room. Thankfully, only a bolster had been flung at the TV set. A flower pot could have blown the screen to smithereens. A flower pot had really been pitched at Gautam who had caught it in time; thanks to the practice street cricket had given him during his childhood. The object had not hurt Gautam but the dart of a false accusation, Kalyani had indirectly thrown at him, had hit home. But what could have been done? There was no convincing explanation. Evidence was deepening the misunderstanding.

The producer of the TV serial, "Chand Chura Kar Laee Hun," Fatima Kadari, had thrown a party that evening. The party went on the whole night. From there, Kalyani came back home at four o'clock in the morning. There was nothing unusual in this. Whenever she returned late she used her key to the apartment and came in silently, without disturbing Gautam or Janki. But tonight she beat and thumped the door noisily. She even pressed hard on the door bell, hard enough for it to emit a shrill, emergency siren like sound. Alarmed, Gautam woke up and came running out.

A furious Kalyani was standing outside. Seeing him she shouted, "You are a liar, Gautam! Together with Janki you hide things from me! Janki was picked up by the police from a rave party, such a scandal you didn't let me know."

This long concealed secret between Janki and Gautam had surfaced in the glamour event held by the TV producer Kadari, which was more or less a filmy party. Many forty plus silver screen heroines were now in television. Besides, representatives of many film producers who had diverted their resources towards TV were also there in the party. A prominent producer, though, was there in person. So when Sami made his entry, people from film fraternity began whispering to each other. So did the group of people Kalyani was present in. They talked about a rave party, Sami taken into police custody from there and media reports related to the matter. Then somebody reminded Kalyani that she should know all this in detail since her own daughter was among the youngsters. Kalyani was shocked. She knew nothing about it. But her face gave nothing away letting people assume she knew about it. Though, it was not in Kalyani's nature to retain her poise whenever such an emotional disturbance occurred, here she tried hard. She moved away from the group of talebearers and headed toward the bar. She picked up a glass of sweet soda-lime and pretended to sip it.

Kalyani's pride made her hide her ignorance regarding her own daughter from her friends. But she couldn't help admitting to Mrs Pasricha that she had missed the media clippings of the incident. Mrs Pasricha immediately informed her that someone had loaded the clippings on the YouTube and if Kalyani was interested she could watch them on the laptop lying nearby.

As Mrs Pasricha ran the clippings, Kalyani to her horror witnessed Janki with Sami and others in many frames. In one, Janki was seen undulating on the dance floor. In another she could clearly be seen with a cigarette in her mouth. A clipping inside the police van also had Janki in it. But the biggest blow was the shot in which Janki was seen emerging from the van in the courtyard of the police station. Here, the continuous flashing of cameras had made Janki cover her face with a stole, but she had put her hand over it. The hand bore the green emerald ring.

This was a double blow. Kalyani had been cheated on two accounts, not just one. She recalled Gautam saying that the emerald ring was with him that he had safely put it in the almirah. "If Janki had worn it, Gautam could have told me that, she is my daughter as well, I was not going to stop her from wearing the ring." With these disturbing thoughts, she was now on the verge of losing her equilibrium. Realizing this she had immediately left for home, where she had banged on the door in a frenzy and pressed the door bell. But at that moment, she did not know a greater shock was in the offing.

Gautam stammered through his explanation. "Kalyani, I was going to tell you about the rave party but since you had come with Taeeji I didn't say anything at the time. I had planned to tell you later on. I have proof of this if you don't believe; come here and see, I have kept a newspaper cutting to show you the media report," he said pulling it from the almirah. Along it something else fell out. This was Janki's photo in which she wore nothing but the emerald ring. Kalyani had picked it up from the floor. She became catatonic when she saw what had emerged from Gautam's cupboard. Paralysed she couldn't move or speak. After a while as she regained consciousness with a barrage of incoherent sentences, she started flinging and hurling objects around the room.

"Look Kalyani, listen to me ··· stop it, first listen to me, I have something to tell you ··· try to understand," Gautam was yelling at the top of his voice but Kalyani went barrelling on without respite. Janki awakened with the clamour and came out rubbing her eyes.

She could clearly see the photo thrown by Kalyani on the floor. She thought her mother was angry merely because Janki had dared to shed her clothes for an assignment or because she was not told about the emerald ring. But Janki did not know that it was a far more serious contention. "Why does a father have to secretly keep his daughter's nude photograph in his possession and try to conceal it," was Kalyani's objection. She found the behaviour extremely disgusting. No reason given by Gautam was now enough to convince Kalyani, even if it was genuine. Because she had to face a series of lies and deceit from her husband which had shaken her trust in him. The reason, that he had seen his mother in Janki because of a mole and that a meeting with a reincarnation researcher had influenced him into thinking that this could possibly be a link with the rebirth of his mother, had cut no ice with Kalyani.

"You claim to be a rationalist Gautam, from when have you begun to believe in rebirth?" The lack of trust was clear in her bitter tone.

If, for Gautam, Janki's nude picture bore the sign of his mother's rebirth, for Kalyani, it carried the seeds of suspicion. She recalled the incident on her first night, when Gautam had suggested that she keep the emerald ring on after she had removed her clothes. This was the same ring. How could she now believe that what she had plainly seen in the picture was not Gautam's idea?

If Kalyani thought what he had done was disgusting, he too, found her accusations equally nauseating. "She could be suspicious of me for cheating and lying, but how could she, even in her wildest fancies imagine something so lewd about Janki and me," thought Gautam.

As Kalyani's eyes fell on Janki, her rage was like a laser focused on the girl. She was, after all, a party to the scandal. "So, eventually, you have proved that you are Ghunghru's daughter, Janki. The great skill with which you stole the ring reminds me of the sleight of hand with which 'your father' used to pick up things," said Kalyani with rancour in her voice.

A stinging reply came from Gautam who was burning with rage and humiliation by the aspersion of theft thrown at Janki and by Ghunghru who was dragged in here, a complete no-no in their family life. "And you Kalyani, you too are true to your DNA. The way you are behaving makes it clear that you have taken after your mad father," Gautam shouted back a retort.

Janki's heart began to sink with the realization that the altercation revolved around her. If she was the reason for her parent's quarrel then she would leave home. She would go somewhere else, she thought. But where, immediately this question simultaneously, crossed her mind. She could not contact Mohan, he had not taken his mobile or laptop along. She could not go to Parizad or Pranita's place; they no longer lived in Mumbai. Pranita had married an NRI Indian and had settled in Australia, whereas Parizad was now in America, having got admission in a creative writing course in San Francisco. Aah! America! Janki sighed, "how lucky Parizad is," she thought wistfully. Janki, too, dreamt about making it to America. She would do any damn thing to go to the country of her dreams. But the route papa suggested was not at all for her. Gautam had always told her to prepare for GRE, score well and get admission in a good US university. This was out of bounds for her. She knew she would not be able to crack such exams. But that didn't mean that she was going to bury her dream. She tried another track. She was going to the US with Sagar Irani's dance troupe. Mummy knew who Sagar Irani was; Janki's parents had no objection about this. She had got their consent long ago. Even her passport and visa were ready, but there were ten days to leave. Yet even ten minutes at home lay heavy on her heart. What was she going to do now?

The night seemed very long for Janki. In the morning, the three had breakfast together, but there was a distance of light-years between their souls. After this, Kalyani went to her work, Gautam left for his. They did not inform each other regarding their destinations. Janki didn't go anywhere. No one asked her why she chose to remain at home on a working day.

After her parents left home, Janki, sitting at the dining table began drafting a letter to them. She opened the letter with the mention of her love and gratitude toward them. Then she wrote about leaving home. She wrote she was going to Dimpy's place for now, from where she would go to London according to her previous schedule. "Don't worry about me. Dimpy would help me to convert the currency," she wrote. Then, along with her passport and some essentials she left home hoping her parents' anger would subside by the time she returned.

Dimpy did not get her visa for the US, but still Janki had to stay with her; she, even temporarily, needed a place to stay.

• • •

London would be a grand, awe-inspiring city where she was going to put up in a luxurious hotel with Bollywood film stars; this was what Janki had imagined before reaching London. But she faced a huge disappointment when she reached.

Both the film stars, Simran and Iman, went to a big hotel, along with their retinue and assorted hangers on. Even Simran's mother stayed with them. The producer, Sagar Irani, had also checked into the same place. But Janki got lodging in an apartment with a hall, a bedroom and a kitchen. She was hardly in a position to enjoy the space; there were others sharing this flat. Janki, Gatha, Shruti and Saeeda were given the hall. Saeeda was a Pakistani. She had no intension of leaving London after the musical tour was over. She never revealed how she was going to do this.

The bedroom had been taken by Keval Ramani. Two people were in the kitchen. One was Akbar a mimicry artist from Pakistan. Along with him was a stand-up comedian Raju Bharatan from Mumbai, who occasionally appeared on the small screen. Bharatan had objected to being put in the kitchen. Then, Keval told him that only option was to stay in the kitchen or go back to India, immediately. And Raju quietly accepted the ultimatum.

Janki did not know where the extras were staying. She could only imagine the kind of compromise that had to be made. They had to commute to rehearsals by bus or tube. Janki too had till now mostly seen London via the underground. Even from Heathrow they had taken the tube. Separate arrangements had been made for stars and producers. These people had been flown by executive class while the economy class was reserved for the others.

When Janki shared her annoyance over this with Keval, he had a good laugh, calling Sagar a stingy idiot with no foresight. "Do you know I have arranged for the apartment with my own money? Left to Irani, he would have made you eat free at the

Akshardham Temple, like those extras he has brought. But I am not that kind of a man. I have taken the responsibility of caring for those included in my group."

"So shall I go back from London without seeing the city in its true splendour?" asked Janki disappointedly.

"Oh, no Janki, you will see London with me, I promise!" Keval smiled patting her back fondly.

Over the weekend, Keval took Janki, Gatha, Saeeda and Shruti for a trip across London. On Saturday evening they went first to a typical London pub in Covent Garden. There each one had her favourite brew. Then they headed for Leicester Square to dine in a restaurant. Keval joined the line to book a table for five; meantime the girls joined the people dancing in the street. This evening London didn't seem damp and gloomy to Janki. It was alive with people dancing, eating, walking and chatting. The girls found this unusual but charming that people were dancing by the side of a road. They were grateful to Keval who was splurging his own money on their entertainment.

Janki was feeling a little guilty because she thought it was she who had expressed her wish to see London, because of which Keval had to take all the girls around. She thought, in return, she should also do something for Keval. Janki had a few pounds with her. So when they were taken to Harrods, she bought a five-pound T-shirt for Keval. After a while, it occurred to her that the piece was very nice and that she should buy one for Gautam, too. Now she was looking for something for Kalyani and her eyes fell on a beautiful leather bag. It was too costly. She began searching for something within her range for Kalyani and zeroed in on a silk scarf. Saeeda smiled as Janki bought this scarf, because she also had bought the same for her mother's hijab.

Janki spent a few pounds on getting her portrait done by a

Japanese girl on a footpath in Piccadilly Circus. She never knew the money she was splurging now would be needed to save her very existence in time to come. She thought she should spend happily, because after the tour to London and the US she had to anyway return home.

Sagar Irani whose acquaintance with Kalyani was thought to be a guarantee, Janki had not even exchanged greetings with him till now. For him Janki would not be more than an extra. Or maybe he didn't even know her. The show was finally over and most of the participants returned to India. Otherwise, too, all of them were not going to America. And the others, who were going, were to board from Mumbai. There were ten days to leave for New York so even Sagar had left for Mumbai. Simran and Iman were not going to the US. A different pair of stars, Puja Jacob and Irshad Khan had been booked for the states. Just now, they were shooting in Switzerland and were to board from London.

In the present circumstances it was not possible for Janki to return to Mumbai for a mere ten days, then to again leave for America. Keval Ramani was a part of Sagar's US troupe; Shruti and Gatha wanted to return home only after making a tour of Europe and they stayed back at Ramani's apartment in London. This was enough reason for Janki to remain there.

With each passing day Janki and Keval were coming closer to each other. At this point of time she was very lonely and had begun to share her sadness with Keval. She even sought advice from him in her personal matters. She said she missed her parents terribly, but had no courage to contact them because of the scene created before she had left for London. She was facing a kind of mental block in calling them, she confessed.

Keval gave her a solution. Janki should send an email either to her father or mother, which could be as simple as informing them about her well-being.

The next day she would go to a cyber café nearby and send a mail. Janki had decided this and felt a bit relaxed by the thought. She was so much at ease with her own decision that she showed the gifts she had bought for her parents to Keval. While unburdening her heart, she divulged her till now carefully concealed history to Ramani. She told him about Saoo, Ghunghru, Laxmi, Tauji and others along with the many things that had happened in her life, but she never mentioned a word about Mohan. She cleverly kept back telling Ramani anything that involved Mohan. Why? Was there a thief in her heart? Yes, and Keval seemed to be attracted toward her. One day the inevitable happened when she went to his room. They surrendered to each other. Janki had totally forgotten what Mohan had told her that the physical union of a couple in love is the most glorious thing on earth and it should by no means be just instant gratification. It ought to be explored without guilt, hypocrisy or duplicity but not without deep love and passion. "I don't say this because this would be ethically right or because the sexual act could be a means of salvation; we leave that to mysticism, but, of course because when the pair unites physically, mentally and spiritually it is even superior to the bliss of union with the Infinite. I think we should wait for the right time to experience that supreme bliss," he had said.

Poor Mohan! The true lover was forgotten. Cut loose from her parents, Janki had tried to find an emotional anchor in Keval Ramani and in a moment of weakness sensuality overtook morality and rationality. Janki had even missed this glaring truth that she was a young girl and Ramani was in his forties.

That day, Keval was going to Manchester. As usual he asked

the girls whether they would like to come along. The girls readily agreed. In Manchester, Keval took them to Jo-Jo's place. This was Jogendra Jumerati alias James Joyce. "James Joyce?" when introduced, asked Gatha, who was the only book lover among the three. "But this is the name of an Irish writer." Keval had laughed over this saying, "One should not worry too much about names, but I can certainly tell you about Jo-Jo's profession, he is a filmmaker. When he was in Mumbai he used to make C-grade movies. I don't know what kind of films he produces now, but he is still making films, that much I know."

Jo-Jo showed a keen interest in knowing more about the girls. He showered them with questions to uncover every detail about them. When he came to know that Gatha and Shruti did not get the visa for the US and that only Janki had it, his focus shifted solely toward Janki. "Oh, lucky mascot, I mean the lucky girl," he said.

They had a full day for themselves and they ate, drank and chatted about various things. It came out that Gatha and Shruti were planning a trip to Switzerland and Paris. "No big deal, it's a routine thing when you are in Europe," Jo-Jo said, "but I have some work for you in Paris," he turned toward Keval, "Please do me this favour. Why don't you accompany the girls to Paris and while you are there do a little work for me. You already have a tourist visa I understand," he said to Keval. Then the two men went inside so that both could discuss the details of the errand to Paris.

Keval seemed convinced, rather enthusiastic, to go as he came out after discussing the matter with Jo-Jo. Janki did not know about the nature of this errand. But one thing she remembered well that when she had sulked Keval pampered her more in return. Yet he never gave her the chance to accompany him to Paris. Keval explained to her that though Gatha and Shruti would make a longer trip, he would return earlier.

"It's a matter of just two days. Then together we will go to the US, for a proper trip," he had said.

Keval gave his mobile to Janki along with many instructions before he left for Paris. (She should always keep her passport with her. A few dollars to be kept in the apartment safe while a couple of pounds and her Cox and Kings flight ticket to New York in her purse, which she always carried.)

That morning, the apartment bell rang. Afraid Janki thought "who could this be?" She peeped through the fish eye in the door. The two boys who had come to clean the apartment earlier were standing outside. Among other things, Keval had instructed her not to let the cleaners come in or to let anybody know she was all alone. So Janki opened the door slightly and through the crack answered them that cleaning was not required.

After sending the boys away Janki took a shower, sat at breakfast, locked the apartment and putting the keys in her purse went out into the city.

The wind was cold; she shivered a little but enjoyed walking aimlessly on London's roads. In Trafalgar Square like others, she fed the pigeons. Then standing in a long queue she bought a ticket to Madame Tussauds Museum. She didn't realize how three hours had passed with her wandering among the wax statues.

She returned long before dusk. At home, everything was just as she had left it. Janki had roamed the streets of London on her own and the fear of being alone had now vanished. Confident, feline like, she stretched her body contentedly. Then she made a large double-decker sandwich, like London's buses, for herself. A cup of hot coffee with the sandwich relaxed her and she sat on a sofa with her eyes closed.

A few minutes passed before the mobile rang. There was Gatha on the other side. She was crying. She couldn't speak coherently, so Shruti took over. Keval Ramani had died instantaneously in a road accident. How, where? Gatha and Shruti were not in a condition to answer. Janki was too stunned to ask anything further.

Everything around her was whirling; her head was in a vicious spin. The ground below her had disappeared like the roof over her head. She descended headlong into a dark pit, her heart in her mouth. Janki ran for the washroom, puked and sat down holding head in her hand. She had lost all sense of time.

Janki cursed her fate as she regained consciousness. She had lost not only a friend and well-wisher in hard times, but also her dream to go to America had been broken half-way. Though she held the visa and ticket to New York she had no idea where she would go after reaching America, how she was going to meet Sagar Irani's troupe there. Here, in London also, she was a stranger who was left to her own devices. What was she going to do with the apartment? Would she run away leaving it empty? Would she handover the keys to the owner and pay the rent? From where would she arrange enough pounds? An apartment on Baker Street was out of pocket.

Whenever Janki was in trouble she had always thought of her saviour, Gautam. "I should call him and say I am coming home immediately," was her first thought. Then she pondered over whether she could remain here but ask Gautam what could be done in such circumstances or Kalyani could contact Sagar Irani and make arrangements for her US tour. She would tell her parents that, she didn't know any details of the trip because

Keval was doing everything. Soon she realized that if she did so, her father would be unhappy with her stupidity that she had left everything to Keval and was ignorant about the planning of the trip. Then how would she explain to him that Keval was much more than a team leader to her.

No, she couldn't risk annoying her parents further. Her nude photo had already annoyed them enough, there was no space for any more scandals, she realized. And she stopped midway, putting the thought of calling Gautam aside.

Whom shall she ask now? She knew nobody in England, except Jo-Jo. But she didn't have his phone number. With the name Jo-Jo it was not possible to trace a number in the directory. There was no Jogendra Jumerati or James Joyce either. But Janki knew where he lived. So she decided to go to Manchester, to Jo-Jo's place.

Janki felt better as she met Jo-Jo. She cried her heart out in his handkerchief. Then she narrated her story to Jo-Jo who gave a sympathetic ear to her blabbering. She sought his help in dealing with her dilemma about choosing between home and America. Janki also spoke of the fear of falling in her parent's eyes if she told them everything that had happened to her. Jo-Jo in turn confirmed her fears and advised her not to confess anything to her parents.

"Have you gone mad, Janki? After all that has gone wrong; there is only one window of hope for you, that is, the visit to America, golden America. Don't be a fool! Till now, whatever happened to you was misfortune, but now it will be like throwing away your own fortune if you will not go despite a visa in your hand and a ticket to America." He waited for a while then continued, "The US is an awesome country Janki, you will forget your sorrows once you are there."

Janki who was almost crumbling got strength from Jo-Jo's pep talk. She liked his advice and had faith in it. "Jo-Jo is right that she should go to America. What was his interest? He was not going to the US with her," she thought. Also Jo-Jo did not ask her to stay with him at his place in Manchester. Janki was distraught and alone, Jo-Jo could have taken advantage of the situation. But he didn't do that, rather he gave her twenty pounds from his own pocket. In panic, she had forgotten to take money out from the digital locker in the apartment. But this much he said he feared that people may suspect Janki's hand in the accident that could have been seen as murder since she was living with Keval.

Janki was never as fearful as she was now. She was terrified to the marrow. Unfortunately, misfortune had closed in around her. That night, coming from Manchester there was only one passenger with her in the tube, who was staring hard at her. The stations were almost deserted. Reaching London, she took a taxi to her apartment. The taxi driver, she realized, had a hard, unsmiling face. But she had already boarded his cab. She told him the name of the street she was to be dropped off and after that they travelled in an awkward silence.

Reaching her destination she looked at the meter. Thirteen pounds, it showed. Janki gave the driver fifteen pounds thinking she was leaving a rather generous tip of two pounds for him. But the driver who was probably a racist, found the amount meagre. He had, it seemed, expected more from his passenger. Peeved, he flung the money on the road. Janki got so scared that she didn't dare to look back at the driver or money, never knowing whether he picked it or not. Head down she walked away.

There was nobody around, even as she took the lift to her floor. Within a few seconds she was at the apartment door, but before she could heave a sigh of relief a new jolt shook her. There was a big hole in the door which was covered by a paper with a notice on it "Under Metropolitan Police."

This time, Janki had Jo-Jo's contact number. She called him and feverishly narrated the whole saga. Jo-Jo told her to go over to an address near Hyde Park, to Jina's place. He assured Janki that he himself would come there the next day and request Jina in person to accommodate Janki.

Again Janki was riding in a cab. This time the driver was cordial. He not only put on music, he also had a friendly chat with Janki. But Jina was a perfect bitch. She didn't let Janki take a sandwich and cola from her refrigerator before paying for them. The second day she told Janki that she would be required to share the apartment rent with her even if she stayed for four days. To make matters worse even Jo-Jo didn't turn up the next day.

The next morning Janki pulled herself together and went to Keval's apartment. Police had till now completed the formalities and had shown Janki around the apartment. The police had no objection about her living here now. But she wanted to keep herself away from this place. She was still afraid of thieves and police too, like any other true blood South Asian. Jo-Jo had stoked her fear by saying that police may question her about Keval's death. "Janki you should now never again set foot in that apartment. They may send Keval's dead body there. Your interrogation would be certain," he had said. Janki was so afraid that she didn't even dare to take dollars from the digital locker in the apartment. And despite Jina's bad behaviour Janki had come to live with her.

Jina charged her for every single thing, even for the bed spread and hot water. So in between Janki had tried finding accommodation in a hotel. The room rent was seventy pounds a day. They needed some identification too; when she said she has come with a dance troupe, they asked for her company's letter. She had none and she returned to Jina's place because there was nowhere else to go.

Janki was not entitled to work in the UK. Then just for a week who would give her work? She could get no work here, not even that of a charwoman. Then, Jina herself showed her a way. She took Janki to a back street, to a general store there. They entered and went into an inner shop, a shop selling sex toys. Jina introduced Janki to a Japanese girl here and she got the work for seven days.

There were only four days to leave for New York. Janki had earned a few dollars working in this shop. Even after paying Jina, Janki had saved a few pounds which she converted into dollars. Now she had everything, from dollars to the ticket to New York but she still didn't know where she would meet the dance troupe after landing in the US. Then Janki called Dimpy in Mumbai. She asked her to find out where she could meet the dance troupe in America and also Sagar Irani's contact number. Dimpy didn't call her back but meantime Jo-Jo contacted Janki. "You should not get worried when I am there to help you," he assured her. "Don't put yourself down by calling Dimpy all the time if she has no courtesy to call you back. Above that I myself am a Mumbaikar, I will give you Sagar's number," he said.

"Then what shall I do?" asked Janki.

For an answer to this, Jo-Jo made a few phone calls to his acquaintances in Mumbai and took some information from them. After looking at the notes carefully he decided that the matter was solved. He told Janki that outside the John F. Kennedy (JFK) Airport she would find Joshua waiting for her. Joshua, the son of a rabbi, had lived in Mumbai for five years and would guide Janki to where the dance troupe was staying.

Jo-Jo then called Joshua and handed over the phone to Janki.

The customs and immigration desks at JFK asked her where she was going to in the US. She gave Joshua's address there. When she came out she found Joshua waiting for her, but Joshua had never been to Mumbai. Forget about five years not even for five days. His accent was so unlike she had heard thus far, that Janki found it very hard to understand him. He, too, had to struggle to explain to Janki that the venue of the dance troupe had been shifted from New York to Dallas and they had to take a flight to reach over there. Since Dallas was far, in deep south, a change of flight at Chicago to Fort Worth was necessary. This was too complicated for a newcomer to America. So she left everything to Joshua.

After reaching Dallas, Joshua left Janki to Mac's tender mercies. This was Janki's dance troupe, a striptease in Dallas. Mac had confiscated her passport; Janki was not hand cuffed, she was free to eat, sleep and dance, but she was cut off from the world outside. The girls were under the mafia's control.

• • • ● • • •

Twenty-one

EVERY NEWSPAPER in the small town was full of the news. "Hijara sardar Hameeda brutally murdered," "Lallan guru's aide Ayub Saki key suspect in murder," "Saki absconds, blood-stained pickaxe found," "Gang war erupts among hijaras," "A dispute over begging turf". ··· There were several ways in which the incident was reported, the sum of all was the same. Hameeda, the newly-elected guru of a hijara clan, was murdered by rivals.

Kalyani was stunned. It seemed just yesterday that she had met the hundred-year old hijara guru and Hameeda at Anguri's place. Events had moved so fast that Vrinda guru and Hameeda appeared and vanished from the scene, all so soon, she thought.

Kalyani was already distressed and these developments increased her sadness. After Janki, Gautam too had deserted her. One evening he said that he was going to his village. But at that point, sullen and resentful, she didn't even ask him when would he return? Next morning when she woke up, she found that Gautam did not take even his laptop and mobile along with him. She was shocked. For the first time Kalyani wondered why she had been suspicious of her husband. Then Janki's nude photograph flashed across her mind and she shook off the momentary guilt, replacing it with a resolve that now she was going to immerse herself in her work. For a while, he put her sorrows into the back burner.

Kalyani took up a few assignments which flopped. Like in an anchoring, because of her disturbed mind she fumbled a lot. Then in a twenty-minute uninterrupted anchoring she thrice forgot her lines. The director said that he would postpone the date of the recording. Later, Kalyani got to know from her sources that after she went home the recording was done the same day with some other anchor in Kalyani's place.

With creeping age, Kalyani's demand was already decreasing. Her personal grief left her dull and restless and to make matters worse her grief-stricken mind affected her articulation. Far from immersing deep in work, even some minor tasks became a challenge for her.

Ultimately, Kalyani took refuge in an old illusion. She began to weave romantic fantasies of herself with Kabir and thought that thankfully she had at least Kabir to occupy with during this agonizing time. With the thought of Kabir something else occurred to her. If he so wished, she could get an assignment. Up to here she was absolutely right. She got an assignment to interview Kabir for a magazine. Initially, the editor shied away from delegating the responsibility to a person unaware of the workings of the print media. Yet as the hero himself had recommended her name he relented. Since the editor was not assured of the interviewer's journalistic skills, he had given Kalyani a questionnaire.

She was now in Kabir's vanity van, sitting upright on a sofa, holding the questionnaire. Kabir was speaking on his mobile, and Kalyani meanwhile had begun to create a file on her I-pod, on which she could record the interview.

Kabir's air-conditioned van was lavishly furnished with all the comforts. Dressing table, refrigerator, washbasin and what not? It had a drawing room, bathroom, bar, and even a small luxury bedroom. It was a home in itself.

As Kabir finished talking over the phone, looking anxiously at his wristwatch he called Kashi, his make-up man. "Come here, Kashi, we have half an hour to finish the make-up," saying this, Kabir moved his hand over his head and, to her great surprise Kalyani saw him removing a wig. Kabir was completely bald.

Kashi moved ahead and cleansed Kabir's face beginning from his neck to his naked head, buffing it with a sponge. While he did his work, Kalyani continued asking the questions from her sheet. "Will you give a shot when the make-up is over?" Kalyani asked off-handedly. "No, no not for a shot, I am readying myself to meet somebody," he answered.

His phone rang again. Kabir lowered himself to pick it up and, as he straightened himself, Kashi's hand bumped into Kabir's jaw. The foundation caked hand's blow knocked Kabir's denture out onto the carpet. The hairless, toothless hero's eyes met with those of Kalyani. He was flustered, though he never cared about his impression on Kalyani until removing his wig or sitting before her without make-up, the loose denture, none the less had left him a little embarrassed. Kalyani was now put off by his physical charm.

Again Kashi had begun to do Kabir's face. Kalyani sat there mute and withdrawn, as if it was her fault, but didn't leave the place because there were questions left to be asked.

After a while, Kabir was again ready to charm his admirers. As if on cue, Kashi went out and sent in a girl. Kalyani had not finished the interview but all of a sudden Kabir shot out, "All right Kalyani, whatever is left can be done later."

With this, Kalyani got up wordlessly. From the corner of her eye she saw that Kabir had slid close to the girl and was now caressing her thighs, without bothering that Kalyani had not yet left the van. As she was stepping out of the door, Kabir was taking the girl into his bedroom.

Kalyani returned home completely disenchanted. The spell was broken. No trace of honey was left in the golden bowl of her reveries. Frustrated, she flung, tossed and hurled objects around the room. But today there was neither Gautam nor Janki to tolerate her tantrums or to clean up the mess.

The next day, wiping her tears, Kalyani herself had to pick up her things and tidy up the room. She was disappointed, angry and sullen. But there was no one around to soothe and pamper her. She missed Gautam and Janki very badly. Now she didn't feel like writing the interview. But she was bound to complete it. The editor had doubted her ability at the time of giving her the assignment. "She won't be able to write it," he had said clearly. Kalyani didn't want to prove him right by turning her back on the job. So, she collected herself to transcript the conversation with the film star.

After a long time, she was once again operating the laptop belonging to Gautam and which she used occasionally. As she opened it, Kalyani found the photograph of Gautam with her and Janki, each one of them brimming radiantly with happiness. Kalyani, at this point, couldn't bear the image of her own happy family so she once again closed the laptop and decided to write by hand.

Writing by hand? But where was a notepad or a blank paper? Her home had become almost paperless, she realized. Years ago, Gautam used to write in diaries, she recalled, hoping she could find empty pages in any old diary.

She looked for it but found only a logbook with one or two yellowed, unfilled pages in it. She could bring a writing pad from the stationery shop nearby, she thought, but dropped the idea immediately since she didn't feel like going anywhere. Ultimately, she called the editor to tell him that in one or two days she would be in the magazine's office to give him her I-pod. The transcription could be done by any of his colleagues. The editor was irked at this suggestion. "Why did you take the trouble of doing the interview if you couldn't handle the task? We didn't invite you. If we had to write it, we could have taken the interview too," he almost scolded Kalyani.

He was right. Kalyani decided she should forget about the interview now. She was not going to write it. The thought itself relaxed her and she stretched out on the couch, her eyes closed. As she resumed a semblance of concentration, it occurred to her that those diaries were missing which she had gifted to Gautam in their courtship days. Gautam used to write in those mole skin diaries with Italian covers, she recalled. Soon she was obsessed with the thought of finding them.

Vigorously searching for the diaries, the whole day, Kalyani left the house in shambles. She pulled out clothes from the cupboards, took out books from the shelves. Scattered socks, hankies and things from Gautam's shaving kit. She even broke open his almirah, hurting her finger with the hammer in the process.

And yes, she found two of his diaries below a brown Turkish towel spread over one of the shelves of his almirah. Those were not simple daily diaries but a detailed account of events in Gautam's life, their dates, people he came across, impressions they left on him. His father, stepmother, half-siblings, teachers, all were there along with the description of his school, college, village and town. Janki and Kalyani were also there in the diary.

What he had written about Kalyani was full of passion. There was intensity in his expression whenever there was a mention of Kalyani. His craziness for her reflected in each word. Kalyani would have been flying if it was some other time. But just now she felt the pang of not recognizing her true lover in time.

That night Kalyani didn't sleep, she was so absorbed in the diaries. Keeping the bruised finger in her mouth to relieve the pain, she kept reading and crying at the same time. The passage which disturbed her the most was the description of Gautam's mother whom he had not seen. With so much speculation, some truth buried therein, a clear mention was made of a breast mole, too. Gautam had also mentioned that he was let into the secret by his father. "So, what Gautam had said about the mole was true, not something he fabricated on the spot in self-defence, but I didn't believe him," regretted Kalyani with a deep sigh.

In the entries before his marriage there was mention of a daughter he had dreamt of begetting. There were many pages devoted to the unborn daughter, even a name – Anuja – was given to her. "I truly and deeply want a daughter. I will ask Kalyani to give me a daughter, as a double gift. I will be able to see my mother also in her," he had written.

After reading this, Kalyani began burning in remorse. For a shallow physical benefit like preventing her stomach from creasing, she had deprived Gautam of a great emotional need and, above all she had doubted him when he found it in Janki. Neck deep in regret, she was now thinking about how could she win Gautam back. How could she earn a hostile Janki's love back? Where could she find them both? Questions were many, the turmoil and quandary even bigger.

• • • ● • • •

Twenty-two

MOHAN WAS BACK FROM the Himalayas but had not yet come to Mumbai. He was, for now, residing in a village in the valley, finding place in an ascetic's empty abode. The hermit would leave his hut early in the morning and no one in the village knew exactly where he went. The villagers had now and then seen him meditating on a rock, right in the middle of the nearby river. Sometimes he was seen roaming in the woods around the village. The sage ate only once in a week, as far as the villagers knew. So he would turn up in his hut, every Thursday from wherever he was. On that day, people brought food for him. A home cooked vegetarian meal.

The same evening he would counsel those who sought advice from him on matters of spirituality. Most of the time he had to solve family disputes and his listeners had faith in his wisdom. He listened to them calmly and dealt with their issues carefully and with justice. Maybe for this they called him Samajhdar Baba.

The arrangement was perfect both for the people and the ascetic. There was no fee for these counselling sessions; the food made up for it.

Mohan was here in the hut, the hermit not being at home. The villagers were busy with their regular works. Finding free time, Mohan opened his bag to arrange the things inside. The bag made up of tiger hide had been gifted to him by Vatsal Guru. It could be used as a mat too. Mohan brought along with him some rare Himalayan herbs. Some curious non-metallic gadgets, formed from nature's bounty, through careful experimentation, were also there. Some were made of tree bark and others from lotus stem; they worked well technically. Snake's shed skin, beaks of various birds and natural colour pigments were in Mohan's collection.

Mohan carried a broadsheet sketchbook with him. He used canvases very rarely. Generally he drew or painted pictures taking a leaf out of the sketchbook or made sketches in the diary itself. He enjoyed working on these thick and smooth drawing sheets.

While leaving for the Himalayas he had taken along some of his drawings and paintings done earlier. So the collection contained the picture which had Laxmi and Meera in it. The day was marked when Mohan and Laxmi had roamed around their settlement riding on Meera's back. After that incident Laxmi had disappeared from the scene. Bherulal spirited her away. So whenever Mohan saw this picture he felt a pang. He had never shown it to Janki because he thought that she had forgotten Laxmi, and her days in the Lord's estate.

Mohan had, however, taken the painting to show it to Vatsal Guru who liked it. Looking at Laxmi and Meera in the illustration, he said that Mohan would find Laxmi and that Meera would be instrumental in this.

When Mohan seemed a bit sceptical about the prediction then Vatsal Guru gave him an apparatus, he himself had designed after many years of experimentation with natural materials. It was a rectangular wooden box closed from three sides. Along with it was a liquid contained in the hollow of the hard-shell of a mountain fruit. One more fruit full of saffron sap was given with it. A hollow lotus stem was set in the box. It was designed in such a way that a slight intonation would be audible after passing through the lotus tube.

Giving this equipment to Mohan, Vatsal Guru told him to meet the ashram's animal language teacher, so that Mohan could understand its working and talk to an elephant through it, when the time came.

Here in Samajhdar Baba's hut, Mohan had taken out this stuff and was tidying up his bag, with the material spread out on a sheet in front of him. The village children were playing in an open space near the hut with a ball which they fashioned from scrapes of clothes.

Once, by mistake the ball shot in and the children peeped into looking for it. Mohan responded with a smile. This encouraged the children and they trooped in. Soon they surrounded Mohan and began touching, seeing and asking questions about the strange things he carried. They squealed in awe to see the painting of an elephant with a girl. But a trace of anguish clouded this happy picture. The elephant had a bloody gash on its neck.

Seeing the picture a teen claimed he knew of a female elephant with a pus-filled abscess on its neck. The elephant and its mahout lived in a village nearby, the child said, and that according to him one of the previous handlers had hurt the animal badly with his prod repeatedly gouging its neck. Only a *kaviraj*'s herbs could help heal the wound.

Hearing this, Mohan sprung to his feet as if jolted by an electric current. He held the teen's hand requesting the boy to guide him to the hamlet.

Mohan took off for the place with the group of children. The boy who had given him the indication was walking along with Mohan; his tiger hide bag slung from his shoulder. The bag contained medicinal herbs and the apparatus to decode animal language.

Mohan's surmise was correct; the ailing elephant described by the teen was indeed Meera. She had aged. Overwhelmed, Mohan broke down and Meera seemingly had tears in her eyes.

The reunion over, Mohan mixed and ground a few herbs into a paste as an ointment for Meera's wound. This must have eased her pain, yet she continued swaying her head. "Meera does not look as calm as she should be, maybe she wants to communicate something," thought Mohan, caressing her trunk. He rested his head on it in order to concentrate on her rumblings. The animal language teacher in the Himalayas had given him some training but here Mohan could guess nothing much except that there was certainly something that was agitating her. He stepped back from her trunk to observe her gestures and try to apply the next part of the training to understand animal language.

Mohan observed that Meera flapped her left ear and waved her trunk several times toward the east. Mohan asked the mahout about these actions; he spoke of a bungalow with red-tiled roof, where Meera often took him.

Only an elephant could understand another elephant. So for Mohan, it was not talking freely to Meera. But Mohan understood something from the patterns. An easterly direction, a girl and a woman, probably the same person, a single-storeyed house; roof thatched with red tiles baked in a brick kiln, a place where the river takes a bend.

The next day Mohan bid adieu to Meera, but with a promise of returning soon.

• • •

"Sharansthali," this was the name of the single-storeyed house with a roof of red tiles. It was like the *dak* bungalows of the Raj era. The house reminded Mohan of the Lord's bungalow in his home town, only a little smaller. "The child of that abode," thought Mohan, looking at it. "Maybe Meera just wanted to indicate the direction of a house similar to the bungalow."

But there was more to it. The place was named Sharansthali because here women, saved from the flesh trade, were given shelter. A non-profit organization (NGO) was running it, which had volunteers from both India and Nepal.

In the office, Mohan met its chief Kalpana Thapa. He asked her whether they had a woman named Laxmi there. But there was no such person. Mohan was little disappointed to hear this. He had not yet mastered elephant language and couldn't comprehend what Meera had to say, but he did not give up. He showed the painting which carried Meera and Laxmi to Kalpana. She had never come across this woman sporting a large bindi and flowing black hair.

An inmate appeared in the office with a mandatory glass of water. The girl was barely eighteen or nineteen-years old. As she came near, she craned her neck inquisitively to peep at what Mohan was showing Kalpana.

Calling for some Khurshid *aapa*, she scurried back into the house. A few days earlier a mahout had appeared with his elephant. Khurshid had brought a coconut and some guavas for it and had cried while putting the coconut on its trunk. Wondering, the girl had asked Khurshid that people who worshipped Lord Ganesha offered a coconut to an elephant, but why was she since she belonged to another religion? At this, Khurshid had smiled, fighting back her tears.

The girl recalled this incident and thought Khurshid *aapa* loved elephants and would definitely be happy to see one in the picture. So pulling Khurshid by the hand she brought her into the office. But Khurshid's eyes fell on Mohan first and she began to cry, sitting down heavily on the floor. Mohan was baffled with this sudden, unexpected outburst. But as he observed the figure closely, she seemed to be somewhat familiar to him. Soon her voice, too, had begun to ring a bell in Mohan's mind, and he finally recognized the identity of the prematurely aged figure. This was Laxmi.

• • •

Laxmi's story was a document of misery. Taking her along forcefully, Bherulal wandered from town to town. Initially, he had some money to buy himself liquor. Soon he needed people to comply him with free drinks. Since nothing came free, his newly-minted acquaintances began demanding favours in return. This meant Laxmi; what else had he to offer, anyway? Soon he loaned Laxmi to "a friend" for a bottle of country brew. Laxmi cried, shrieked and bit the man in protest but she couldn't save herself. Bherulal gave her an extra thrashing that day for biting his friend.

In the next town the number of Bherulal's friends increased from one to four. And gradually he left his friends with Laxmi on the pretext of obliging them to get a drink. He would bring strangers to the house and take money from them for his wife Laxmi. In one particular town the business flourished so well that Bherulal decided to settle down there. But here his stratagem failed and his ploy took a beating. As the pimps in the town got wind of it, they demanded their cut.

Hukum ka Patta, a local goon who was an extern from the region, but lived there under the nose of police, had threatened Bherulal. He said that every woman in the town was his property and only he had the right to sell her, so he needed the lion's share of Bherulal's earnings. He would otherwise take Laxmi forcibly.

Bherulal was so terrorized by the bully's threat that taking advantage of the dark he slipped away that very night with Laxmi.

In the new town he had arranged for a few customers. He had bought a cot and basic things for the kitchen. That day he had been drinking heavily from early evening. When he got hungry, he ordered Laxmi to cook a meal for him. But there was no kerosene for the stove. When Laxmi said she could not cook because of this, Bherulal thrashed her. Then he sent her out to bring a packet of bread.

Laxmi walked to the market, tears rolling down her face. When a woman in the neighbourhood saw her crying, she stopped and asked Laxmi what was bothering her. Already in turmoil for a long time, Laxmi took this opportunity to relate her plight to the woman.

After listening to her story, the neighbour suggested an escape route and Laxmi saw liberation in it. It involved the neighbour Saeeda's brother. Irfan had a job of collecting cow dung from the streets and burying stray dogs. He was married, childless and unlettered. Irfan thought it was his wife's inadequacy that they couldn't have a child. The wife was equally ignorant in thinking it was never a man's fault and she bore the guilt of not bearing a child. This guilt kept her badgering Irfan to take one more wife, which was normal, going by their faith. But legitimate or not was not the only question here. Poor Irfan's profession was so disgusting and his social standing so weak that he had got his first wife with great difficulty. Nobody was ready to give his/her daughter's hand in marriage to him. For years Irfan collected money for the *mehar*. Still, the woman he got was short, had a pock-marked face and dark skinned. This was Nafisa whose father had died. Saeeda thought, Irfan would be fortunate if he could marry a woman like Laxmi.

"There is just one thing you need to do, you will have to change your religion," Saeeda said. "I had to cast all morality aside, I have no religion now," a crying Laxmi replied. And they agreed to a plan.

"Sneak over to my house when he is asleep, I will keep the small gate on the right ajar. At four in the morning, bus no. 14 halts at the stop near the tea stall. We will take that bus to Irfan's village. Both of us will wear burka, I will arrange one for you too, so you will not be recognized; just come to me," said Saeeda.

"That hog doesn't sleep so easily," said Laxmi nervously.

"We have to take the four o'clock bus. So come whenever you are sure he is asleep," said Saeeda.

That night, Laxmi could not run away. Not even the second, third, fourth or fifth night. The opportunity came after ten days. One night, when Bherulal was fast asleep after drinking heavily, Saeeda threw a clod of earth at Laxmi's window at midnight. It smashed against the window but Bherulal remained inert. Still Laxmi couldn't gather courage to open the door and escape. She went toward the lavatory at the back, where Saeeda hung a ladder along the boundary wall, for Laxmi to jump across to freedom.

Irfan turned to be a good husband. He did not torture Laxmi, whose name was now Khurshid. On the contrary he loved and pampered her and would even press her legs when she asked him to, something unheard of in Indian society. She had a little discomfort because Irfan reeked of cow dung. But Laxmi had to endure drunkards and rough men in the near past so she could at least tolerate this small matter of stench from Irfan.

Irfan's first wife Nafisa was a nice woman. Far from being hostile toward Laxmi, she was caring. She deeply wished that Khurshid would become a mother. For this, Nafisa took Khurshid from place to place to pay obeisance at the tombs of Sufi saints and to the doors of fakirs for their blessings and the threads and amulets they gave so that her *saut* could bear a child. Almost one year passed but Khurshid didn't get pregnant. They never realized that it was Irfan's inadequacy, not that of his wives.

This practice of Nafisa, taking Khurshid from one dargah to another for blessings, turned disastrous. Not far from their village was a town where Nafisa heard a pir would come visiting; his blessings were a guarantee of fertility. That day Saeeda was also there at her brother's place. The trio took a ramshackle government bus for this town. That day Hukum ka Patta was also in the same town to get an amulet from the pir. There at least three times, due to her old habit, Saeeda called Laxmi by her real name instead of Khurshid. Hukum ka Patta who was nearby heard this and got suspicious as to why a woman wearing a burka was called Laxmi. Now she was on his radar.

Hukkum ka Patta and his gang now chased them following their every movement. After ten days a group of motorcyclists came to their village and abducted Laxmi. With this she found herself in a deeper pit than ever before.

Hukkum ka Patta had sold her to a brothel in Mumbai. There she got pregnant thrice but every time her owner forcefully had them terminated. Once when no nurse or doctor was available, the foetus was brutally dug out. Laxmi bled profusely and an infection followed. But mercy was not a word to be found in the red light area.

Laxmi didn't recover sufficiently to make for the Mumbai market. She was sold again to a man from Bengal. There was no cash transaction this time. The pimp had brought along a frightened, sixteen-year old Nepalese girl; she was left behind and Laxmi was taken instead.

This was the border area between India and Bangladesh. Here the red light area had no buildings. The settlement was a formation of shacks and shanties. Customers came seeking sex in these shanties. At a little distance away was the highway, where some of the women went to find work. Here too some shanties and cabins had been erected and rented out for prostitution.

Most of the women here came from the other side of the border, from Bangladesh, without official documents, usually by bribing security personnel from both sides with their bodies. To mingle with these women Laxmi decided to continue as Khurshid. Here it was already difficult for her since they spoke an alien language.

Like every other woman Khurshid, too, had a "babu", who was her husband-pimp. Khurshid's babu's name was Mushtaq. Due to fear of him, she never revealed her real name.

Six months after her arrival at this place, Khurshid became weaker and took to never subsiding illness. She felt sick and feverish all the time and would lie coughing in her shanty. Even in this condition Mushtaq brought an endless stream of customers to her. Given the proximity to the highway, customers would come during the day, mainly truck drivers.

In the adjoining shanty lived Amina, a Bangladeshi and her thirteen-year old daughter Mahru. Pimps did not spare even

Mahru; she was sodomized, raped and offered to customers since she was just ten.

For Khurshid, Amina and Mahru were a big help in the time of her sickness. Either one would give her food or tea when required. When Khurshid felt she was too weak to clean her hut, Mahru would come and sweep her floor and wash her utensils. Khurshid loved Mahru. She reminded Laxmi of her own beloved sister Janki.

"Dear Janki! How is she, where is she, she must have grown into an adult," Laxmi would often wonder! Many a time she asked herself, "who did she love the most?" The answer from inside was always Janki. Laxmi often thought of ending her life, but never took the step because of the hope that someday she might meet her sister Janki.

That day when Mahru was washing dishes in Khurshid's hut, Amina's babu came rushing in looking for Mahru. Finding her there, he ordered her to hide somewhere immediately. Not waiting for her to follow his instructions but holding her by hair, pushed her behind a stack of firewood.

There was chaos and everybody was scampering around in the settlement. People from an NGO had come to distribute condoms. They were going from door to door and explaining to women that they should insist that their customers use condoms. "You will be ruined if you don't do that. You don't want to contract and spread AIDS," they were told. Women from the NGO also explained how they must maintain hygiene and keep themselves infection free.

Amina's babu was afraid that the NGO worker's eyes might fall on Mahru and that they would surely object to the presence of the teen in the settlement. And they would certainly not stop just at informing the police; no "caught today and freed tomorrow." So if they found Mahru they were going to file a petition in the court for a permanent solution. This and other NGOs had done this before; they had freed one or two teens from the settlement. That was why Amina's babu had rudely pushed Mahru behind the heap of logs.

Barely a few minutes later the "didi" from the NGO and her colleagues were at Khurshid's door. As she came in, a group of people, including two policemen and a doctor, entered.

The doctor saw ailing Khurshid lying on a cot and came to check her up. He asked her how she felt and what her problems were; the doctor's assistant took the patient's blood sample. The result of the blood test was awaited but the doctor spoke to the volunteer in a low voice saying it seemed the woman on the cot had AIDS.

While they were discussing the matter, a woman's muffled cry was heard from behind the logs in the shanty. Heartened by the situation, Laxmi told them that a girl was hidden behind the heap of the firewood. The police found Mahru and took her along.

That night, Amina's babu, with two other men, entered Laxmi's shanty and beat her severely. Bruised and half conscious she lay on the floor, crying intermittently but nobody in the settlement even came to give her water. The second day, the volunteer and the doctor came to visit her, along with the police. Laxmi was found HIV positive. They had moved her to Sharansthali, so that she got proper treatment. This was Laxmi aka Khurshid's story.

• • •

"Now I have just one desire left in me that before I die I want to see my sister Janki." When dabbing her eyes Laxmi said this,

Mohan smiled.

"What makes you smile when she is crying," asked Kalpana Thapa, the chief of NGO, with surprise.

"Yes I am smiling, because finding Janki is no reason to be worried. I know Janki, rather very well," said Mohan. And he narrated the whole saga of the adoption of Janki by Gautam and Kalyani, and about his own closeness to the girl.

"Will she recognize me?" asked Laxmi apprehensively, "and acknowledge her poor and unfortunate sister if she ever recognizes her," she said with a shudder in her voice.

At this Mohan, reassuringly, put his hand on Laxmi's trembling shoulder, said, "Let's call Janki now. I also need to inform her that I am back from the Himalayas, but I don't have a cellphone," he said and looked at the mobile peeping from Kalpana's shirt pocket.

But Mohan was wrong when he said they were going to talk to Janki. On Kalpana's handset this massage appeared repeatedly, "This number does not exist." Then he tried Gautam's mobile. It rang continuously but was not picked up. He tried calling on the landline at Kalyani's home in Mumbai. This, too, received no response. At last, when Mohan called on Kalyani's mobile, her voice came through to his relief.

• • •

Kalyani went to Gautam's village, but couldn't find him there. Unexpectedly, she found someone else. She saw this person, his face painted blue, disguised as Lord Shiva wandering down the village lanes. A group of children laughing and hooting followed him. The man was new to the village, Kalyani was told. He had come here the previous week. The man was a *bahurupia*; he portrayed a different character every day. One day he wore the get-up of a tiger, the next covering his head with green leaves and twigs of a banyan tree, he turned into a forest deity. The third day he was God Brahma with a beard of white cotton wool. On some other day, he acted as a transgender. People said this was the best of his performances. He acted so well that he could easily be confused for a hijara. "Probably he was really a hijara," they thought. His height, singular gait and his voice seemed to them the tell-tale signs. The villagers observed that the man spoke English, especially when he was angry.

Gautam was never honoured in his family. They never bothered about him. But somehow they welcomed Kalyani. She was served her favourite meal. They called her *bhabhi* and she was put up in a large, airy room at the front of the house. One day sitting near the window looking out she saw the *bahurupia* entering the courtyard. Today, he was dressed as a hijara. He seemed so familiar to her that Kalyani came out to watch him close up. She asked him who he was and from where he had come. Instead of answering he began to cry, embracing Kalyani all the while. Shocked by his reaction, Kalyani began to scream, "Leave me alone!" she yelled. Hearing the commotion family members rushed out and villagers passing by crowded around in curiosity. Then, suddenly, Kalyani recognized her. This was Rani, a member of her hijara friend, Anguri's, group. Kalyani immediately called Rani inside the room. She was concerned and wanted to know what made Rani wander from village to village begging, in disguise.

Rani began to recount her story from how she was born as Raja, had an affair with a same sex person and how the hostile lover had given him to drug pedlars, who, after emasculating, sold "her" to Chameli hijara. A period of some comfort ensued when Vrinda guru took Rani into her fold. But Vrinda died and Hamida was anointed as the new guru. Hamida was very understanding and promised Rani to help realize her dream of sex change through surgery. But Hameeda was murdered by Ayub Saki, a hijara of Lallan group. Lallan then forcibly took Vrinda guru's home, property and everything else.

"Oh! Yes, I remember coming across this news. The local papers were full of it," Kalyani said.

But Rani, as if hearing nothing, continued her story desperate to tell Kalyani everything, here and now.

"Let me tell you, didi, Lallan is not a hijara. He is a man. He took on the guise of a hijara to extort money by bullying people. From a long time he kept an eye on Vrinda guru's property, and also on me and Anarkali. He pushed both of us into prostitution. I fled and wander from village to village in disguise. Poor Anarkali remains in the trap. One day at a Shiva temple I came across Ramila, she said Anarkali had contracted AIDS."

"AIDS! How come this devil knocked on her door?" shocked, Kalyani asked.

A family member had purposefully trained his ears on the conversation. As the word AIDS entered it he got into the alert mode and began to shout, calling others in the home to come out. "Look, what Kalyani *bhabhi* is doing here. "She has let a street-roaming hijara in and is talking dirty to him, AIDS, sex, prostitution . . . ."

Those who had earlier welcomed her all of a sudden turned against Kalyani. They told her to quit their home immediately along with her "dear guest". Kalyani could now infer how they had treated Gautam. "If they couldn't love and respect their own blood Gautam then how could they love and accept me," she thought as she left the place with Rani.

Kalyani promised Rani that one day she was going to help fulfil her dream of transforming her into a girl. "I will get your sex change surgery done in Mumbai and foot all the bills. You should stop worrying now," she reassured Rani. "Is there a way that we could meet Anarkali?" asked Kalyani.

"It seems impossible to release that ill-fated girl from the clutches of those barbarians," replied Rani, "look at me, how I am running around to get away from their wrath. You have offered me to come along with you to Mumbai, but I am really frightened. Lallan may catch me on the train itself. You don't know his reach," continued Rani without a breather.

"Don't be afraid, I will take you by air and we won't board the flight from the airport in our town. You are coming with me, now, in my car to Bhopal. From there, we will go to Mumbai," said Kalyani with an unexpected calm.

"But you had said you plan to meet Milarepa in our home town; now you say you are going to Mumbai directly," said Rani careful not to show the happiness she was feeling about going to Mumbai, that too, on a flight. It seemed unseemly to her to look happy when Kalyani had to sacrifice something.

"I will come back next week to meet Milarepa," said Kalyani, "and it's not going to make much difference even if I return next month. Just now my priority is to take you to Mumbai," she concluded.

• • •

The sun was going down. Twilight was setting on Milarepa's ashram, casting a cerise hue over its already crimson set-up. All the visitors had gone except one. Kalyani was the last visitor who remained with the ashram-dwellers.

A mouth-watering fragrance of asafoetida, fenugreek, ginger and a mixture of powdered spices filled the air. It was, after a long time, that the aroma of food began tickling the hunger spot inside Kalyani's head. After analysing her dreams Milarepa would eat his dinner and go to sleep. A woman in a red sari had put on all the light bulbs, which were wrapped in red, see-through paper, throwing a reddish stream of light.

Milarepa gestured to Kalyani to sit on the red mat spread before him. While sitting down, Kalyani glanced at the empty coffin lying to one side. Milarepa told her quickly that she was not required to lie in it. "You just have to sit quietly with your eyes closed. Open them to answer the question and shut them again."

The midget who was to read aloud the dreams from Kalyani's diary was ready, wearing his red beret. He began to read: "I am visiting a farm. Its rolling acres are full of a lush green, healthy crop of gram, interspersed by cucumber creepers. A peasant wearing a fluorescent pink turban is guarding the crop. I ask his permission to eat some cucumbers. He says there is no knife to slice the cucumbers and peel their skin covered with thorns. I assure him that I am going to peel the cucumbers and cut them, too, using my teeth. The only thing I need is his permission."

"The peasant gives me cucumbers. I take them and step up on a machan in the field. Sitting there, I begin to eat the cucumbers."

"A little girl comes and asks for those tasty cucumbers. I don't give her any. She insists but I don't relent then she gives me a tight slap. Her little fingers leave an impression on my cheek. I am disturbed, thinking that if the impression lasts, it will mar my beauty. The print of her hand may become wrinkles."

As the reading of this dream was completed, the midget

stopped for a while and looked at Milarepa. He knew that these little interspaces were required so that Milarepa could cross-question the dreamer. So, as the midget stopped, Kalyani opened her eyes and Milarepa threw his first question.

"You had this dream only once or is it a recurrent dream?"

"No, this is not a recurrent dream, but the little girl appears every time, whatever I am dreaming about."

"Can you guess who the little girl is?"

"Yes," said Kalyani and went silent.

"Are there any other things, which you see again and again?" As Milarepa asked this, Kalyani's hand went spontaneously over her short cropped hair and she said, "Yes, I often see in my dream, my long, black, silky hair cascading like a stream down my back, like it used to be in my childhood and my youth. The same hair Taeeji used to braid in two long plaits. I become so happy that at last I have found my crowning glory. But, alas, as I wake up I realize it was only a dream and I become sad."

"Regret, I can see the symbols in your dreams indicate regret; regret and insecurity. They indicate the fear of losing, too," said Milarepa and simultaneously nodded at the midget to read the next dream.

"I am in the Alps. Hefty Swiss cows are grazing on hemp leaves. Ghunghru is there, mounting one of these cows. He has grown hemp here and there, amid the fodder. Ghunghru's hair has turned white. He reaches his hand over his hirsute chest and plucks a strand of hair from the root, only to sell it off to a cow. Soon the cow transmogrifies into an airplane. An Asian man boards this plane. The man is robust but his face is full of wrinkles. The flight is about to land. The man says he is going to pull all the wrinkles off his face."

The midget stops. Baba asks Kalyani, "Is this, too, a recurrent dream? Do you see this again and again?"

"No, never, I had this dream only once. And let me tell you, I have not seen Ghunghru for many years," confessed Kalyani.

Milarepa didn't tell the midget to read the next dream. Instead, he probed further, "So, it was not a recurrent dream, you say, but was it indistinct or very sharp and clear," he asked.

"It was sharp and clear. It was so vivid that I thought I had actually reached Switzerland," replied Kalyani.

Milarepa closed his eyes. After ten minutes he said this was not a regular every day dream. "There is so much going on in the cosmos that we know so little of. We are very small in the larger scheme of things. It is possible that the events in dreams come to us in a time capsule long before they occur," said Milarepa.

"So, can you interpret this dream for me?" asked Kalyani.

"I am Milarepa, not Brahma or Vishnu. I will delve deep into your life and then attempt to interpret your dreams accordingly, but there is a limit. I can't do this on your behalf; I can do it only while I am sitting with you. You attempt to interpret now or some other time; with me or singly, but don't forget one thing that this is an important dream; a sparkling diamond lying in a heap of rubbish. Don't let this dream fade from your memory. The hidden clues may help you in the future. But it's your life after all and only you know it," saying this he smeared freshly rubbed sandalwood on her forehead and Kalyani understood that it was a sign for her to leave.

• • •

Kalyani returned home disappointed. Milarepa's dream interpretation did not help her solve the complications of her confused life. "I am already aware of the repentance and regret

I have over certain issues. I regret Gautam and Janki's going away. I regret losing my youth. So there is nothing new in what Milarepa indicated," thought Kalyani and came outside, in the veranda of the Lord's bungalow, disillusioned.

She could not sit in the veranda for long. It was no more the place it once was. The peaceful, private avenue leading to the farm had almost turned into a public path. Kalyani had sold a part of the farm over which a mall and multiplex had been built. The first mall in the town, it was always bustling with eager visitors, not all of whom were shoppers or movie goers.

The entire scenario made it impossible for Kalyani to sit here for relaxation. Frustrated, she went in.

"A watchman is required outside the Lord's bungalow; now it cannot be left unguarded while I am away in Mumbai," thought Kalyani. To sell it was something she could not even think of. These days she felt a pang of regret for the piece of land she had already sold, where once Ghunghru's hut stood.

She had forgotten her mobile phone inside the house when she went out to the veranda. As she came back she found it ringing incessantly. She rushed toward it wishing the call was from Gautam or Janki. But it was from Mohan. He was back from the Himalayas and showered a storm of questions on Kalyani. Where was Janki? He had been calling Janki but the only reply he received was, "this number does not exist." "Had Janki changed her number?"

Then Kalyani narrated the whole saga to him. He was disturbed when he heard all this and said he was leaving for Mumbai immediately. Kalyani told him that she was at home in Shivnagar and would be reaching Mumbai post-haste.

In the course of the conversation, Mohan informed Kalyani

that he had found Laxmi in Sharansthali, and that he was speaking from the mobile belonging to Kalpana Thapa, chief of the NGO, Sharansthali.

• • •

Where would she find Gautam? What could have happened to Janki? Was she still alive? Dread was killing Kalyani, her heart rending from distress. Before leaving for the small town, she had reported Janki missing to the police. But the police was unwilling to register the case. Town Inspector Radheshyam Verma was sceptical of the whole affair. He said that when she herself took months to report her daughter missing, how an FIR could be lodged with any alacrity. "You never know. It is possible that the girl has eloped with someone. We also hear she was into drugs," he added vaguely.

Kalyani was all the more disappointed when she had returned from the police station. Her spirit was at its lowest ebb. There was no one she could talk to about this. Now as Mohan was back, she thought of calling Mohan. But she thought again. She was to reach Mumbai soon and would meet Mohan in person. Where was solace now, when she really needed it? Her thoughts wandered once again to Milarepa. Her earlier meeting with him left much to be thought about, yet she decided to see him once again.

It was noon, when she reached the ashram. The place looked deserted. But the woman she had met during the previous visit was there, this time too. She received Kalyani and informed her that Milarepa would come to the antechamber after his sleep for a dream. Only a few minutes might have passed before the midget came out and announced, "Baba is now recording his dream. You are all invited for a round of herbal tea after that." Then grinning for no reason he added, "Sister you, too, come along." This was for Kalyani.

"Thanks Gulgul," said the woman and for the first time Kalyani came to know the midget's name. She turned to the woman and asked her name. "Dharti," she replied.

"Dharti! You mean earth? What kind of name is this, I have never heard anything like this before," said Kalyani, laughing.

In response, Dharti let out an almost Homeric but cordial laugh. "Actually my name was Usha. But Milarepa had rechristened me Dharti."

"Why was the name Dharti chosen for you, did it mean you had to endure a lot of grief, like mother Earth?"

"Yes. I had gone through a lot, but that was not the reason for him to give me a new name. It was given so that I would forget the sorrows of my past and start life afresh," answered Dharti.

"Do, you mean Milarepa can make you forget your sorrows, that he is not merely a dream-interpreter or a soothsayer," asked Kalyani, like a child who had not yet encountered matters of rationality.

"Look sister, you are right when you say he is not merely a soothsayer. He is believed to be a *trikaldarshi*, a man who can look beyond time. But my own perception is that he can look beyond your heart and spirit to touch the core of your being, to reach your soul and share with you your sorrows and malaise. If he doesn't present himself as a clairvoyant, people will not be able to use his attributes of a perceptive psychiatrist," as she stated this, Dharti realized her mistake and bit her tongue in a "what-have-I-said" gesture. She had unknowingly spilled the beans.

As Dharti finished speaking and looked up, she found that Gulgul was staring at her angrily. Damage control was required immediately. Her guru was not a charlatan. So Dharti decided to elucidate further. She began to explain, "Please don't get Milarepa wrong. Before forming an opinion about him you need to know more of him. Milarepa in fact holds many degrees in psychology, from universities at home and abroad. He had been a practising psychiatrist in Benares. He had chosen psychology because he had seen his own mother suffering from an acute mental illness. She and the others around her were ignorant and illiterate. Nobody had thought of giving her proper treatment. She was taken to witch doctors and *ojha*s. Her son decided to become a psychiatrist. He was bent on fighting ignorance and superstition," said Dharti and paused to seek Kalyani's reaction.

"If his ideal was so great, why didn't he continue serving as a psychiatrist in Benares?" asked Kalyani sharply, despite the feeling of empathy she had for the man. She knew the pain of a child whose parent suffered from a mental illness.

"I was coming to that, sister Kalyani," said Dharti, "yes, he should have continued with that, but providence had some other ideas in store for him. His beloved wife and twin sons died in an accident. He was disenchanted with life so he left for the Himalayas. He spent three years in an ashram there, coming across some fantastic methods and lines of psychiatric treatment developed by people of spiritual wisdom. He realized that what he had learnt, if clubbed with his academic knowledge of medicine and counselling, could give wonderful results in the field of psychology and spiritual well-being."

"But that still doesn't answer my basic question, as to why he did not practise as a psychiatrist and why he is masquerading as a mystic," asked Kalyani with a touch of suspicion.

Dharti began in the same tone, "I was coming to that. You know in India, people with psychological problems remain untreated. They don't go to a psychiatrist, but to a pandit, fakir and ··· *ojha*. Milarepa wants to lend his services in whatever form they are received so that as many people as possible get treated. It's free of charge, so the question of deceiving anybody does not arise."

"But the grief of losing wife and children ···," Kalyani tried to put the question.

Dharti interrupted again with her stock phrase "Yes, I was coming to that only. There is no cure for grief, only time heals, gradually, at its own pace. But Milarepa had learnt a few methods during his sojourn in the Himalayas that helped him continue postponing the arrival of pain."

Before she could complete the sentence Gulgul announced, "Milarepa has now entered."

Sitting before Milarepa, Kalyani did not discuss her diary of dreams. Her sorrows, grief and regrets were the themes she shared with him. When she asked him how she could come to terms with her tormented mental state, Milarepa answered, "You have to work to dissolve yourself in···."

"You mean I should begin fasting and other austerities. Or starve myself, be ready for penance and atonement or meditate myself into a trance?" asked Kalyani.

"No, no nothing like that," he answered with a broad smile, "don't force yourself into any state of being ··· let it submerge you physically and mentally so that you forget hunger and thirst, forget the time of day. Forget everything until only the core remains."

"What you have suggested is too complicated. I don't know how to go about it," said Kalyani.

Milarepa replied, "What you are suffering from is not a

normal depression. If it was, I would have given something to quieten you. After a period of restful sleep you would have recovered. But your problem is born out of a situation, which you cannot alter now. You should certainly try to find your husband and daughter. Meanwhile, internalize with a clear conscience and chasten yourself."

"To make an inward journey, do I have to meditate and go into a trance? I can't do that. There is so much tumult in my head that I am unable to concentrate," said Kalyani.

Milarepa didn't reply, instead he called Dharti who came quickly. Then he said to Kalyani, "I will prescribe medication to correct the chemical imbalance in your brain but for now, if you want, you may join Dharti, she is going on a circumambulation of the Govardhan Mountain. I am confident this will help you to a large extent."

"I am not at all a religious person then how can a pilgrimage give me the peace of mind one gets from such an exercise …," before Kalyani could complete the sentence, Milarepa interrupted, "You yourself have answered the question. For some this is a pilgrimage but for others it is merely an activity which is good for your physical, mental and spiritual well-being. What is pilgrimage anyway? It seems humankind might have invented it to ward off sorrows for a while. Forgive me for my extreme views; I think we have invented God and religion to fight our miseries. It is a different matter that all this had become a mindless tradition and the tradition of making a pilgrimage has lost its significance."

Milarepa continued, "I can only suggest that you go. Only the experience will show you the difference it will make to your disturbed mind … difference, I said, I don't say the pilgrimage would lead to the complete elimination of your sorrows. When you return, take up some good cause and serve others. When we dissolve our egos and begin to empathize with the downtrodden, we will surely forget our sorrows," said Milarepa and got up from his seat. Then he turned his head and said, "Do meet me when you come back, and let me know how you felt."

• • •

Birds began to chirp. A soft orange-red sun emerged from behind the mountain. The mountain was somewhat rocky but looked majestic as the sun spread a layer of molten gold over it. It was a lovely morning but Kalyani remained unenchanted as if nothing could please her.

Now it was time to set out for the *parikrama.* Everybody in the group was ready to go. When Dharti told her to come along, Kalyani was all prepared with her shoes on, dressed in orange salwar-kameez. She had slathered sunscreen on her face, covered it with her dupatta wearing a peaked cap.

When Kalyani thought she was ready to move, she looked at Dharti and asked, "You were asking me to begin the journey, but you yourself are not ready. You have not yet put on your shoes."

Dharti laughed softly at this and answered, "I am ready. It is just that that I am going to walk without shoes."

Now Kalyani looked at others in the group. It was not only Dharti, but there were others, too, who were ready to leave barefoot. Some had a wooden pole in their hands; others wore a saffron dupatta across their shoulders. Some held musical instruments like cymbals and *manjira.* Slogans praising the Lord of Govardhan Parvat ranged through the air as the pilgrims left the camp singing bhajans. Some simply clapped their hands in time. Shortly the group reached the starting point from where the *parikrama* path began.

On one side was the holy mountain, in the middle was a wide trail and, on the other, was an open ground interspersed with an occasional public washroom facility or a tea stall or a food vendor's shack. Toward the mountain side, forget about urinating, even sitting a while to rest was prohibited.

Kalyani walked along like a robot. The first stretch was effortless because she was used to exercise on treadmills. There was no effort in this and she did not find herself involved physically or mentally. Painful thoughts of loss and repentance were still droned through her mind. She could forget nothing, so was it worth it to come here on Milarepa's suggestion? She questioned herself and answered too, that if she had come, she should complete the *parikrama*. If the process didn't turn out to be absorbing, she could talk to Mohan while walking to keep her involved. But this wasn't possible since they had to leave their mobiles at the camp. What anguish Mohan must have been going through, he loved Janki so much, she thought. Just then, she saw something unusual.

A man was going the distance not by walk, but prostrating himself and crawling. He would lie on his stomach, stretch his hands above his head and fold them as in a *namaskar*. Then he would rise and repeat the whole process once again. This way at one time he could cover only the distance equivalent to the length of his body. He had no need for speed, it seemed; he literally inched forward not caring about people who stared at him curiously.

Instead of becoming tired, people got more enthusiastic as they went along. Chanting slogans and singing devotional songs, they began to dance to the tune of their musical instruments. The atmosphere was charged with a new fervour, as if a wave of ecstasy was set in and engulfed the pilgrims.

Meantime, Kalyani came across so many people fulfilling their difficult vows, that nothing surprised her any more. There were people who covered the distance by doing somersaults on the rough road. Then there was this man who did sit-ups at one point, lie down there and again perform sit-ups at the place where his head had reached last. Dharti turned to Kalyani, "Didi, the pilgrimage which we are going to complete in seven days, this man, in this way, will complete in six months."

Just then, a girl went crawling on her stomach and a foreigner, creeping on the ground, slowly moved forward.

"Why are these people putting themselves to such severe torture? What do they think that God would be pleased by their stunts?" Kalyani asked Dharti. But the answer came from another quarter, not from Dharti. Before she could answer an old woman walking along broke in, "No dear sister, whatever promise they made, they had made to themselves, not to God, maybe they have done this in the name of God. What has Govardhana Nath to do whether somebody chooses a bed of roses or a bed of thorns?"

Night was fallen. Despite the floodlights, a resplendent moon in the sky shed a pure and heart-warming glow. Millions of stars in the ink-blue sky made it irresistible. With a sigh Kalyani thought, "Gautam loved so much to watch the sky when it was full of bright stars." He used to tell her, "Kalyani, in Mumbai we miss sleeping on terraces and watching the stars from our bed."

Kalyani looked around. The big ground served as their bed. People curled up in whatever space they found. Some were preparing to sleep, some were dozing already. A few lay at the edge of the path without worrying about those who preferred to walk during the night.

Kalyani took off her shoes to slip them under her head

as a pillow. She was so tired that she lay down on the uneven ground without any hesitation and covered herself with her dupatta. Just then it occurred to her that she had forgotten to bring her sleeping pills. But she need not have rued this. After a few minutes of discomfort on the rough surface she went into a deep slumber without the pills. At about four o'clock Dharti woke her up and both of them joined the public toilet queue for the morning ablutions. They had to be ready by six o'clock to resume their journey for the second day.

The morning was going into day. Kalyani found it different even as people around were full of enthusiasm to begin the trek. Nobody seemed to bother how they looked. Kalyani didn't bring out her make-up kit from her tote bag. But she thought it would be wise to use the sunscreen at least. She was rummaging through her bag just as a palanquin passed by. Two porters carried an obese, middle-aged moneybag sitting leisurely in it.

The old woman who had earlier commented that what we promise we promise to ourselves, what has God got to do with it, was present on the scene and pointing toward the man in the palanquin, said to Kalyani, "Look at him daughter, riding in a palanquin. That man would certainly be able to complete the formality of a *parikrama*, but neither he nor his legs will ever know how and when it had been performed."

Seemingly light in tone, the remark carried such a deep philosophy that Kalyani looked at the old woman in surprise. She perhaps did not have a formal education. Kalyani didn't know how it affected her but, at once, she put the sunscreen back into her bag without using it.

The group was now ready to trek and everyone was waiting for Kalyani to go through her ritual of wrapping a scarf across her mouth and putting on her cap and shoes. But she did nothing of this. She felt a new spark after the day and-a-half with her companions. She looked at their feet. No one had worn their boots and Kalyani, too, decided to hit the road barefoot.

Yesterday she had walked many kilometres, barefoot at a stretch and now Kalyani felt feverish. Her body ached, the soles of her feet sore, her face got reddened by continuous exposure to the sun. But Kalyani did not care. It was someone else's body; it seemed not her own. There was a kind of detachment from her physical self while her mind was ecstatic with a newfound wave of energy so big that all else became small. Maybe, it was an adrenaline rush. Whatever it be, Kalyani was walking, her body only a medium. It was no more her main concern to save it.

Again as night fell and as her group decided to stop, she lay down at that point at the edge of the trek, and was immediately lost in slumber, on the rough ground without even a sheet spread on it. In the middle of the night she woke up for a while and looked up. There was no limit to her enchantment like the boundless sky above her, so clean that the stars sparkled like diamonds. Surely, the stars appeared every night in the sky, but today it seemed unique to Kalyani. It was late and there was a nip in the air, so she took out her petticoat from the tote bag, covered herself, and went back to sleep.

• • •

As Kalyani landed at the Mumbai airport her phone rang. It was Rani, "Kalyani didi, there are great tidings, the news is so big, I couldn't wait for you to come back. I tried calling you repeatedly but your phone was switched off. . . ."

Rani was sounding so happy that Kalyani thought it must be about Janki and she interrupted the former in mid-sentence, posing her own question, "Great tidings, what great tidings, did somebody find Janki? Where is she?"

With this, Rani realized her mistake. There were no tidings, other than finding Janki, which could have been great for Kalyani just now. Rani thought she ought not to have acted so hyper. She lowered the volume of her voice to an "acceptable" level of enthusiasm and delivered the news again, "Sorry didi, what I am going to tell you may not be the greatest news but certainly it is important. Remember, you once introduced me to Mr Vivek Arora from Mayo TV. One day he called me to sit in the audience of one of his shows. There I asked two-three questions. People's eyes fell on me and, just two days ago, Vivekji called me to tell that on Electra TV a show, anchored by a third gender person, Shabana, is getting very popular. Mayo TV needs to beat the competitor at its own game. They wanted me to give an audition. I got selected because I speak both Hindi and English well, I can dance . . ." there was no end to Rani's enthusiasm.

"This news is big and heart warming. I am happy for Rani," thought Kalyani, loading her luggage onto a trolley. "Now the next step is to do something for her sex change operation," her train of thought continued as she walked.

Kalyani took Rani to a plastic surgeon, Dr Raman Sankhala. According to him, it was possible to do sex change operation in India, but as it was a complicated procedure, it could be a gradual process. "For, at least two years hormone treatment is needed. Then, breast augmentation is done. For a few months thereafter the patient has to get used to the weight of her newly-formed bosom. Some minor surgery and hormone treatment still remain before the most important part of the female anatomy, the vagina, is constructed. All this will lead to many mental and physical complications," he warned. "Rani is already in a tumultuous mental state just now. She is taking psychiatric treatment right now, so obviously this is not the right time for a sex change surgery. She should wait for some time," Dr Sankhala suggested.

• • •

The eleventh floor, again. Kalyani was there, after a long time, at her Mumbai apartment. She did not have to use the keys. It was already open; Mohan and Kalpana Thapa were putting up there. She was also there, Ghunghru's elder daughter ··· no-no, Kalyani corrected herself, she should rather think about Laxmi as Janki's sister, not as Ghunghru's daughter. Never make that mistake again, she reminded herself.

Mohan opened the door with Laxmi just behind him. Along with Kalpana they were waiting behind the door for Kalyani. Mohan touched Kalyani's feet and then stood aside with tears in his eyes. Kalpana folded her hands and with a smile introduced herself, "I am Kalpana Thapa." Now it was Laxmi's turn. She came near Kalyani and before she could bend to touch her feet, Kalyani stopped her and pulled Laxmi into her arms. And both of them cried in each other's embrace.

Now they were sitting in the drawing room making out a strategy, absent till now, to launch a search for Janki. Kalyani missed her terribly and Gautam too, but suggested to her colleagues that there was no point in searching for him down the legal path because he was not really missing, but had left home on his own. Besides, the police could deride them or follow a dead-end lead if they lodge a complaint about the missing father and daughter. So they concentrated on search for Janki. Also because Kalpana feared that Janki could have fallen prey to human traffickers, it would be necessary that police take the case seriously. And, for the first time, police registered a complaint without any fuss, perhaps because this time Kalpana was also there with Kalyani.

Kalpana had sent Janki's photographs to all centres of Sharansthali with the message that if anyone who came across the girl should report to her.

After two days, Kalpana received a call from the Chennai centre. But this was not regarding Janki. Kalpana was visibly disturbed after this. When she told the others what the matter was, everybody got shocked. A boy named Mutthu was to be brought to Maharashtra from Tamil Nadu. He was only ten years old but had AIDS. The disease had not been transmitted from his parents but from a customer.

A short distance from Madras there was a small town on the coast. Many tourists visited the place and Mutthu's father also came here frequently bringing his son along. Here he would first approach a tender coconut vendor, Shreenivas, who in turn introduced him to a foreign or a desi tourist. The tourist would give a hundred rupees to Shreenivas, who kept twenty rupees and passed on the rest to Mutthu's father. The boy would then be sent off with the customer to some hotel nearby. In the beginning Mutthu had cried a lot, but his screams were always drowned by the roar of the sea.

However, Mutthu was not the only one who was trapped in this black alley of criminals. There were many more children like him. One day, on the complaint of an NGO police raided a hotel in the town. But only two children were found with customers that day. One was Mutthu, who was sent to the Amaravati centre of Sharansthali. Now living in Maharashtra far from his home he could get treatment and an education and start a new life without fear of his father. The other child was sent to Madurai.

Knowing about Mutthu's plight Kalyani became saddened. Concerned, she asked Kalpana, "What will become of Mutthu now?"

"Sharansthali will arrange for his education and treatment. In the meantime; we will try for his adoption. But···," Kalpana's voice trailed off.

"But what?" asked Kalyani.

"I said but because to give such children in adoption is not the solution," replied Kalpana, "You can never say, people adopt children happily, but in the course of time, they may become insensitive and non-caring toward the kids." The last sentence slipped involuntarily from Kalpana's mouth but what could be done about an arrow already released from the bow? She regretted her own comment when she saw Kalyani's face suddenly paling. For a few seconds there was a silence in the room. Then Kalpana spoke again. In an effort to handle the awkward situation she changed the topic, "Kalyani, I want your perspective, rather your help in a problem. In our small towns and villages, people are not completely AIDS literate. We want to run an awareness programme. Can you introduce me to a producer who could make a strong documentary on AIDS for Sharansthali?"

Kalyani paused a little then offered her services if Kalpana agreed. "We can possibly take the first few shots in Amaravati to begin the documentary with. I would prefer to go along with you to Amaravati," said Kalyani. While suggesting this Kalyani had many thoughts on her mind. The first was that Milarepa wanted her to take up a project through which she could serve and enhance the lives of the underprivileged. Somewhere inside she held on to a feeble hope that she may find Janki in the process. Within the week Kalyani left for Amaravati with Kalpana Thapa.

Mohan also thought that for him now there was no point in being stuck in Mumbai. And he, too, set off on his own mission to find both the father and the daughter. He asked his mind about where they could possibly be. Gautam had no relatives and had cut all ties with his village. Above all, Gautam was an intelligent, self-reliant man; he could settle anywhere in the world. It would be difficult to find him. Mohan looked for a thread along which he could trace Gautam's route. Meantime, something else occurred to him. He remembered that Gautam had introduced him to Dr Karun Prabhaker, a researcher into reincarnation in the Khushi Centre. Mohan had observed that otherwise a rational being, never ready to accept unreasoned situation, Gautam that day looked a different man. Though he had denied that the doctor could have had any influence over him, one could see that Gautam was under the spell of this scientist. Wordless, he had remained seated in his chair, for a long time after Dr Prabhaker leaving Gautam. This too Mohan knew that he had invited Gautam to visit his Centre for reincarnation research. "So it is possible that Gautamji could have gone to the Centre," Mohan thought, "or he might still be there." With this in mind Mohan left Mumbai for Dr Prabhaker's town.

• • •

In the AIDS ward of a government hospital in Maharashtra, Kalyani was seated next to Dr Batra, head of the department. At his suggestion, she had put on a white apron to appear as a doctor herself so that patients would not shy away from giving their case histories to the doctor, in her presence. This left her free to make observations for her documentary.

The first patient was a woman from a town nearby. Her carpenter husband had given her the disease. The doctor wrote out a prescription explaining to the woman how she might get these medicines for free from a help centre, nearby, run by an NGO Sahayata. The next patient to enter, a man, was a vegetable vendor was going every week to Mumbai to sell the produce grown in his village. He got infected during such visits.

Then it was another woman with her six-year old daughter Farida. Farida was a fidgety little girl. Instead of sitting with her mother, she kept running about touching things with her childish curiosity. She took a couple of somersaults before her mother could stop her. Kalyani turned her eyes several times toward Farida feeling a river of fondness flowing in her heart.

Soon the mother's turn came. She pulled Farida along with her to the doctor's desk. Kalyani was shocked when she came to know that the kid was an AIDS patient like her mother. Rather, it was transmitted to her while she was still a foetus. This made feel Kalyani rotten. But this was not the ultimate jolt. It was Anguri who now came in. Life in Lallan guru's gang threw this misfortune into Anguri's quarter.

It was a moment of happiness now for Kalyani to find Anguri again, marred by the knowledge that the dreaded disease had infected her. Kalyani offered to take Anguri to Mumbai with her. Anguri declined, horrified by the thought of living in Mumbai again. The terror of Kamathipura still haunted her. She requested Kalpana to place her in any branch of Sharansthali.

They were now waiting for Mutthu's arrival. In comparison to the child her own anguish looked trivial to Anguri. Along with Kalpana she apprehended the hand of human traffickers in Janki's disappearance.

"These big-bellied monsters swallow innocent girls and don't even burp," said Kalpana who had come across many such cases.

When Kalyani showed Janki's photographs to Anguri she said she had seen a girl resembling the one in the picture in Mumbai's Kamathipura area. Kalyani was now eager to go to

Kamathipura and run a search for Janki there. For Kalyani there was no one better than Anguri who could help her. Anguri came out with a resounding no, albeit in a trembling voice. She was really scared. Clarifying the reason for her refusal she said, "Kalyani, we don't know evil minded people there. They are ruthless. I fled from there, a crime in those men's eyes. They will not spare me if I am found. I don't want to be seen by them." She urged Kalyani never to try wading in those shark infested waters.

Kalyani was hurt by Anguri's flat refusal to accompany her. She also was scared. But it did not deter her from setting up a search there. The thought had entered her mind and she was adamant to go all the way. Kalyani approached the police in Mumbai with a request to dragnet the area. But the police was in no mood to oblige. They had raided the place a month ago and had uncovered nothing. Otherwise also the clue provided by Anguri about her seeing a young woman similar to Janki was not sufficient. Something more concrete was needed for them to move. They said that since the FIR had been registered the department was not sitting idle. Kalyani was advised to keep this in mind.

Kalyani could not push the police and though she said nothing further the horror remained that Janki might be there somewhere. It ate her like a worm. She was now obsessed by the thought of going personally in search of Janki. Even Kalpana Thapa who had seen the world of sex workers up-close said there was no point in going into the fires of hell on a small possibility of finding Janki. But this was a state of mind where logic had abandoned Kalyani. Kalpana was surprised at her behaviour simply because she was unaware that Kalyani had inherited this stubborn irrationality from her father. It ran like a rogue elephant through her genes. It ruled her DNA.

Laxmi, who till now was silent over having spent time in Kamathipura, opened her mouth when she found Kalyani repeatedly accusing the police. It astonished Kalyani to know that even Laxmi had lived there for some time.

"Police raids don't make much sense," warned Laxmi. While in Kamathipura she witnessed one such "khaki invasion." An informer had forewarned brothel owners to shift the girls; in those four or five hours what they had to go through was worse than anyone's fiendish nightmare. Laxmi herself had to hide in a dark narrow hole dug into the wall under their cots. After packing the girls in, the mouth was covered by a wooden plank. Laxmi could hardly breathe, tightly curled up as she was in that ridiculously cramped space with four other unfortunate girls.

"Otherwise also, these pimps have no mercy. They hand down severe punishment to girls who dare to escape. You will shudder just hearing about it," said Laxmi.

Kalyani was horrified by this account. It fed into her system where the idea of searching for Janki became even more stubborn. She needed a pretext to troll the place. She applied to a private TV channel to be commissioned for a documentary even as she heard people talking about the subject being so played out. Kalyani decided to go ahead with the documentary on her own steam. Whether the TV channels ran it or not, she at least could begin taking shots as a screen for her mapping out the area.

She first chose noon time to shoot, not the evening when customers would begin visiting their "things" for the night. Kalyani had Laxmi go along as a guide. She could not refuse Kalyani as Anguri did. She was Janki's own sister and the one who had been obliged to live on the Lord's estate. Or so she thought. Laxmi acquiesced to Kalyani's thinking going along with what she thought was a whim.

Kalyani picked up a cameraman Ajay with only a hand-held camera. He suggested that this would lower the quality of her documentary. She had to explain to him that she needed only a few shots of the real world, the shooting would be done in the studio with actors. The shots would be mixed in later on. No further convincing was needed and Ajay was ready to move.

Laxmi went as far as she was able with Kalyani, her courage running out as they entered the area. She was trembling, her clothes sweat-sodden. Still she could not back out. Seeing Laxmi's face drain of blood Kalyani herself suggested that she should remain at a corner tea stall and wait for her and Ajay to return. Meanwhile, Laxmi could ease the tension by indulging in sandwiches and tea.

It was just another afternoon like a settlement anywhere else in the city. A woman filling her bucket at the community tap, a small boy at the front steps of a *kholi* was whirling a top.

Two boys shouted at each other, a woman was hanging a sari to dry on her balcony. Lattice work covered the porch of a house from which two girls peeped out. This was where Kalyani thought a shot could be taken. Ajay caught her signal and positioned himself immediately. The girls scared by the camera ran inside.

From a side door Kalyani entered the house through a damp, dark corridor which led to a staircase. In the narrow alcove below, a *kholi* had been carved out with barely enough room for a single cot. Mumbai's humidity had never been as unbearable as it was here. There was no fresh air, the atmosphere loaded with a peculiar stench. Kalyani was overcome with nausea and could not stop retching. Hearing this, a middle-aged woman came out from one of the rooms, her eyes falling on Ajay who was right behind Kalyani, the presence of people with camera angered the woman. In a loud rasping voice she asked Kalyani, "Eh, Bai! What do you want from us? Who gave you permission to crash into our space?"

Kalyani was dumfounded by this sudden battery. She could not answer the woman's brazen questioning and became tongue-tied with fear. Before Kalyani could say anything the woman barked out again, "will you go from here or shall I call Ganesh?"

Whoever he was, this Ganesh must have been a goon. Ajay was shaken scared, the first to run out. Kalyani followed him. In the lane Ajay refused to take shots within the settlement any more. He said he would go into the building at the corner from where the settlement began and take some shots of the lane there. Otherwise also Kalyani was mixing real shots with those of actors. When Ajay suggested this Kalyani accepted immediately. As Kalyani hit the corner, Ajay reached the balcony of a nearby building. The morsel of bread which Laxmi had put in her mouth seconds before became stuck in her throat. Paralysed, she could not move a finger. Standing a few steps away was Hukkum ka Patta twirling his moustache, staring at Laxmi with blood-shot eyes. He had a water bottle in his hands which he had probably bought only a few minutes earlier from a store nearby.

As Kalyani reached her, Laxmi, regaining her senses, shouted, "Run didi, run!" Kalyani never asked why. And both, holding hands, began to run. But they were running in the opposite direction to where there cab was parked. Kalyani realized this in a flash and waved down a cab. The driver downed the meter and opened the door for them. Laxmi leapt in first, Kalyani was able to put one foot in when the unthinkable happened.

• • •

Ajay was a traitor. He had given the bites of the incident, along with other shots from Kamathipura to his channel that had run the story – two teenage girls looking out from a caged balcony, a portly woman in petticoat and blouse washing clothes outside a *kholi*, two boys fighting with each other, a pushcart tea stall at the corner, Laxmi riding in the cab, Kalyani rushing to follow her, and acid attack on Kalyani.

Mixed in together were some old shots from Kalyani's anchoring days and the advertising films. Not only Kalyani, they targeted her daughter. They dug up shots in which Janki had been held by an anti-narcotics team. Ajay was an insider and he knew why Kalyani had gone to the red light area. He leaked this to his channel to spice up the story, bytes from the police regarding Janki's disappearance was spliced in to bulk up the sordid tale.

The acid attack had not touched Kalyani's face. Instead, the bottle hit her shoulder and fell to the floor and shattered, spewing out the fuming liquid. The horror of the incident was enough for Kalyani to lose consciousness. She slumped toward the taxi even as Laxmi pulled her in and slammed the door. The taxi driver was taken completely by surprise yet his reflexes made him floor the accelerator speeding them away from the danger. Ajay's shots never really said what had happened there. It was unclear who had thrown the bulb. It was a coincidence that while he was panning the camera across the red-light area that Kalyani came into view with the bottle flying in her direction. No one had a clue that this would happen except Laxmi who suspected the villain as Hukkum ka Patta and that she was the real target, not Kalyani.

Probably Patta had spotted her in the area much earlier when Kalyani had left her at the corner tea stall and had entered the *gali*. Laxmi realized his presence quite late; by that time he would have bought the acid. Finally, when she did see him standing there twirling his moustache, there was already a bottle in one hand, which Laxmi thought was a water bottle, could have been the murderous liquid. Laxmi sifted through all this in her head not daring to share her thoughts with anyone, not even Kalyani, forget about the police.

After watching the news, many people came to visit Kalyani in the hospital. Kabir came, too, to enquire about Kalyani's condition. His visit drew a large crowd at the hospital gate. The news value of the acid attack shot up immensely and other channels bought shots from Ajay. Kabir allowed his secretary to speak on TV about the film in which he had worked with Kalyani which had now been dumped. Kabir as a producer now was working on a remake of the film *Satyam, Shivam, Sundaram* as his first film, where the lead lady has half her face scorched in an accident. Here Kabir found ready publicity in Kalyani's fate. Kalyani, in her previous avatar, would have gone crazy with joy at Kabir's visit. The acid burns on her shoulder would have taken an added grace. They had brought Kabir to her bedside. Not now. The new Kalyani was almost unmoved by his courtesy. Though Kabir had come, for whom was she waiting eagerly! She, like musk dear, could not recognize the one she loved when he was near, and pined for him when he was away. She realized then how much she loved Gautam.

Gautam was back. When he got to know about the acid attack on Kalyani, he was devastated. He realized how superficial his anger for Kalyani was and how deep his love for her. She was in his whole being.

Now Mohan came along Gautam. He had correctly guessed that Gautam was at Dr Prabhaker's Centre. He found Gautam there involved in research along with the doctor.

Either the incident was big or was made out of proportion by the media. Anyway, Kalyani's wounds were not serious, and she was soon at home. The day she returned she received a call from Rani, "Didi I have some good news."

"Good news? The only good news for me is of the whereabouts of Janki."

Rani was embarrassed by Kalyani's reaction. She was going to tell Kalyani about herself. Now she spoke softly and to the point. "Didi I am going to America. The American government has chosen me for a leadership programme. They will help us study human trafficking, which is a three-week programme."

A saddened Kalyani did not want to wet-blanket her friend's enthusiasm. She answered with an edge of excitement in her voice, "Rani, I am really happy for you. Please share everything with me when you return. We can meanwhile keep in touch."

• • •

After leaving a long journey and the formalities of travelling to the US behind her, Rani came out of the airport at Washington DC. She saw a girl approaching her and as she neared she extended her hand. "Hi, I'm Emily. You are Rani from India, right?"

"Right, right," smiled Rani in return.

All the tiredness and fear of how she was going to survive in an alien country vanished when she saw Emily who had already arranged for a cab.

The two left for the hotel and this was the first foreign trip of Rani. From the cab window she looked around eagerly and felt as if she had entered somewhere, a place seen only in dreams. She turned to look left and right and wanted to devour everything with her eyes. In the bright sunlight, cherry trees were in full bloom. The roads were broad and clean, houses almost picture book beautiful. Rani looked around spellbound. Emily knowing her guest's mood, preferred not to strike up a conversation. She politely took Rani's permission and turned on the walkman's earphones.

Through the heart of the city a river ran clean and broad. Rani looked around in awe. "There in India, a river like the Ganges is considered sacred but it is highly polluted," she thought with deep sadness. She asked Emily the name of the river, though she hesitated a bit wondering how the American would take the question. Rani had not studied the cities of America she was going to visit. The American Center had sent her some books, maps and other reference material while she was in India. Finally, curiosity won and she looked at Emily questioningly. Taking the cue the girl took off the earphones.

"This is the river Potomac," said Emily. They began chatting and Emily did not put on the earphones again.

"Apart from attending the sessions on trafficking in persons, do you wish to do anything special here?" asked Emily.

Rani was quick to reply, "Oh yes! I want to see a Broadway show."

"Good," said Emily, "you have mentioned it now. Broadway tickets need to be booked quite in advance. New York is the last in our four city schedule; we must book the tickets today."

Soon they were at the hotel Lincoln where, in the lobby, Karma, Usuf and Zhing were waiting for Emily. From the State Department, Emily had been appointed as their group leader for three weeks. Karma was from Bhutan. She was a police officer there. Usuf was from Bangladesh, the chief of an anti-trafficking

NGO based in that country. Zhing, a Chinese man, lived and worked in Kolkata for a newspaper; his beat was South Asian issues. Zhing's parents ran a Chinese restaurant in the city.

Emily handed over the traveller's cheques, given by the State Department to each person. And they booked rooms for themselves. A meeting was fixed for the same evening in the lobby.

The delegation was to first meet with the Department of Homeland Security. Here they were given an overview of the role and function of the Office of Immigration and Custom's Enforcement. They discussed anti-trafficking initiatives, Rani sitting peacefully through the PowerPoint presentation about how to save a victim of trafficking. Rani found the case histories disturbing. The agony of those women and children was an acute reminder of her tortuous past. The truth began to revive in her the horrors she went through as a casualty.

The feeling was overwhelming and Rani felt like crying. She went over to the water cooler thinking who else could understand this terror that is in her, how people trap you in the name of love. They misuse your trust in them. They betray you.

The case histories being discussed was of a Chinese girl. Her trust had been twisted to push her into the flesh market. Rani wanted to talk to somebody, but here in an alien country, there was nobody with whom she could speak of the storm within tearing her up, "it must be midnight in India," she thought with a sigh. She pulled herself together within a few seconds deciding to call Kalyani later and recount how people cheat girls after becoming the blood brothers. The thought calmed her feelings and she returned to the meeting.

At lunch they went to a mall. As soon as she saw a food joint with the signboard "Bombay Stall" she raced toward it like a famished soul, thrilled to see Indian food here in DC. Karma was with her and laughing at Rani's madness for Indian cuisine, she broke into Hindi, *rani aap soch rahe hain america mein dal roti mil raha hai to dal roti khao, prabhu ka gun gao!*

"Oh Karma! You know Hindi!" Exclaimed Rani, pleasantly surprised.

"In our place people are crazy about Bollywood movies. They sing Hindi songs ··· even elders in our homes watch Hindi serials ··· Rani, tell me is it true that your *sas–bahu*s live in a state of eternal combat?"

This question made Rani laugh. "This happens only in serials. In real life they have to adjust to each other ··· what is shown here is a distortion of reality," explained Rani.

They saw Emily and Zing coming toward them. Emily had bought a pair of denim trousers for a hundred dollars.

Lunch time was almost over; there next station was the US Department of Justice. There they were to meet a trial attorney and deputy chief of the criminal section to learn about investigation and prosecution of trafficking-in-persons cases.

That night following dinner, Rani called Kalyani, "Do you know didi, what blood-brother means?"

"Real brother, the biological one, a blood relative, what else?" answered Kalyani, yawning, as she warmed up to Rani's call.

"No, not a real brother. Blood brother means the one that plays with your trust and ultimately breaks it ··· now how can I explain it to you ··· ?" Rani stopped for a moment, then continued without waiting for Kalyani.

"I need to tell you about 'M'."

"M?" asked Kalyani.

"Yes M. They don't speak of the victim's identity, narrating instead the case history for the sake of creating awareness. M was looking for a job while she was in China. The kidnapper took his time in building a bond with the girl. Then the time came when he told her he was like a brother and would certainly help her find a good job. To win the girl's trust he made a blood oath with her. He pricked his index finger and let a drop of blood fall into a cup of water. He made the girl do the same. The water was stirred so that the blood was mixed and each of them drank from the concoction. The boy was now M's blood brother but in time he raped and sold her."

"Oh Lord, this was pure cheating ···" sleep fled Kalyani's eyes.

"What do they say, what would have happened to M now?" asked Kalyani.

"It is too complicated a legal procedure for me to understand. Still I will try and give you the information I have. On a tip off, the police raided a massage parlour where they found M with some other girls."

"In the criminal division of the US Justice Department they introduced us to a trial attorney. Human trafficking is modern-day slavery and the government and the NGOs fight cases for the victims. If the victim is a foreign national they help to send the individual back to her country of origin. If she feels it is dangerous to return she gets a special visa and shelter in the US."

Rani suddenly changed the topic. "How are you didi? Aren't you considering plastic surgery for your shoulder?"

"No, no Rani, I am alright this way. My only concern is Janki now. Gautam has placed ads in the missing person's columns in some newspapers. And, for the first time, we have got a response from the police. They have informed us that they had received a call that Janki was seen in London," said Kalyani.

"So didi are you going to London?" Rani shot back.

"No, no foolish girl, London is not so small that I can go looking for Janki. All this is not breaking news, going to London was in her schedule. The question is whether she came back to India or went to the US from London. Gautam will be visiting the American Consulate and present them the whole issue. . . ."

The phone disconnected midsentence, abruptly ending the conversation.

• • •

Mr Roger Lang, an officer from the NYPD, had asked Janki, if she wished she could be sent back to India. Did she have a family there? A home perhaps? Janki told him she had no family to go back to.

Janki was in a shelter in New Jersey. On a lead given by an NGO in New York, US Immigration and Custom Enforcement had raided slave driver Mac's den in search of undocumented migrants. What they found was something much bigger. There were six girls caught up in his net. One of them was Janki, whose visa had long expired. To help these girls, Sakhi, an NGO in New York, had also come forward.

"South Asian girls fear uniforms. It strikes terror in them. The girls would not talk openly, let alone pour their heart out before the police," said Sakhi's chief Komal Bindra whose presence was meant to avert such a crisis. Along with her was UNIFEM head Jiyang, a woman of Chinese origin. They assured Janki that they would try for special T-visa for her if she felt there was any danger for her in going back to India. She was strongly encouraged to help dismantle the ongoing racket.

The idea of helping the prosecution alarmed the young

women. The girl from Bangladesh was so traumatized by the thought of becoming a witness that she began crying. She thought of the goons attacking her family back home if she said anything against them here.

"It is better that you send us back," she said tearfully.

After assuring the girls that they would return and hear their problems Komal and Jiyang left them.

This was not Janki's worry. She concluded that Indians were not involved in this sprawling criminal enterprise. She had been brought in from London. Jo-Jo was her handler, in cahoots with Joshua. "This would not have happened if Keval Ramani had not died," she thought. Then, too, if she returned to India, how would she face her parents was the question. ··· She had lost her face. This way she really had no one in India to go back to. The only option was to remain in the US. Janki was in a conflict. Deep within, she wanted to return to her country. She argued with herself that the girl from Bangladesh was illiterate, therefore helpless; no choices were open for her. Janki thought she was, if not highly, sufficiently educated to find a job and settle in any part of India.

Janki's mind juggled with contradictory thoughts even when she was feeling a little secure as she was in the shelter now. The fear, suffocation and turbulence of living in the dead embrace of goons were over. With the luxury of idle hours on hand and a comparatively quietened mind, thoughts of Mohan softly came to her. Mohan loved her truly and passionately. Keval too was a good man lacking Mohan's intensity. She realized that for herself Keval was only the harbour in bad times.

Twenty-three

"DIDI PLEASE OPEN your laptop," this was Rani over the phone.

"Have you gone mad Rani? It's two at night in India. I am switching off my phone," said Kalyani going back to sleep.

The next morning at about seven Kalyani remembered that she had abruptly cut Rani's line. Why would she have called that late? Kalyani began wondering. Had she gone to New York from Dallas? May be the time zone change had confused her. Kalyani recollected that tickets had been booked for *Producer* showing at Broadway. Rani may be gone to watch the play and must have been so excited to share the experience that she forgot about time. She must have posted her Time Square photographs and was eager to show them, thought a bemused Kalyani opening her mailbox. What appeared along with the description was so strange and unexpected that she called Gautam.

"Who is this old Englishman, why has Rani sent his photograph to us?" he asked querulously.

Reading the accompanying text his expressions gradually changed to amazement and he asked Kalyani, "Didn't a man similar to him once come in your dreams Kalyani? Maybe that's why Rani sent you this picture."

"Definitely yes," she said taking a printout of the mail. Together they began to read from the same leaf.

"Yesterday morning," she wrote, "we went to Brooklyn to visit an NGO named Safe-Horizon. There a case history was presented to us. The account included something so unbelievable by which we were so stunned. We were compelled to think it was a wonder greater than the Brooklyn Bridge. You will pardon my exaggeration in comparing it with that technical phenomenon. I am all the more surprised by the extent to which people can go to infiltrate the US. Now no more riddles, let's talk directly about this case.

"An elderly Caucasian man boarded an Air Canada flight from Hong Kong. He had an extremely creased and a wrinkled face. On the flight he would visit the bathroom quite frequently. A few times he got up from his seat to visit one or two other passengers a little away from him. One of the persons he met was a South Asian girl. After an hour or so this girl took the old man's place. They might have exchanged seats and after telling the girl to sit in his place he went to the bathroom. The person who returned to the seat vacated by the girl was not the Caucasian but a South Asian middle-aged man."

"According to the Canadian Border Alert Force this was a case of travelling in disguise. This was not a simple case. The way the man had disguised himself was unbelievable. This was certainly not the work of a single person. There must have been a gang behind it, members working perfectly in close unison. Yet their cleverly laid out plan was ultimately exposed."

"The man in disguise had exchanged papers with another Caucasian, mimicking his posture and gait, wearing the same attire as he had. He used a near perfect silicon mask of the old man's face, complete with wrinkles and skin tone. The real person must have himself completed immigration formalities and acquired the boarding pass. In the transit lounge, it seemed, they exchanged their boarding passes through a willing collaborator. The transformation was effected by the South Asian man in the washroom of the Air Canada flight."

Kalyani and Gautam, reading this account, got astounded. Their eyes fell on the line Rani had written. "Please click to the next mail I have sent which contains the real face of this South Asian man."

Kalyani and Gautam followed Rani's instructions. There was a photograph, carrying a caption "This is the Indian man who was trying to escape to Canada under an assumed name and identity. His real name is Keval Ramani. Two girls are also seen in the picture; one is wearing a burka. Her name is Zubaida, real name Shruti. The other girl's name is Dimpy, her real name. Dimpy had a valid American visa. It seems Keval Ramani had a plan to infiltrate the US from Canada with Dimpy. She could be the vehicle with an American visa. Canada's International Alert Force has passed on this information."

"This was what Janki had written in her letter – I am going to Dimpi's house," shouted Kalyani excitedly.

"And yes, this Keval Ramani is the person who had thrown a rave party where Janki was found by the police," said Gautam and bit his tongue.

"Yes. You had hidden this even from me," answered Kalyani reproachfully. She could not afford to sulk, for, a significant clue was about to reveal itself. Kalyani steadied her voice and told Gautam, "Gautam, I know who Keval Ramani is. I will call Sagar Irani right now."

"And I am going to the American Embassy," said Gautam.

"American Embassy? But what Janki had a touring visa ··· the Americans do not let anybody stay on after that period," said Kalyani.

"You are right Kalyani. The likelihood of Janki staying over in the US is almost nil. That's why we never paid attention to this possibility. But now we should think it over again and seek help from the American Consulate," said Gautam.

"Shall I call Rani ··· it must be night there." When Kalyani said this Gautam quipped, "So what do you think, Rani is the American Police that you want to inform her regarding this matter, or what?" Gautam tried to smile though his lips were dry and flaked.

Gautam called Mohan and briefed him about the turn in events.

Sagar Irani gave Kalyani an appointment and met her briefly. When the conversation shifted to Janki he clarified his position. There were many extras in his troop to London; there was no way he could know them all. But participants brought by Keval Ramani were not lodged in the hotel booked by Irani. The former on his own had arranged accommodation for the people of his group; it was difficult for Irani to say who the girl was. He said he could have helped by giving Kalyani rough shots of practice sessions, has his editor not deleted them.

As far as Dimpy was concerned, Irani said he knew nothing about her, denying he had ever heard her name. Irani's secretary came up with Keval's office address which he gave to Kalyani.

Kalyani followed it up but found it locked. The neighbours said it had been three years since it was shut, the property being in dispute. Kalyani knew that the police could give Keval's farm house address though it seemed futile to her now. She knew that Keval was in Canadian police custody. So she stopped trying to get further details from this lead.

Mohan with Kalpana Thapa went to the police station concerned in Mumbai where Kalyani had lodged the FIR regarding Janki going missing. Here Mohan came to know that they had established communications with Scotland Yard and got the address where Keval had rented an apartment. A case of theft was registered at that location. When the police recovered the stolen goods they found the portrait of a girl, probably done in London by some street artist. When this was compared with the photograph given by Kalyani to the Indian police, it looked like it was the same girl. It became clear that the girl who stayed in that apartment with Keval Ramani was Janki. From London, Keval Ramani moved over to some place in Europe. Janki had left for New York from Heathrow; they did not leave London together.

Twenty-four

When people visit New York they go to see the iconic Empire Estate Building. Now Rani was here, inside it, looking over the Big Apple. Awed by the splendour of the city of skyscrapers, Rani told Anita that she wanted to remain forever by this window; the sight of this grand city had taken her under its spell.

Anita laughed and said, "You have come here only for a few days, you do not know the struggles one has to go through to survive in this 'grand city.' When I changed my home I myself had to load and drive the removal van, not to speak of carrying my belongings up without a porter. From painting the walls to sewing curtains, you have to do everything yourself."

They were on the fifteenth floor of the Empire State, in the office of the United Nations Development Fund for Women. Earlier, Anita Zaidi was in the organization's Delhi office, shifted six months back to New York. The two had been in a meeting in the UNIFEM office and had come out for coffee from the vending machine.

"Yes, here you have to do everything on your own, like we have had to come out to drink our coffee. It's not that you merely press a bell on your desk and the peon comes along to take your order," said Rani.

Anita became serious after this comment from Rani, replying, "They do not keep peons here. South Asian people don't understand this. A few days back a husband and wife from an Indian family were in serious trouble. Their Indian house help had reported to the police that the owner made her work ten hours a day; she was not allowed to open the refrigerator for food without permission. She was made to sleep on the floor and such like. Here it is considered modern-day slavery, human trafficking ··· the owner will certainly get a long term in jail."

"Oh Lord!" said Rani. Then as if she had remembered something, she asked Anita, "you look after matters related to South Asians, right? I am going to forward you a mail after reaching my hotel. This came yesterday from India."

"Okay, let's return to the meeting," replied Anita.

• • •

The next day, Anita called Rani. "I saw the photographs forwarded by you and read the accompanying text. I will certainly discuss the case of your niece in the UNIFEM meeting. Then there are some NGOs who work on South Asian issues. I am going to forward this mail to them too. But we cannot expect much. Maybe, your niece is not here in the US. She might be somewhere else in the world or may have even left this world. ···"

At the other end of the phone Rani said nothing in response, except for a long soft "Hmm".

Anita thought probably Rani did not like the last bit, that her niece may have left this world. To lighten the air she changed the topic, "Rani, you mentioned earlier that you miss Indian food. I know of a place where you can enjoy authentic Indian cuisine. A few minutes from your hotel in Manhattan there is a Pakistani restaurant – Baluchi - let's go there tomorrow. I will pick you up. From there, we can walk down to the restaurant."

"Anita, in front of the hotel as we cross the road there is a supermarket. I have bought some nans, a can of kidney beans and a few tomatos from there; very close to the taste my Indian tongue is used to, so now there is no need to. ···" Before Rani could complete her sentence Anita broke into Hindi, "*to ameriki sarkar ke paise par aish kar rahi ho rani* ···" and began laughing. Rani replied in baritone laughter.

Anita continued, "We will not go on an eating spree ··· my plan is that we invite the heads of some NGOs to have lunch with us. The one who works on issues related to South Asian women. I will forward your mail to the guest beforehand. We can continue discussions over lunch.

"You are doing so much for me Anita, a person you are barely acquainted with," said Rani.

"Why should you be surprised Rani, look at yourself. You, too, are doing so much for a niece you have never met ···," replied Anita.

"This is because of Kalyani didi, Anita. You do not know how much she has helped me. I would not be here or anywhere else leading a respectable life if it were not for her. You know very well Anita what it means to be a hijara in India. It is a curse you live with your whole life. Kalyani didi had lifted the yoke from my shoulders," said Rani.

• • •

There was a bit of snowfall sometime back. Now it is raining. Rani did not realize it in the hotel that outside it was very cold. When she was leaving for America, Kalyani had bought a leather jacket from Tata Exports for Rani to take along. Today she realized it was useful in the true sense. Up to now she had been wearing a long woollen coat which was quite sufficient. But New York's biting cold pierced her bones. A one and a half kilometre distance seemed an eternity. Rani could not speak, her teeth chattering inside her head.

They entered the restaurant; its cosy warmth was a great relief for them.

Sajan re jhoot mat bolo, khuda ke pas jana hai, a Hindi film song sung by Mukesh was playing. While they looked around for a table, a waiter with a food tray passed leaving a waft of *tarka dal* in Rani's nostrils. She sucked it deep inside and smiled at the prospect of eating a good dal-biriyani. The waiter turned to give her a hard stare.

Anita went over to a table where a woman sat. They hugged each other. Rani joined them. This was Komal Bindra, Sakhi's chief. Ordering food they opened the mail on Anita's laptop. After seeing the photograph and text Komal said, "I am not sure, but I think I have seen a girl similar to this one in New Jersey."

Can we go to New Jersey?" asked Rani.

"It's not possible for me to accompany you today, but I will give you the address," said Bindra.

Anita looked at Rani, "Can we leave for New Jersey after eating?"

They went down to the tube station nearby, took the blue line, walked some distance and were soon at a wharf on the Hudson River, from there they took a ferry. They could see the Statue of Liberty from a distance. On the opposite side, the city of New Jersey stood glistening in the light.

Getting down on the other side they walked on a bit and

entered the basement car park of a building, where one of Anita's friends had left a car for them. Their journey began toward the address given by Bindra. It was seven in the evening but the sun was not yet set.

Looking at the wide-eyed Rani, Anita explained, "Here the sun sets very late."

"Will they allow us to meet the girls in the shelter?" there was a trace of doubt in Rani's voice.

"They might not. But I have texted our chief Jiang and she has managed to get permission for us. In fact, Jiang frequently visits this shelter to meet the girls here.

"But after seeing Janki's photograph Jiang said nothing and gave no sign of recognition, like Komal Bindra had done," said Rani in a voice trembling with doubt.

"It's possible that for Jiang all Indian girls look alike, like for us all Chinese girls look similar." They began to laugh as Anita said this.

They reached the shelter, a house just behind a Catholic Church. An African-American girl guided them in. At the reception there were messages, regarding their visit to the shelter, both from UNIFEM and Sakhi. There was one more message for Rani and Anita. The Indian Embassy had sent an account, along with a photograph of a girl who looked like someone named Jane living in this shelter. The Embassy in America had received the photograph and the case description from the American Consulate in Mumbai, where Gautam had put up Janki's case.

The dots were being joined, completing the chain of events and making the tangle comprehensible. The moment they had waited for so long was at hand.

After much fear and reluctance Jane admitted she was Janki. Embracing Rani, she cried her heart out. Rani explained how much Kalyani and Gautam loved her. She should not be apprehensive of or shy away from returning home. But Janki did not want to talk to her parents over the phone. Rani could do so if she wanted. So she called Kalyani on reaching her hotel, "Didi there is good news."

"Good news! Janki is found?" Kalyani bit her tongue – it was unnecessary this time. Yes, this was the best news ever, Janki was found.

• • •

Your heart pounds when you are happy and when you are fearful. Here it was a mixed feeling. Ecstasy, because Janki was coming! But there was strange feeling in Gautam and Kalyani wondering how to face her and how would they face each other in Janki's presence?

There was happiness all around. The air at home was full of excitement, as if it was Diwali. Kalyani took down all her photographs from walls. Mohan painted over those portions in pink and was now using it as a canvas to draw Janki's portrait. Seeing this, Kalyani began to put up Janki's photographs from where she had removed her own. The collage was not as glamorous as Kalyani's pictures ··· there were no close-ups either of her face or kajalled eyes. No pouted mouth. Janki's pictures were comparatively simple but photographs from every age were there. When Gautam saw Kalyani arranging Janki's photos he thought of something. He opened his drawer and took out the photograph in which Janki was seated on a teapoy, wearing a red sari with a jari border. The sari-bindi was strangely combined with a necktie and a hat ··· how could he forget that it was the photograph of this series which had created the huge misunderstanding?

While setting up this picture, Gautam looked at Kalyani and she turned toward him, their eyes meeting and lowering. Then a moment came when they held each other's gaze for a long while, with no hint of self-consciousness that they were husband and wife, and dawned on them a slow-growing smile. The moment of awkwardness which would have otherwise appeared between the two, finding Janki before them, instantly vanished. Now Gautam came forward and took Kalyani in his arms. Then both separated, wiping their eyes. It was a moment of tremendous release.

Laxmi was also preparing in her own way, for Janki's welcome. She had told Kalyani that she would like to celebrate the big occasion by lighting earthen lamps using pure ghee. She had bought some from the bazaar, had washed and dried them. She had rolled out some wicks from cotton. Now her heart was throbbing with apprehension. The moment she had been waiting so long for was at hand. She was going to meet Janki. Anxiety overpowered her. Would her sister who had been separated from her in childhood recognize her? These thoughts constantly crossed her mind as she removed pits from the dates. She had requested Gautam to bring a packet of dates so she could make a sweet mouthful of dates and jaggery that Saoo would once prepare for her girls. Laxmi wanted to celebrate Janki's home coming, but this apart she had chosen this particular dish because somewhere inside her she believed its taste would bring back childhood memories in Janki.

• • • • • • •

Twenty-five

AT LAST THE MOMENT came. Janki was at the door of her parent's home. But she stood there like a stone, quiet and inert. Laxmi was the first to come forward and welcome her with a plate containing a diya for her sister's *arati*. After the ritual she put the *arati thali* aside and took her sister in her arms. To her disappointment Janki did not respond remaining rooted to the spot. Scared, Laxmi stepped back and began to cry. Now Kalyani came forward to hug Janki. There was still no response. So Kalyani held her in a tight embrace, the petrified young woman did not respond. Mohan who had gone to the airport to fetch Janki knew very well that she was strangely benumbed. "After a long journey she must be tired, maybe that's why she is silent and listless. She will be alright after reaching home," Mohan had reassured himself.

Now it was Gautam's turn. He put his hand on Janki's head. She remained as lifeless as before but a drop of tear rolled down her cheek. Just one drop of tear as an indication of the floodgates of grief would open soon. Looking at this portent, Kalyani and Laxmi started weeping. Now Gautam took Janki in his arms and began to sob. And a miracle happened. The till now lifeless statue began heaving. Gautam separated himself and

Kalyani took his place, mother and daughter crying and clutching each other. The wall between them is no more. Embracing each other they felt as if they were talking to each other with their entire being.

After a few moments, when they parted, Kalyani pulled Laxmi to the front and asked Janki, "Do you know her Janki?" for a few seconds Janki fixed her gaze on Laxmi and then asked, "how can I forget her?" Hearing this answer from Janki a river of tears flowed from Laxmi's eyes. To hide this involuntary show of emotions, she stuffed her sari in her mouth and ran into the kitchen to ready the plate of sweets for Janki. It was enough for Laxmi that her sister hadn't forgotten her.

Yes, Janki forgot nothing. There was nothing she could delete from the disc of her memory. Repeated rape by Mac, customers who clawed, pinched and bit her flesh, thrashings that left blue scars, Maria who kept her hungry for refusing to dance in the nude, the bald Tom who inflicted frightening pain on her by sodomizing her again and again, how could she forget these all? Above all, Keval Ramani the deceiver. While in the shelter when she was told that Keval Ramani was very much alive and that he was the villain, she went mad with anger. She had been grossly cheated. That Keval had died was the impression she had all along. She had not been cheated by Jo-Jo; the mastermind behind the plan was Keval. Jo-Jo was only an agent acting on his master's direction. Dimpy's job was to lay the trap, something she had done both smartly and subtly. The realization of this deceit gift, wrapped in the silk of love and friendship, made Janki's blood boil with rage. So when the American government sent the message through Sakhi that they wanted her help in the prosecution of traffickers she readily agreed.

This was the same Mumbai in which she had been brought

up. Mummy, papa and Mohan were there the way they had always been, still Janki felt as if something had changed. Yes, it had. Inside her she felt as if the previous one had died and a new Janki was trying to take birth ··· but not so easily. The labour pain was long and severe. Her loved ones were trying to put life into her, to rejuvenate her and make her the Janki they once knew. How could this happen as long as Janki held on to her anguish? How could she be liberated from the shackles of a recent painful past unless she shared her suffering with her loved ones?

Laxmi and Kalyani slept with her in Janki's bedroom. They did not dare leave her alone. Mohan visited the place every day to meet Janki. Gautam tried in various ways to make Janki smile. She did everything except smiling. Laxmi wanted to take Janki to a god man who would chant sacred incantations, putting his hand on Janki's head. Gautam took Janki to a psychiatrist who began counselling and a line of treatment.

They took Janki to Mahabaleshwar thinking that a change would cheer her. They even went to Khandala and Lonavala. No Sunday went without such a trip. But nothing changed Janki. She did not smile.

That day Anguri had come to Kalyani's place. Like everybody who had their ideas Anguri suggested, "Didi, *chokri kee nazar utaro*, sometimes you need to fend off the evil spirit from the person. You do this and I am sure Janki will begin to smile."

When Anguri said this, it was Laxmi who got excited at the thought of the formula being accepted and said enthusiastically, "Yes, yes! I too feel like that and I have suggested this to them before."

But Gautam, Kalyani and Mohan looked at Laxmi in a way as if she had said something improper.

Seeing their reaction, Anguri became a little cautious but did not drop her suggestion and tried to push the point, this time even more strongly.

"You do not know Kalyani didi, like the blessings given by 'us' fructify we help ward off evil too. Please bring some salt and mustard seeds and a piece of cloth, I will do this for Janki and then wish her eternal good luck."

When Anguri demanded this no one refused what she asked for, but then no one went in either to bring them.

That her suggestion was not taken did not discourage Anguri from laying out more plans. Her concern for Janki ran deep. This time she addressed Gautam not Kalyani, "Gautam babu, a lot of silt has been deposited in your daughter's heart like the sediment at the bottom of a pond. It needs to be removed to make a fresh-water lake again. As soon as this happens graceful swans of happiness will burst upon its surface."

"You are right Anguri. Janki will regain her happiness only when she is cleansed of the memory of the bad experiences she had been through, that is why we have begun taking her to a psychiatrist ···change does not come overnight; it will take some time," said Gautam.

"That's all right, Gautam babu. What you are doing would remove the thorn that has pierced your daughter's heart ··· but what about the nail that remains in her soul? That will come out only when she opens the window of her soul to her loved ones," remarked Anguri.

"A sharp nail stuck in one's soul?" Gautam began pondering over this thought. Anguri continued talking about how their group gathers in a cemetery, on the last day of the dark half of a month, choose and anoint their new guru from amongst themselves. In the cemetery sitting around a bonfire, each recites a disturbing account of their life. While doing this they weep, wail and pound their chests to get rid of the sorrows of the past.

"Interesting, very interesting," said Mohan sarcastically. "So you people throw a 'catharsis party,' laying out thorn apples as a special dish ··· listen! this is not going to work here. Janki had already cried enough. We don't need to make her cry any more, we need to make her laugh and smile. While pouring out her heart to us she will surely cry all the more."

This time Anguri became really angry, clapping her hands in the singular fashion of her ilk she said loudly, "that is the point I want to make! Laughing and crying, both will purge the pain from her system. But if she needs to be liberated from her past neither tears produced by smelling onions nor a laugh induced by a glee club will work. Once the nail in her soul is removed she will laugh and cry with all her heart."

"So we should start thinking about having a meeting to precipitate and outflow of passion," Mohan was smiling now. Gautam agreed that this was a point to be considered. A gathering of this kind will help in removing the weight from their hearts; it was about a soul to soul communication making them understand each other better.

• • •

They all gathered in the drawing room of Gautam and Kalyani's apartment. The TV was switched off. Mohan, Kalyani and Gautam had tried to chalk out the agenda for this meeting. How they should go about it, where they should all gather. Certainly it could not be in a place like a cemetery, as in the case of Anguri's group. There was no rite waiting to be performed, a formality would be contraindicated. If they decided that today they should and pour their hearts out to each other and this premeditated action did not bring a single word from their mouth what could be done?

The venue could be the antechamber of this apartment. But who will sit where? And who will start? How would the subject be moved? The biggest question was once Janki realizes that this was all planned she may not open up or be ready to speak a single word.

What could then be done to make it look informal? It could be that while Laxmi oiled Janki's hair, Gautam could come and sit on the sofa with a book and would try to make it seem he was reading. Kalyani would then come and switch off the TV after which she would start rearranging the flowers in the vase that kept on the TV. Mohan would ···! It was all too artificial, too contrived. The proposed meeting was finally called off as it was too ridiculous. The whole idea was given a silent burial.

Then, one day the thing worked out in its own way.

Mohan's mobile rang. It was a Sunday and everyone was at the dining table for an elaborate holiday lunch. It was fixed that Mohan would come every Sunday, but today Anguri had also joined the family.

Nobody was sitting in front of the TV, though it was on and could be heard. The other voices were of people eating lunch. And here Mohan started speaking on his mobile over the noise. It went on for a few seconds before Mohan suddenly dashed toward the TV and switched it off. Now Mohan's words became clearer to everyone eating and conversing leisurely at the table.

Mohan's voice rang out, "O Lord no! May God give peace to her soul! It is my fault. I am the culprit. I deceived her."

For whose soul was he seeking peace? Who died, and whom did Mohan deceive? The ambience turned heavy as these questions propped up in everyone's mind. At the dining table everybody was silent, morsels remaining uneaten.

The conversation was over and Mohan came back to the dining table. He did not start eating; instead, he rested his elbows on the table and covered his face with his hands. After a while he moved his palms to wipe the tears off his face. Then he looked at others and addressed them without being asked for. He was in fact talking to himself, a man filled with guilt.

He said, "Meera passed away. I had promised her that on my way back I would meet her again. But when I called Kalyani didi from Sharansthali and came to know about Janki went missing I was out of my wits. I hurried to Mumbai."

"Meera? Which Meera?" asked Gautam and Kalyani simultaneously? Janki too looked at Mohan questioningly. Anguri, who was sitting leaning against the back of the chair sat up straight. Laxmi's eyes were full of tears. Only she knew who Meera was.

"I have lost one of my sisters," said Laxmi, removing tears from her eyes with her sari *pallu*.

"But for me she was like my mother, or you may say *mousi*, she reminded me of my mother," said Mohan.

Mohan began explaining to the perplexed listeners that this mother, sister and *mausi* were none other than a cow elephant. Looking at Gautam, Mohan began speaking, "neither siblings nor mother, nor kin. I only had a father whom I hated with all my might. It's never easy to hate your own father, Gautamji. So it was only Meera in those times of emotional bleakness came to my rescue."

"I can understand how it feels to fall in hate with your own father," said Gautam. "I too hated my father intensely.

But perhaps that was the reason I always tried to find solace in thinking about the mother I had never seen. I had always pined for her but since Janki came into my life, I have no repentance. Her presence has given me emotional gratification and strength."

This was a wondrous moment. Listening to Gautam's words, a smile spread across Janki's face. It was a good sign. This was the first ever smile on her face, since she came back from hell.

Kalyani was thrilled to see Janki smiling. But from what Gautam had said a question sprang up inside her. She did not keep it to herself. Posing it, instead, to Gautam, "My presence never gave you emotional strength Gautam, I know. But today I also want to open my heart and bare it before all of you. Both of you said 'it's not easy to hate one's own father'. I would say for me it was not easy to love my father. I had feelings for him but shied away from accepting them. The feeling of shame I used to have regarding his mental illness always surpassed the daughterly love for him. Being a selfish snob I had always put this question, "what will people think," above my own feelings. My father was not an awe-inspiring gentleman; he was a mad man in the perception of this world, this society. And I cared more about society and less about him. Rather, I treated him as a non-entity, this was my fault. Now I repent," said Kalyani tearfully.

Laxmi came forward and wiped Kalyani's eyes with her sari's edge, saying, "Don't lose heart didi, in a situation like this it becomes difficult naturally to accept your mother and father as they are. Look at me; my own father sold me off. Can there be any truth bitter than this? I, too, hated my father with all my heart, with all my soul. But whatever be the truth, you learn to live with it." Laxmi shifted her *pallu* from Kalyani's eyes to her own.

The atmosphere was heavy and Laxmi's statement had stirred up a storm in Janki, who was almost in a state of paralysis. After all, the father Laxmi was talking about was also her biological father. Laxmi was her real sister. The same blood ran in both their veins. Janki too hated Ghunghru. But because of this charged atmosphere whatever came from her mouth was different.

Janki began to speak and everybody listened to her in complete silence. "All of you talked about your suppressed hate or suppressed love toward your mother or father. What I am fighting with is my own disgust for my body. I am burning with hate with myself. So many men violated me. God had given me such a decent father and mother but I deceived them. I deliberately put aside memories of my mother who had given birth to me and nurtured me with her soul during my childhood, just because she was poor and it did not suit my new-found status. ··· I fell into greed," saying this Janki began sobbing uncontrollably.

"No, no my dear daughter, you neither cheated nor deceived us. When one is at a certain age, hormones all of a sudden pick up the reins. That was not your fault, not at all," said Gautam putting his arms around Janki's neck.

"But my body was violated, I feel desecrated. I feel sinful and guilty." When Janki said this Kalyani came over to her and said: "You haven't committed any crime; why should you feel guilty? This is a wrong kind of conditioning Indian girls are hardwired for and they call it *sanskar.* This is a misconception. By some wrong notion of sacredness and virginity, in our society, the victim suffers guilt and infamy while the criminal roams free, rather honourably acquitted. You don't have to accept this notion, Janki. You have done no wrong. Just try and root out this worthless guilt from your heart."

"Yes Janki, put the past aside. Now you are present among us with a new body and a new soul." When Mohan said this the crying Janki began to smile. As everybody else began smiling, catharsis broke loose.

"When everything is falling out of the cupboard I, too, want to tell you a secret, why should I hold it back now?" said Kalyani.

"Yes, yes tell us, what you want to say, our ears are ready to listen," said Gautam. Now his tone was lighter.

"My Taeeji ··· my Taeeji," Kalyani stammered.

"Yes, yes, your Taeeji what ···," Gautam encouraged her to continue.

Kalyani tried again and this time she spoke without faltering, "My Taeeji died a virgin. The marriage had never been consummated."

"What?" everyone screamed in surprise!

Now Anguri was speaking, "I, too, have a secret with me. ··· My hundred-year old guru had once told me that she used to send one among us to massage your Tauji. Your Tauji had no interest in women."

Kalyani was smiling despite the obvious embarrassment. Janki, perhaps in order to change the topic said, "I want to meet Lantarani *bua* at least once. Where is she, how is she, I really want to know."

Laxmi said she was also thinking along the same lines. They all decided to visit their home town and stay there for a few days.

• • •

Oblivious to all this, at the same time, Lantarani was strolling along a footpath in the small town, mumbling to herself. Nobody knew where Ghunghru was. He had disappeared long ago. Lantarani's husband had died. There was no one Lantarani could talk to. Everybody was gone but her habit of spinning yarns was not. She kept busy talking to herself all the time. She was one person who never needed a formal catharsis.

• • •

As a postscript, Janki had no mole on her breast. It was a tattoo made for the occasion.